Language Arts *for*
Upper School
by Katherine Weitz

POETICS & PROGYM I

Student Book

Acknowledgements

The art on the cover is taken from the nineteenth century painting "Ulysses and the Sirens," by British artist John William Waterhouse, courtesy of Wikimedia Commons (commons.wikimedia. org). Other images courtesy of The Graphics Fairy (thegraphicsfairy.com) and Dreamstime (dreamstime.com). Most selections at the beginning of lessons are in the public domain, besides the full length excerpts of the progymnasmata translations, which are used by permission of the Society for Biblical Literature in Atlanta, Georgia (see Bibliography).

I owe a debt of gratitude to several folks for their help on the Cottage Press Language Arts Curriculum. The gorgeous cover designs are the craftsmanship of my friend Jayme Metzgar. Many other dear friends have helped with both editing and content: in particular, Cheryl Turner, Kimberlynn Curles, Dovey Elliott, Kathy Whitmore, Hannah Taylor, Melissa Turner, and all the other exceptional teachers, moms, and students of Providence Prep. My daughter Grace Weitz has spent many hours editing the project, and contributed significantly to the content of Teaching Helps. As always, the main source of help and encouragement in myriad ways – from design consultation to field testing to laundry, dinner, and dish duty – has always come from my dear husband and my wonderful children.—kpw

Printed in the United States of America.

Poetics & Progym I

Contents

Writer's Journal

Commonplace Book

Vocabulary Study

Theon's Six Narrative Elements

Narrative Plot Observation

Example Narrative Plot Observation

Figures in Poetics & Progym I

Eloquent Expression Through Copia

Grammar Terms & Definitions

The Academic Essay, Classically Considered

Proverbs & Anecdotes for Additional Elaborations

Prose & Poetry Handbook Sample Pages

Bibliography

MATERIALS NEEDED FOR POETICS & PROGYM I

Materials, resources, and links listed below are available at Cottage Press
cottagepresspublishing.net

Required Books and Resources

❦ POETICS & PROGYM I TEACHING HELPS Features a full answer key for grammar (Diagramming and Parsing) exercises, tips on teaching, and additional notes and enrichment ideas. Please note that if you are using this in a co-op situation, each teacher at home will also need a copy of the Teacher Manual.

❦ SENTENCE SENSE The grammar handbook from Cottage Press for terms & definitions, sentence diagramming and parsing. Lessons from the 1878 classic *Harvey's Revised English Grammar* are included in *Sentence Sense*, scheduled in *Poetics & Progym I* and *II*, and referenced in *Poetics & Progym III*. This comprehensive and concise grammar reference is also used throughout *Bards & Poets* (*Language Arts for Intermediate Students*).

❦ THREE COMPOSITION BOOKS Each student will need three sewn composition books (100 pages). These lay flat, and pages tend to stay in better than they do in spiral-bound notebooks. One will be used for a Commonplace Book, one for a Prose & Poetry Handbook, and one for a Writer's Journal. See instructions for setting up and using these in the Appendix.

Required Literature

❦ THE ODYSSEY OF HOMER A classic with which every student should be familiar is the literary centerpiece of *Poetics & Progym I*. Choose the translation by Richmond Lattimore or by Robert Fitzgerald, both of which retain much of the beauty of Homer's original language and form.

❦ COMMENTARY ON HOMER'S ODYSSEY An invaluable aid for the teacher in guiding the student through *The Odyssey*. The best, simplest, and least expensive commentary we can recommend is Leland Ryken's *Homer's The Odyssey: A Christian Guide to the Classics*. We have scheduled readings from this commentary for students and teachers in the *Poetics & Progym I* lessons.

❦ POETRY ANTHOLOGY Students will be prompted in each lesson to read and copy poems into their Commonplace Books. There are several excellent anthologies linked from the Cottage Press website; a favorite for this level is *Committed to Memory*, edited by John Hollander.

Recommended Literature

❦ BULFINCH'S AGE OF FABLE Thomas Bulfinch's classic guide to Greek and Roman mythology will provide an excellent foundation for Homer's *Odyssey*. If possible, read this aloud with your student in the summer before beginning *Poetics & Progym I*. Several chapters are required reading for the first few lessons of *Poetics & Progym I*, but these may be accessed online at gutenberg.org for free if you prefer not to buy it. Make sure you purchase or access the original version by Bulfinch, not the one revised by Rev. E.E. Hale.

❦ BOOKS, BOOKS, BOOKS! Excellence in writing is inextricably linked to excellence in reading choices. Cottage Press has long-term plans to republish worthy books for students. Visit us often to check our progress!

Recommended Resources

❦ BOOK OF CENTURIES A blank timeline book for students, from Cottage Press. We provide suggestions in the lesson for entries that should be added to the Book of Centuries. When adding entries to the Book of Centuries, students should include authors and works of literature as well as events and other historical events. For works of literature, format the work properly (poems in quotations, book titles underlined) and include the name of the author and date of compositon and/or publication.

❦ QUIZLET An online flashcard review site. Cottage Press provides free flashcards at this site for *Poetics & Progym* to use online or to print. Access this resource from our webpage.

❦ HARVEY'S PRACTICAL GRAMMAR ANSWER KEY An answer key for the exercises required in *Poetics & Progym* is included in Teaching Helps, but you may wish to access this free online answer key for the rest of the exercises in case you want to use them for extra review. Look for the link on the *Poetics & Progym I* page at cottagepresspublishing.net. This is the correct key to the exercises from *Harvey's Revised English Grammar* in *Sentence Sense*, even though the name is slightly different.

❦ A PRINT DICTIONARY Vocabulary studies are best completed with a big, old-fashioned comprehensive dictionary—the fatter, the better. I recommend an older collegiate dictionary. These generally have not been afflicted with the modern malady of political correctness, and better yet, can often be had for pennies at a used bookstore or thrift store.

❦ A THESAURUS Indispensable for Vocabulary Study and Eloquent Expression lessons. Free online versions, like thesaurus.com work well also, but beware the ads!

❦ A RHYMING DICTIONARY Very handy for Poetry Analysis and Classical Composition lessons. Also look for free online versions, like rhymezone.com.

Introduction for Students & Teachers

My heart overflows with a pleasing theme;
I address my verses to the king;
my tongue is like the pen of a ready scribe.
— Psalm 45:1, ESV

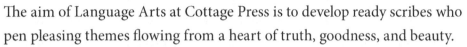

The aim of Language Arts at Cottage Press is to develop ready scribes who pen pleasing themes flowing from a heart of truth, goodness, and beauty. Our methods are based on a classical tradition beginning with the ancient Greeks and Romans, and embraced in the educational practices of Western Civilization—Christendom—over the past two thousand years. The ancient Greek and Roman orators and rhetoricians, who developed and articulated many of the methods that we have adopted, considered training in effective communication to be inseparable from training in virtue. We agree wholeheartedly.

Our methods are inextricably linked with the Great Books, a.k.a. the classics, those that contain the best thoughts of the best minds of Western civilization. They are the very foundation upon which the culture of the West stands. Every truly educated person must have an understanding of this great body of thought. Because of this, literary selections in Cottage Press Language Arts are culled in large part from the Great Books.

Many lists of THE Great Books have been compiled through the years. These lists vary somewhat according to the listmaker's preferences and biases, but there are probably a hundred or so books that must be on any worthwhile list. Works like Homer's *Iliad* and *Odyssey,* Virgil's *Aeneid,* Augustine's *Confessions,* Dante's *Inferno,* Milton's *Paradise Lost,* and of course, the very greatest of all great books, the Bible, must be included if the listmaker wishes to be taken seriously.

The Great Conversation naturally rises out of these Great Books, as great minds in each age respond and refer to the thoughts of the great minds of previous ages, transcending the boundaries of time and place. As we sit at the feet of these remarkable men and women, listen to them, ask questions of them, answer them back (pen in hand!), we become participants in this enduring exchange. Who knows? A *Poetics & Progym* student may even make a contribution of his or her own someday.

Cottage Press Language Arts courses are organized around the ancient Greek Progymnasmata (Progym) because it is a comprehensive pedagogy, aimed at developing rhetorical skill and love of virtue. Students trained by the Progym are prepared for ALL of life's writing requirements including—but not limited to—academic and college-level composition. Literature and poetry studies along with a strong emphasis on grammar round out our Language Arts instruction.

The Greek word *progymnasmata* (pronounced proh-jim-naz-MAH-tuh) literally means *exercises before*. These fourteen successive exercises are designed to train students in elegant and effective composition. As they worked through these exercises progressively, ancient Greek and Roman scholars imitated great orators and authors of their past. With the knowledge gained from each level, they would then write their own compositions. This training was intended to produce virtuous men who were able to think and speak persuasively on any given topic in the public forum and in the court of law. The need for virtuous and persuasive articulation of truth is certainly as great today as it has ever been.

For a more detailed explanation of each level of the Progymnasmata, visit the Cottage Press website: cottagepresspublishing.net.

The composition exercises in *Poetics & Progym I* first review the Fable and Narrative exercises of the Progym (covered thoroughly in *Fable & Song* and *Bards & Poets*). The rest of the lessons are based on the Anecdote and Proverb exercises of the Progym. In these exercises, you will learn to elaborate (examine and explain) an anecdote or a proverb. This leads naturally into the modern expository essay. The writing sequence is emphasized: Plan, Write, Revise. The aim of poetry lessons in *Poetics & Progym is* first and foremost to delight in the poems. In addition, you will learn to scan poems, identify rhyme and stanza forms, and recognize other literary devices.

In all lessons, you will practice a variety of applied grammar and vocabulary exercises, including extensive sentence diagramming. You will learn to identify figures of speech and figures of description, and to use them in your own writing. All of these exercises are designed to supply you with copia—an abundant stockpile of language, ready at hand. Read more about this in Lesson 1.

In all lessons, you will practice a variety of applied grammar and vocabulary exercises, including extensive sentence diagramming. You will learn to identify new figures and you will use them in your own writing. All of these exercises are designed to supply you with copia—an abundant stockpile of language, ready at hand. Read more about this in Lesson 1.

One word of caution: All of our Language Arts books) are intended to accompany your broad and generous curriculum of reading. We teach you to observe these particular stories and poems in a very detailed way, but please do not attempt to do this with every poem and story you read. Most of your reading should be unencumbered by analysis and "comprehension" exercises, which are often little more than busywork. Instead, you should form the habit of narrating (telling back) what you have read with very little intervention from your teacher. For more details on this, consult the many excellent resources online that explain Charlotte Mason's completely classical method of narration.

Another word of caution: Our literary studies presuppose that you are regularly in church hearing the Bible read and preached, that you are pursuing a regular course of Bible reading on your own, and that you are actively studying Christian doctrine and practice. These habits provide a solid foundation from which to understand and evaluate the texts we encounter, many of which are not written from a specifically Christian perspective, and some of which are written from a distinctly anti-Christian perspective. Those which are written from a Christian perspective will often have theological difficulties or even outright errors. Doctrine is essential. In classroom settings, we should not gloss over doctrinal questions or differences, but fully explore them, particularly by seeking the counsel of church leadership.

Especially when reading literary works, we should approach them first as works of imagination, not as works of theology. The classic literary canon has much to teach us about our common humanity as image-bearers as well as our common depravity in Adam. At the same time, we have a duty as believers to "take every thought captive" in submission to Christ; so a thorough theological foundation is absolutely necessary. Quite honestly, we would be hesitant to encourage a study of certain Great Books under any other circumstances.

Poetics & Progym I is designed for the needs and abilities of an advancing writer, from 8th grade and up. Adjust the pace according to the needs and abilities of the student.

The instruction in the Student Book is written directly to students, yet the material is intended to be actively taught by a teacher. *Poetics & Progym I* works well in home-school, classroom, and co-op settings. In any case, the student should have either parental or teacher oversight for **each day's** work. For composition lessons, students are instructed to work with a writing mentor. This is the person who works one-on-one with the individual student. It may be the teacher, the parent, or an outside tutor employed for the purpose. There are even online services that provide writing mentorship. See the Cottage Press website for links.

STUDENT PREPARATION

Poetics & Progym I contains twenty-eight lessons. Each lesson is centered around a classic literary selection—either a poem, or a retelling of a historical or literary narrative. Each lesson has five sub-lessons and a review section. The format is flexible, so that each sub-lesson may be completed in as little as one day, or at a more leisurely pace over several days. This may also be varied from lesson to lesson.

Lesson components include:

- ♦ Commonplace Book
- ♦ Prose & Poetry (literary analysis)
- ♦ Language Logic (word usage and grammar)
- ♦ Eloquent Expression (developing style)
- ♦ Classical Composition (retell a fable or parable)

You will be instructed to complete most written work in your Writer's Journal. You will also enter passages from literary selections into your Commonplace Book. The Appendix has instructions for setting up and using these composition books. These images indicate that the work is to be completed in one or the other:

Work to be completed on the computer is indicated by this image:

This image indicates grammar lessons to be completed in *Sentence Sense* (See Materials Needed for *Bards & Poets*).

Accompanying literature readings are indicated by these images:

Grammar terms and definitions will be added throughout the lessons, and should be reviewed regularly. There is a complete list of Grammar Terms & Definitions in the Appendix. Cottage Press also maintains a classroom at Quizlet (quizlet.com/class/1650721/) for *Poetics & Progym I*. From there, you may review, practice, quiz, and test online; you may also print flashcard sets there. This symbol indicates that flashcards are to be reviewed and quizzed, or that new flashcards are to be added.

Before you begin Lesson 1, gather and set up your materials. First, read each of these sections in the Appendix; then, follow the instructions to set up your notebooks and flashcard review system.

- ◆ Writer's Journal
- ◆ Commonplace Book
- ◆ Grammar Flashcards

Familiarize yourself with the layout of *Sentence Sense*:

A. Read the Preface and Introduction.

B. Study the Table of Contents.

C. Turn to each of the five chapters and get a bird's eye view of the content of each.

Lesson 1

ℭℜ

The Dog and His Master's Dinner

from Aesop's Fables, A New Revised Version From Original Sources

A Dog had been taught to take his master's dinner to him every day. As he smelled the good things in the basket, he was sorely tempted to taste them, but he resisted the temptation and continued day after day to carry the basket faithfully. One day all the dogs in the neighborhood followed him with longing eyes and greedy jaws, and tried to steal the dinner from the basket. At first the faithful dog tried to run away from them, but they pressed him so close that at last he stopped to argue with them. This was what the thieves desired, and they soon ridiculed him to that extent that he said: "Very well, I will divide with you," and he seized the best piece of chicken in the basket, and left the rest for the others to enjoy.

He who stops to parley with temptation, will be very likely to yield.

ℭℜ

Lesson 1.1

Prose & Poetry

AESOP AND HIS FABLES

Aesop was a Greek storyteller who lived sometime around 620-564 B.C. According to the ancient Greek historian, Herodotus, Aesop was a slave. As a reward for his wit and wisdom, Aesop's master gave him his freedom. To further his learning, Aesop visited the rulers of many countries, especially those who were known to be patrons of learning. His keen wit is reputed to have caused his death at Delphi. He so offended the people there that they hurled him from a rock into the sea.

The characters in Aesop's fables are often *anthropomorphic* animals—those who speak, act, and have the characteristics of people, while still retaining their animal traits. Fable plots are brief and often conclude with simple, commonsense truths that are usually called morals (or proverbs). Aesop's fables are so famous that they are often quoted or alluded to in literature. For example, a liar is commonly referred to as someone who cries wolf, as in Aesop's fable *The Shepherd Boy and the Wolf.*

LITERARY ELEMENTS OF THE FABLE

The steps listed here for studying the literary elements of a fable or narrative will be familiar to *Bards & Poets* students. We will be building on this basic list of questions throughout *Poetics & Progym* as we study literary selections in depth.

1 **Read**
   ♦ Listen carefully as your teacher reads the selection aloud. **Delight** in the story.

2 **Inquire**
   ♦ Does the **title** give any hint as to the content or message of the story? If this story was published by the author in a larger book or an anthology, does that title give any hint?

◆ Discuss the meaning of these words in the context of the story: *temptation, parley*
◆ Are there any unfamiliar persons, places, or things mentioned in the narrative? Discuss these with your teacher.
◆ Was there any part of the narrative you did not understand? If so, discuss this with your teacher and classmates.

3 Observe the Content

◆ **Setting** When and where does this story take place?
◆ **Characters** Who is (are) the main character(s) in this story?
◆ **Conflict** What is the main problem or crisis for the character(s)?
◆ **Resolution** Is the problem solved? If so, how? If not, why not?
◆ **Point of View** Who is telling the story? Is it first-person or third-person?
◆ **Figures** Look for figures of speech and figures of description. (see Appendix for the list of figures taught in *Poetics & Progym*). Why did the author choose these particular figures?

4 Investigate the Context

◆ Identify the story's **Literary Genre**
  ▪ **Genre by literary period** – In what century (time period) and country was the work written?
  ▪ **Genre by narrative category** – Is this narrative primarily **non-fiction** (a story that really happened) or **fiction** (a story told as if it really happened)?

5 Connect the Thoughts

◆ Does this story remind you of other stories with similar plots, messages, or characters?
◆ Does this story remind you of any proverbs or other well-known quotations? If so, make a note to enter these in your Commonplace Book once it is set up in Lesson 1.5.

Commonplace Book

6 Profit and Delight

◆ **Delight What are the sources** of delight in this story?
◆ **Wisdom What wisdom** does this story furnish? Aesop's fables had a very clear message, usually stated at the end of the fable as the moral. Discuss the moral of this fable.
◆ **Read** a portion of the narrative aloud to your teacher with expression and with proper pauses.

PROSE & POETRY HANDBOOK

Every *Poetics & Progym* student will construct a Prose & Poetry Handbook. This is a self-made reference book covering all of the most important concepts of our literature and composition studies. Many lessons in this book will include instructions for adding information to this book under the various headings we will create today. Take care with this book and keep it neat and organized; it will serve you for many years of literature and composition study, even in college and beyond.

🏵 Set up your Prose & Poetry Handbook. You will need a sewn composition book with 100 leaves.

1. Number the pages of your Prose & Poetry Handbook in the upper right corner from 1-100. *Number only the right hand pages.* The left hand pages are left blank for extra space in case you need to add more notes in the future.

2. The Prose & Poetry Handbook has four main divisions. Centered in the top wide margin, write these division names in large capital letters on the page indicated. Embellish these headers if you wish, but do not write below the top line. Mark each of these sections with a removable post-it note or flag for easy navigation.

PAGE #	DIVISION HEADER
1	RHETORIC
30	LITERATURE
55	POETRY
70	FIGURES

Take a minute now to turn to the Appendix and locate the example Prose & Poetry Handbook pages that model the formatted notes and information you will add to your own handbook. These are provided to make the task of constructing your handbook easier. Please do not use these to simply copy the pages all at once, but add the information as you are instructed throughout the course, so that you have context and will better understand what you are writing down.

WHAT IS LITERATURE?

Literature, belles-lettres, and *letters* (all) refer to artistic writings worthy of being remembered. In the broadest sense, literature includes any type of writings on any subject . . . usually, however, it means the body of artistic writings of a country or period that are characterized by beauty of expression and form and by universality of intellectual and emotional appeal.[1]

Middle English *litterature* < Old French < Latin *litteratura,* "writing, learning" < *litteratus* "learned, literate"[2]

The ancient author Horace wrote an instruction manual for poets and playwrights entitled *Ars Poetica* (The Art of Poetry). He said, "Poets wish either to profit *(instruct)* or to delight." His use of the word *poetry* is similar to our use of the word *literature* today. All worthy literature ultimately grants us both **delight** and **wisdom**, as it points our souls to truth, goodness, and beauty. Authors and poets through the ages have echoed Horace's words. One of the most beautiful expressions is this:

[Literature][3] is a fountain forever overflowing with the waters of wisdom and delight. — Percy Bysshe Shelley, *A Defence of Poetry*

Make the entries indicated below in the Literature division of your Prose & Poetry Handbook (P&P). The page number where the items are to be added is listed in the format P&P X (*X = page number*). Enter both of these at the top of the page, leaving additional lines for future lessons. Remember, you will find example pages for the P&P Handbook in the Appendix with all of the information you need to add.

Prose & Poetry Handbook

- ◆ Literature definition and etymology, P&P 30.
- ◆ Shelley quote, P&P 30. Whenever you are instructed to copy a quote, make sure you use quotation marks and attribute the quote.

LITERARY CONTEXT

The **context** in which any work of literature was written give many clues to how we should understand and interpret it. The literary context includes the work's **title, author,** and **rhetorical situation**.

Always begin with the **title** that the author gave to his work. This may give some clues to the author's purpose or message. When you are presented with a work of literature, it is well to learn something about the **author**. Research the author's **origin**, including his or her ancestors and/or homeland. Research the **historical time period** in which the author lived. Research the people,

---

1 Literature. *Random House Unabridged Dictionary of American English,* 2019, *s.v. "literature."*
2 *The American Heritage Dictionary of the English Language,* 1975, *s.v. "literature."*
3 Shelley's original "A great poem" is here replaced by "Literature." In this work, he is discussing the great literary works of the past, most of which were poems; this substitution fits the spirit of his *Defence of Poetry.*

events, books, and ideas that were **influences** on the author and his/her message. For a retelling or a translation, consider both the original author and the person doing the retelling/translating.

🏆 Enter the following item in the Literature Section.

♦ Literature, P&P 30: Subtitle LITERARY CONTEXT and the first two elements Title and Author.

LITERARY GENRE

The word **genre** means type or kind. Classifying things is something we humans love to do—after all, it was the first job man was given in the Garden. The larger category of literature itself is often divided into the very broad genres of **poetry** and **prose**. But there are many other ways to classify a literary work. One very common way to classify literature is by its **literary period**, such as ancient Greek or late nineteenth century American. As we have seen, understanding the historical context helps us better understand the work itself. One way to classify literature is to simply name the century or time period, and the country of origin. For example, Homer's *Odyssey* is Ancient Greek literature. But the selection at the beginning of this lesson is taken from a late 19th century American summary of that Ancient Greek work. In speaking about *The Story of the Odyssey*, both of these classifications are accurate.

The genre of a literary work may be based on:

- ♦ Broad Categories
    - Prose & Poetry
    - Fiction & Non-Fiction
    - Nation of Origin and Historical Time Period
- ♦ Specific Categories
    - Language
    - Subject Matter
    - Style

🏆 Enter the following items in the Literature section.

♦ Literary Genre, P&P 31: Subtitle LITERARY GENRE, then Braod Categories and Specific Categories with their subpoints.

INTRODUCTION TO HOMER'S ODYSSEY – THE AGE OF FABLE

Homer's *Iliad* and *Odyssey* are foundational to all of western literature.

This is why we have chosen his *Odyssey* as the primary literary selection for *Poetics & Progym I*.

We will savor it slowly, one book at a time, beginning in Lesson 3.

We recommend that you read *The Age of Fable* by Thomas Bulfinch before beginning *Poetics & Progym I* (see Recommended Literature, p. vii) to give a firm foundation to understanding Homer's *Odyssey*. *Age of Fable* is available at gutenberg.org, so if you do not have your own copy, the required chapters can be accessed there for free.

Nota Bene: Bulfinch uses the Roman names for the gods. Throughout the book, when he introduces a new god or goddess, he gives the Greek name in parentheses. Every scholar needs to be familiar with both names. *D'Aulaire's Book of Greek Myths* has a beautiful listing in the back of the book. If you need help with mastering these, search Quizlet for a set of flashcards.

⚜ Read or review the chapters indicated below in *The Age of Fable* by Thomas Bulfinch.

♦ Chapter XXVII: The Trojan War—The Iliad

♦ Chapter XXVIII: The Fall of Troy—Menelaus and Helen— Agamemnon, Orestes, and Electra

⚜ Discuss this week's reading with your teacher. Narrate the main action of the selections, and discuss any parts you did not understand.

Lesson 1.2

Language Logic

GRAMMAR TERMS & DEFINITIONS: REVIEW PARTS OF SPEECH

For students who completed *Bards & Poets*, the grammar concepts assigned in the first few lessons of *Poetics & Progym I* will be review. *Sentence Sense* from Cottage Press provides explanations and examples of the grammar terms and definitions covered in all levels of Cottage Press Language Arts. Grammar Terms to Master are available in the free online Quizlet classroom (see Recommended Resources in the Introduction).

⚜ Grammar Terms to Master: Parts of Speech (Review from *Bards & Poets*). In the online Quizlet classroom, review or print flashcards from Parts of Speech – *Bards & Poets* Review. You will also find a list of these in the *Poetics & Progym I* Appendix. You may use these to make your own flashcards, if you wish.

- ◆ Parts of Speech
- ◆ Noun, Noun Classes, Noun Properties, Property – Person, Property – Gender, Property – Number
- ◆ Pronoun, Pronoun Classes, Pronoun Properties, Antecedent
- ◆ Verb, Verb Classes by Use, Verb Classes by Form, Verb Properties, Verb Tenses, Auxiliaries, Linking Verbs
- ◆ Verbal, Verbal Classes
- ◆ Adjective, Adjective Classes
- ◆ Adverb
- ◆ Preposition, Common Prepositions
- ◆ Conjunction, Conjunction Classes
- ◆ Interjection

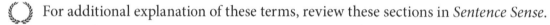

For additional explanation of these terms, review these sections in *Sentence Sense*.

I. Etymology – The Parts of Speech

- ◆ The Parts of Speech – An Introduction
- ◆ 1.1-1.6 Nouns
- ◆ 2.1-2.4, 2.5A, 2.6, 2.7, 2.8A Pronouns
- ◆ 3.1-3.5, 3.6A, 3.7A-3.7H, 3.8 Verbs
- ◆ 3.11A-3.11B Verbals
- ◆ 4.1-4.3 Adjectives
- ◆ 5.1 Adverbs
- ◆ 6.1A, 6.2 Prepositions
- ◆ 7.1-7.3A Conjunctions
- ◆ 8.1-8.2 Interjections

V. Exercises (Note that these Exercises, located in the final section of *Sentence Sense*, are taken from the original lessons in *Harvey's Revised Grammar*. Answers to all exercises assigned in *Poetics & Progym I* are found in the Teaching Helps Lesson where they are assigned.)

- ◆ Optional Review in recognizing the Parts of Speech: Complete the following exercises: 19.5, 19.6, 19.8, 19.9, 19.10, 19.11. An Answer Key for these exercises is found in the *Poetics & Progym I* Teaching Helps Appendix.

Lesson 1.3

Eloquent Expression

COPIA

The great 15th century classical scholar Erasmus of Rotterdam was one of the most influential rhetoricians[4] of the late Middle Ages. He stressed the importance of developing **copia**, by which he meant an abundant stockpile of language, ready at hand. In his book *Copia: Foundations of the Abundant Style*, Erasmus illustrated the concept of **copia** by showing how many different ways could express the idea contained in the simple sentence *Your letter pleased me greatly.* He rewrote that sentence in other words more than 150 times. Here are a just a few examples:

> Your letter was very sweet to me. By your letter I was mightily pleased. Your lines conveyed to me the greatest joy. I was singularly delighted by your epistle. How overjoyed I was by your letter! Heavens, what causes for joy your letter did provide! I rejoiced greatly at your letter. Your missive showered a wealth of gladness upon me. Not unpleasing to me was your letter. Your by no means disagreeable letter has come to me. Your writing, in no way displeasing to me, has come.[5]

Not all of his rewritten sentences are excellent, clear expressions, but the exercise itself is still beneficial, even if some of the variations are less than eloquent. Writing is a process, and in the process, all writers sometimes write duds! The important thing is to practice constantly and diligently.

In Cottage Press *Bards & Poets*, you learned quite a few devices for employing copia in your own writing. We divided these devices into into broad categories: **Copia of Words** and **Copia of Construction**. Copia of Words devices substitute equivalent words or phrases into the original sentence or add words for clarity and description, while preserving the basic meaning of the original sentence. Copia of Construction devices change the grammatical pattern or structure of a sentence, while also preserving the original meaning. In both cases, the end result is a **Paraphrase** of the original. In this lesson we will review Copia of Words. For now, you will just make a list of the devices, and then we will review a few of the most basic ones. Do not worry if you cannot remember or have not yet learned all of these, as we will review all of these in upcoming lessons. But do feel free to use this list as a prompt for revising sentences in your writing.

---

4 A rhetorician is one who studies and practices the effective use of language.
5 Erasmus, *On Copia of Words and Ideas*, 38-42.

❧ In the *Poetics & Progym I* Appendix, study Copia of Words on the Eloquent Expression Through Copia chart.

❧ Enter the following item in the Rhetoric Section.

Prose & Poetry Handbook

◆ Copia of Words, P&P 26: Title CANON OF STYLE (ELOCUTION), subtitle COPIA and then the definition of copia from Erasmus. Write the next subtitle COPIA OF WORDS, then copy the chart from the Appendix. Do not copy the Lesson #s where we will review or learn each device.

COPIA OF WORDS: VOCABULARY STUDY

Excellent writers typically have a wealth of words in the storehouse of the their minds. Our first task in developing eloquence of expression is to observe and analyze this wealth by studying **vocabulary** taken from the literary selection. If you have not already done so, acquaint yourself with the organization of your print dictionary.

❧ Review and discuss Vocabulary Study in the Appendix with your teacher. When instructed to complete vocabulary studies, work in your Writer's Journal.

Writer's Journal

❧ Choose several words from the literary selection at the beginning of this lesson to study. One of the words should be *parley*. The others may be words that are unfamiliar to you, or they may be words that you find interesting or intriguing. For *parley* and at least one other word, complete all of the Vocabulary Study steps (see Appendix).

COPIA OF WORDS: SYNONYMS AND ANTONYMS

These are foundational treasures for your "storehouse" of copia. Erasmus used quite a few synonyms even in our short sampling of his sentences. For example, in place of the word *letter*, he used the **synonyms** *missive, epistle, note, lines, communication, word*s, and several others. Several of Erasmus's example sentences also use antonyms in order to express the idea of how pleasing the letter was to him, Erasmus takes the antonyms *unpleasing, disagreeable*, and *displeasing*, and he **negates** them. This is actually a type of **litotes**, a figure of speech that we will study in *Poetics & Progym II*.

Antonyms used in this way will not always provide the best sentences, so it is a device you should use sparingly in your writing. However, it is an excellent exercise for building copia.

To find a synonym or an antonym for a particular word, start by making a list of those that come to mind ("brainstorming"). When you have exhausted your own supply, look for more in the dictionary and/or the thesaurus. Look up synonyms for your "brainstormed" synonyms and antonyms also. Aim to have at least five or six strong synonyms and/or antonyms for each word—this is copia! As you write your own compositions, you will be glad to have this ready supply of synonyms at your command.

In choosing synonyms and antonyms, you should consider both the word's **denotation** (dictionary meaning), and its **connotation** (suggested or implied meaning based on cultural, historical, or emotional associations). For example, the words *frugal* and *cheap* are adjectives with similar denotations, but you would want to be careful in choosing which one to use to describe your friend! *Frugal* carries the connotation of ecomony and prudence, while *cheap* connotes stinginess and miserliness. As Mark Twain once observed:

> "The difference between the right word and the almost right word is the difference between lightning and a lightning bug."

COPIA OF WORDS: DIALOGUE TAGS

Choosing **dialogue tags** is a further application of copia with synonyms. *Said* and *asked* are the most frequently used dialogue tags, and therefore they are comfortable (or even "invisible") to most readers; good writers use them freely. But the occasional use of a synonym for *said* or *asked* can bring extra emphasis to a direct quotation. Study the sentences below. Using different tags creates a slightly different feeling in each sentence. Writing dialogue with varied tags requires you to exercise your imagination. You may even want to get up from your desk, and act out the scene, and put yourself in the place of the person speaking. Then, choose your dialogue tag considering the likely facial expression, body language, and voice inflection of the speaker.

Copy each sentence below in your Writer's Journal. Paraphrase each using synonyms and antonyms, and varying dialogue tags. You should use more than one device in each sentence.

Writer's Journal

1. As he smelled the good things in the basket, he was sorely tempted to taste them, but he resisted the temptation and continued day after day to carry the basket faithfully.

2. At first the faithful dog tried to run away from them, but they pressed him so close that at last he stopped to argue with them.

3. They soon ridiculed him to that extent that he said, "Very well, I will divide with you."

4. "He who stops to parley with temptation will be very likely to yield," said Aesop.

COPIA OF WORDS: NOUNS

You will often need several different ways to refer to the same person, place, thing, or idea in your writing. Look at the various ways the author refers to the blacksmith and the dog in this passage:

> A Blacksmith had a little Dog, which used to sleep when his master was at work, but he was very wide awake indeed when it was time for meals. One day his master pretended to be disgusted at this, and when he had thrown him a bone as usual, he said, "What on earth is the good of a lazy cur like you? When I am hammering away at my anvil, you just curl up and go to sleep: but no sooner do I stop for a mouthful of food than you wake up and wag your tail to be fed." — Aesop's Fables

Writer's Journal

With your teacher, choose one paragraph from a narrative or essay you wrote in your younger years that could be improved with varied, clear, specific, descriptive nouns and pronouns. Copy the original, and then revise the paragraph accordingly. (This exercise is optional for students who have successfully completed *Bards & Poets*. Check with your teacher to see if this is required for you.)

COPIA OF WORDS: VERBS

Choose verbs that are vivid, precise, strong, and fitting. Consider the verbs (and verbals) in this beautifully descriptive passage:

> In the valley of the river Nile, bathed in glittering sunshine, lay the ancient land of Egypt, a narrow strip of green in the midst of the sands of the desert. From the tall mountains of Central Africa, the Nile cut its way between tall cliffs that glowed rose-pink and lilac, flecked with passing shadows, and lifting clear cut outlines against a bright blue sky. Six times the river, flowing down on its long way to the sea, halted in its course to swirl in foaming cataracts around obstructing rocks, jagged heaps of black granite, that lay as though hurled by giants across the bed of the stream. — Olive Beaupre Miller, *A Picturesque Tale of Progress, Volume I*

With your teacher, choose one paragraph from a narrative or essay you wrote in your younger years that could be improved with vivid, strong, precise, fitting verbs. Copy the original, and then revise the paragraph accordingly. (This exercise is optional for students who have successfully completed *Bards & Poets*. Check with your teacher to see if this is required for you.)

Writer's Journal

COPIA OF WORDS: MODIFIERS

Adjectives (including participles) can bring additional clarity and description to your sentences. You may wish to describe a character's emotions, appearance, virtues, or vices, and what kind of moral character he or she has. Or you may wish to add descriptive details about a place, thing, or idea. Once you have come up with a few adjectives, check the dictionary for synonyms (or antonyms!)

Adverbs can bring better understanding of a particular action in a story by helping us see how? or when? or to what extent? or where? the action occurred. In your own writing, look at the verbs you have used, and think of appropriate adverbs that could help make the action of your story more clear or interesting. Once you have a short list, check the dictionary for synonyms.

A word of caution: Do not use adverbs as a substitute for strong verbs. Before adding adverbs, check to see if you have used strong and vivid verbs. If you find that you have a good number of adverbs in your writing naturally, you will probably need to make sure you use them more sparingly.

 With your teacher, choose one paragraph from a narrative or essay you wrote in your younger years that could be improved with modifiers. Copy the original, and then revise the paragraph accordingly. (This exercise is optional for students who have successfully completed *Bards & Poets*. Check with your teacher to see if this is required for you.)

Writer's Journal

Lesson 1.4

Classical Composition

THE ART OF RHETORIC

One of the primary aims of Cottage Press Language Arts is to instruct students in the art of expressing true, beautiful, and virtuous thoughts in winsome words. This is no new idea or aim— it is the essence of the ancient Greek art of rhetoric.

Rhetoric (literally, *art of the orator*) is the faculty of discovering in a given case the available means of persuasion. — Aristotle[6]

THE CANONS OF RHETORIC

The ancient Greeks divided rhetoric into five parts, called **canons** (make sure you spell it with only one *n*, or the results could be explosive!): **Invention (inventio)**, **Arrangement (dispositio)**, **Elocution (elocutio)**, **Memory (memoria)**, and **Delivery (actio/pronuntiatio)**. We will focus most heavily on the first three, as the last two are more specifically directed towards public speaking.

Those first three canons simplify the process of writing. They address the three things every writer must consider when pen is put to paper:

Invention—*what am I going to say?* The word itself is derived from the Latin *invenire*, literally *to come upon* or *to find*. Have you had the agonizing experience of staring at a blank piece of paper (or a computer screen) with no idea what to write? Maybe "what am I going to say?" has been a doleful lament for you instead of a delightful quest. If so, we aim to change that! **Invention is discovering the important ideas**.

Arrangement—*in what order?* Once you have your ideas in place, you are faced with more decisions. What should come first? What comes next? How should you end your composition so that your reader remembers your main point? **Arrangement is establishing the optimal order**.

Elocution (Style)—*in what manner?* Every lesson in Cottage Press Language Arts begins with a worthy selection from literature or history or poetry or Scripture as models to imitate and/or analyze. These excellent prose and poetry selections will imprint elegant patterns of language, shaping and encouraging your own eloquence. **Elocution is employing winsome words**.

The canons of rhetoric will help you communicate important ideas (Invention) in the optimal order (Arrangement) with winsome words (Eloquence).

THE PROGYMNASMATA

The Greek **progymnasmata** (literally "exercises before") are fourteen successive exercises designed to train students in elegant and effective rhetoric. As they worked through these exercises progressively, ancient Greek and Roman scholars analyzed and imitated great orators and authors of their past. With the knowledge gained from each level, they would then write their own compositions. The ultimate goal of this training was to produce persons well able to discuss and defend truth, goodness, and beauty in the public forum.

6 This definition combines the translations of Aristotle's *Rhetoric* by Robert Rhys and John Henry Freese.

All fourteen exercises together are referred to as the **progymnasmata** (plural); each individual exercise is a **progymnasma** (singular). Ancient teachers of rhetoric held various opinions on the number and names of the progymasmata and the order in which they should be taught. Most modern curricula based on the progymnasmata agree on fourteen, although the names of each and the order may vary somewhat. Alternate names for each progymnasma are indicated in parentheses.

- **Fable** (Mythos, Logos) – retell and amplify a short fictional story illustrating a moral point
- **Narrative** – retell an account or story, either fictional or non-fictional
- **Anecdote** (Chreia) – elaborate a brief remembrance of a person's words or action (Quintilian) following a format of specific topics
- **Proverb** (Maxim) – elaborate an adage following a format of specific topics
- **Refutation** – refute a fable or narrative as "unclear, implausible, impossible, illogical or inconsistent, inappropriate, and/or inexpedient"[7]
- **Confirmation** – confirm a fable or narrative as clear, plausible, possible, logical or consistent, appropriate, and expedient
- **Common-Place** (Common Topics, Topos) – either condemn a certain type of criminal (such as a murderer, a tyrant, or a thief), or commend a certain type of benefactor (such as a statesman, a patron, or a war hero) following a format of specific topics
- **Encomium** (Praise) – laud a subject (a person, a place, a thing, or an idea) following a format of specific topics
- **Invective** (Vituperation, Blame) – censure a subject (a person, a place, a thing, or an idea) following a format of specific topics
- **Comparison** (Synchrises) – combine two Encomia, two Invectives, or an Encomium and an Invective, in consideration of two subjects (persons, places, things, or ideas)
- **Speech-in-Character** (Characterization, Personification) – portray a particular person (or place, or thing, or idea) speaking in a specific circumstance
- **Description** (Ekphrasis) – describe something vividly, bringing it "before the eyes" of the reader[8]
- **Thesis** (Theme) – logically examine a general proposition, including social, political, religious, or theoretical (speculative) issues
- **Law** – defend or attack a law (proposed, current, historical, or fictional)

The Progym and the first three canons of rhetoric work in perfect harmony:

Invention—*what am I going to say?* The content of each exercise in the Progym is fixed, so

---

7 Gibson, *Libanius' Progymnasmata*, 107.
8 Gideon O. Burton, "Description," Silva Rhetoricae, http://rhetoric.byu.edu/

the question is already answered for you in each assignment. Throughout the exercises of the Progym, you will write about ideas that matter, and that incline your affections to those things that are true, good, and beautiful.

Arrangement—*in what order?* The structure of each exercise in the Progym is also prescribed, so again, the question is already answered. By following well-fashioned ancient outlines, you will develop orderly thinking, logical arguments, and a cohesive whole, even as the exercises become longer and more complex.

Elocution (Style)—*in what manner?* The personal style of an apprentice under a great master will come forth in time, but that style will be informed by the brilliance of the master. In the same way, your own style, or voice, will come forth in due time, but it will reflect the great masters under whom you have apprenticed. Immersion in well-written and enduring works of the past fosters eloquence.

Fable & Song focused on the Fable exercise; *Bards & Poets* focused on Narrative. In this lesson, we will review the Fable exercise, and in the next few lessons, we will review the Narrative exercise before going on the the Proverb and Anecdote exercises that will be the main focus of *Poetics & Progym I*. The other exercises will be taught in successive levels of *Poetics & Progym*.

Enter the following items in the Rhetoric Section.

Prose & Poetry Handbook

- Rhetoric Definition, P&P 1: Aristotle's definition of rhetoric (with attribution)
- The Canons of Rhetoric, P&P 1: Subtitle CANONS OF RHETORIC in capital letters. Record the names of the five canons, along with their Latin names.

Lesson 1.5

Reflection & Review

Commonplace Book

COMMONPLACE BOOK

Review instructions for using your Commonplace Book in the Appendix. Each week, there will be at least one entry in your Commonplace Book, usually from your literature reading. Enter in your Commonplace Book:

- a favorite passage or two from the reading assigned in this lesson in *The Age of Fable*

BOOK OF CENTURIES

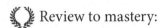 For more information on the Book of Centuries, and how to add entries, see Materials
Needed for *Poetics & Progym I* in the Introduction. Record in your Book of Centuries:

   ◆ Aesop, Horace, Percy Bysshe Shelley, Erasmus of Rotterdam

MEMORY WORK

In this section of each lesson, you will be prompted to review terms and definitions that you must
memorize. For the first several lessons, these will be grammar terms only. In later lessons, we will
add figures of speech as well. You may conduct your review in the free online Quizlet classroom
(see Recommended Resources in the Introduction), or with physical flashcards printed from the
classroom or constructed on your own. For grammar terms, you may use the list in the Appendix
to construct these; for figures of speech, use your Prose & Poetry Handbook.

Review to mastery:

   ◆   Parts of Speech – *Bards & Poets* Review

CR

from THE STORY OF THE ODYSSEY
by Alfred John Church

Three thousand years ago the world was still young. The western
continent was a huge wilderness, and the greater part of Europe was
inhabited by savage and wandering tribes. Only a few nations at the
eastern end of the Mediterranean and in the neighbouring parts of Asia
had learned to dwell in cities, to use a written language, to make laws
for themselves, and to live in a more orderly fashion. Of these nations
the most brilliant was that of the Greeks, who were destined in war,
in learning, in government, and in the arts, to play a great part in the
world, and to be the real founders of our modern civilization. While they
were still a rude people, they had noble ideals of beauty and bravery, of
duty and justice. Even before they had a written language, their singers
had made songs about their heroes and their great deeds; and later these
songs, which fathers had taught to children, and these children to their
children, were brought together into two long and wonderful poems,
which have ever since been the delight of the world, the *Iliad* and the
Odyssey.

The *Iliad* is the story of the siege of Ilium, or Troy, on the western
coast of Asia Minor. Paris, son of the king of Troy, had enticed Helen,
the most beautiful of Grecian women, and the wife of a Grecian king,
to leave her husband's home with him; and the kings and princes of the
Greeks had gathered an army and a fleet and sailed across the Aegean
Sea to rescue her. For ten years they strove to capture the city. According
to the fine old legends, the gods themselves took a part in the war, some
siding with the Greeks, and some with the Trojans. It was finally through
Ulysses, a famous Greek warrior, brave and fierce as well as wise and
crafty, that the Greeks captured the city.

The second poem, the *Odyssey*, tells what befell Ulysses, or Odysseus,
as the Greeks called him, on his homeward way. Sailing from Troy with

his little fleet of ships, which were so small that they used oars as well
as sails, he was destined to wander for ten years longer before he could
return to his rocky island of Ithaca, on the west shore of Greece, and to
his faithful wife, Penelope.

He had marvellous adventures, for the gods who had opposed the
Greeks at Troy had plotted to bring him ill-fortune. Just as his ships
were safely rounding the southern cape of Greece, a fierce storm took
them out of their course, and bore them to many strange lands—lands
of giants, man-eating monsters, and wondrous enchantments of which
you will delight to read. Through countless perils the resolute wanderer
forced his way, losing ship after ship from his little fleet, and companion
after companion from his own band, until he reached home friendless and
alone, and found his palace, his property, and his family all in the power
of a band of greedy princes. These he overcame by his cunning and his
strength, and his long trials were ended.

As you read these ancient tales, you must forget what knowledge
you have of the world, and think of it as the Greeks did. It was only a
little part of the world that they knew at all,—the eastern end of the
Mediterranean,—but even that seemed to them a great and marvellous
region. Beyond its borders were strange and mysterious lands, in which
wonders of all kinds were found, and round all ran the great world-river,
the encircling stream of Ocean.

In the mountains of Olympus, to the northward, lived the gods. There
was Zeus, greatest of all, the god of thunder and the wide heavens; Hera,
his wife; Apollo, the archer god; Athene, the wise and clever goddess;
Poseidon, who ruled the sea; Aphrodite, the goddess of love; Hephaestus,
the cunning workman; Ares, the god of war; Hermes, the swift
messenger; and others still, whom you will learn to know as you read. All
these were worshipped by men with prayer and sacrifice; and, as in the
early legends of many races, the gods often took the shape of men and
women; they had their favourites and those whom they hated; and they
ruled the fate of mortals as they chose.

If you let yourselves be beguiled into this old, simple way of regarding
earth and heaven, you will not only love these ancient tales yourself, but
you will see why, for century after century, they have been the longest

loved and the best loved of all tales— beloved by old and young, by men and women and children. For they are hero-tales,—tales of war and adventure, tales of bravery and nobility, tales of the heroes that mankind, almost since the beginning of time, have looked to as ideals of wisdom and strength and beauty.

Lesson 2.1

Prose & Poetry

THE STORY OF THE ODYSSEY

In the ancient world, and even the modern, all literary roads seem to somehow lead to Troy, or at least pass through it. The *Iliad* details the final year of the Trojan War. The *Odyssey* primarily tells the tale of Odysseus's journey home after the war—a relatively short trip that turns into a ten year "odyssey." Some of the most famous tales from ancient Greece are found in the lines of this epic poem. The Trojan War occured sometime around 1200 B.C. Homer's epics date from around 850 B.C., and most scholars agree that these tales were passed down from generation to generation by the bards and poets of ancient Greece. Homer is so influential that he is sometimes simply called The Poet.

The engaging introduction to Homer's epics at the beginning of this lesson was written by Reverend Alfred J. Church (1829-1912), a professor of Latin in Victorian London. His first published works were translations of Latin authors for a scholarly audience. In the 1870's he began to write stories from the ancient and medieval world for a more general audience, including intermediate and high school level students. These proved so popular that he began a writing career spanning thirty years and producing more than fifty books. Church's love for history and attention to detail, coupled with his engaging narrative style, have delighted and educated generations of children and adults alike.

 The selection at the beginning of this lesson was written for students by late 19th century British classical scholar Alfred Church. Read and enjoy!

THE AGE OF FABLE

We recommend Leland Ryken's *Christian Guide to the Classics* for Homer's *The Odyssey*, or a comparable literary guide (see *Poetics & Progym I* Introduction). Usually, your teacher will be the one reading this commentary, to help guide your discussions. But for this lesson, you should read the assigned section for yourself.

🏅 Read or review the chapters indicated below in *The Age of Fable* by Thomas Bulfinch.

♦ Chapter XXIX: Adventures of Ulysses: Lotus Eaters—Cyclopses—Læstrygonians—Circe—Sirens—Scylla and Charybdis—Calypso

♦ Chapter XXX: Adventures of Ulysses: Phæacians—Fate of the Suitors

🏅 Read Ryken's guide to *The Odyssey*: The Book at a Glance—The Author and His Faith—*The Odyssey* as Epic (or research the characteristics of epic poetry).

🏅 Discuss this week's reading with your teacher. Narrate the main action of the selections, and discuss any parts you did not understand.

WHAT IS NARRATIVE?

> Narrative is language descriptive of things that have happened, or as though they have happened. — Aelius Theon, Ancient Greek orator and teacher[1]

In other words, narrative is just another name for a *story*. A fable, therefore, is included under the broader category of narrative. Synonyms for **narrative** include *tale*, *account*, or *chronicle*. Narrative is distinct in its purpose from **exposition**, writing that is intended mainly to explain or describe something. Essays, articles, speeches and sermons, technical manuals, and travel guides are types of expository writing. Yet even most of these types of exposition incorporate narrative in some way. This is one reason that narrative is the first building block of writing. Master the art of narrative, and you are well on your way to being an excellent writer.

🏅 Enter the following item in the Literature Division.

Prose & Poetry Handbook

♦ Narrative, P&P 34: Title NARRATIVE, then copy Theon's definition of narrative, synonyms for narrative, and distinction from narrative with examples of exposition.

1. Kennedy. *Progymnasmata*, p. 136

NON-FICTION NARRATIVE

Language descriptive of things that have happened. — Theon

Non-fiction is usually written by an eyewitness or retold from an eyewitness account. Non-fiction is comprised of actual people (characters), actual times and places (setting), and actual actions, events, and dialogues (plot). To be truly classified as non-fiction, a story should contain no fictional elements.

The purpose of non-fiction is to provide a factual account of something that has happened. Subcategories of non-fiction include:

- Biography
- Autobiography
- History
- Journalism (Narrative)

Enter the following items in the Literature division.

- Non-Fiction Narrative, P&P 35: Title NON-FICTION NARRATIVE. Copy Theon's definition (attributed); then list the five characteristics of non-fiction.
- Purpose of Non-Fiction, P&P 35
- Subcategories of Non-Fiction Narrative, P&P 35

Prose & Poetry
Handbook

FICTION NARRATIVE

"Language descriptive of things . . . as though they have happened." Theon

Fiction, on the other hand, is not strictly factual, but includes invented characters, invented settings, and/or invented plots, which the author will sometimes place right alongside historical characters, settings, and plots. Laurence Perrine divides fiction into two categories that correspond to the purpose of the work. The first is **escape**, "written purely for entertainement," and the second is **interpretative**, "written to broaden and deepen and sharpen our awareness of life . . . (to give) keener awareness of what it is to be a human being . . . " He carefully makes the point, however, that these are not two exclusive purposes, but two ends of a continuum. A particular work may fall anywhere along that continuum.[2]

2 Perrine, *Story and Structure*, 4.

Subgenres of fiction include:

- Fable
- Myth
- Legend
- Fairy Tale
- Historical Fiction
- Science Fiction
- Fantasy
- Allegory
- Novel

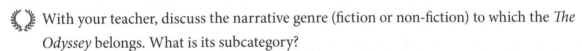 Enter the following items in the Literature Section.

Prose & Poetry
Handbook

- Fiction Narrative, P&P 36: Title Fiction Narrative, then copy Theon's definition (attributed); and then the four characteristics of fiction.
- Purpose of Fiction, P&P 36: Attribute these purposes to Perrine.
- Subgenres of Fiction Narrative, P&P 36

Nota Bene: Our definitions of fiction and non-fiction do not include the word *truth*. That is because works of fiction may (and often do) contain more truth than works intended to be non-fiction. This is a concept we will explore more fully in future levels of *Poetics & Progym*.

With your teacher, discuss the narrative genre (fiction or non-fiction) to which the *The Odyssey* belongs. What is its subcategory?

NARRATIVE AND THE CANONS OF RHETORIC

In Lesson 1.4, you learned that the canons of rhetoric help any author communicate important ideas (Invention) in the optimal order (Arrangement) with winsome words (Eloquence). Narrative is no exception to this. The following chart is a sort of bird's eye view showing how narrative and the canons of rhetoric are related. Some of these concepts have already been introduced. For the ones that are new to you, details are coming in future lessons, both in this book and in future levels of *Poetics & Progym*.

Invention
- Characters, Motivations (Person, Cause)
- Setting (Time, Place)

- ◆ Plot (Action, Manner)
- ◆ Theme (Message)
- ◆ Literary Devices

Arrangement

- ◆ Chronology—the order in which the story is told

Style

- ◆ Point of View
- ◆ Diction

Enter the following item in the Literature division.

Prose & Poetry Handbook

- ◆ Narrative and the Canons of Rhetoric, P&P 38:
  Title NARRATIVE & THE CANONS OF RHETORIC, then list
  Invention, Arrangement, and Style with their subpoints. Do
  not worry if you do not understand all of the terms now.

Lesson 2.2

Language Logic

GRAMMAR TERMS & DEFINITIONS: REVIEW SENTENCE TERMS

Grammar Terms to Master: Sentence Terms (Review from *Bards & Poets*). In the Quizlet
classroom, review or print flashcards from Sentence Terms – *Bards & Poets* Review. You will
also find a list of these in the *Poetics & Progym I* Appendix.

GRAMMAR FLASHCARDS

- ◆ Sentence, Subject, Predicate
- ◆ Declarative Sentence, Interrogative Sentence, Imperative Sentence, Exclamatory Sentence (Sentence Classes by Use)
- ◆ Phrase, Clause
- ◆ Principal Clause, Subordinate Clause
- ◆ Simple Sentence, Compound Sentence, Complex Sentence, Compound-Complex Sentence (Sentence Classes by Form)
- ◆ Capitalization Rules, Basic Comma Rules, Direct Quotation

For additional explanation and review of these terms, review these sections in *Sentence*

Sense.

II. Syntax – The Sentence

- ◆ 9.1A Sentence Definition
- ◆ 9.3, 9.4A, 9.5A Subject and Predicate
- ◆ 9.6A, 9.7A and 9.7B, 9.9, 9.11A, 9.12A Phrases, Clauses, Elements
- ◆ 9.14A, 9.15A Sentence Classification by Use and by Form
- ◆ 9.16A and 9.16B Quotations
- ◆ 11.1A and 11.1B, 11.2A and 11.2B, 11.3A and 11.3B Capitalization & Punctuation (also review 11.3C Rules I, II, X, and XI.

PARSING THE PARTS OF SPEECH

 Review this chapter in *Sentence Sense*. Beginning in the next lesson, you will have parsing exercises along with diagramming. If you are new to parsing, practice using the Harvey's exercises in the Appendix of *Poetics & Progym I* Teaching Helps (answer key included). Parse a few sentences orally each day until it becomes familiar.

IV. A Method of Parsing - Parsing the Parts of Speech

- ◆ 27.0 Steps to Parsing
- ◆ 27.1-27.9 Parsing Each Part of Speech (skip gray sections for now)
- ◆ 27.10 Examples of Parsing

Lesson 2.3

Eloquent Expression

FIGURES OF SPEECH

Figures of speech are a traditional subject of study for students of rhetoric. The sheer number of figures has given rise to various classification systems to keep them straight in the teeming brains of students and teachers. At Cottage Press, we follow the system set forth by Edward Corbett, with some additional categories adapted from *Silva Rhetoricae*, an excellent online resource provided by Dr. Gideon Burton (rhetoric.byu.edu).

The ancient teacher of rhetoric Quintilian defined a figure as "speech artfully varied" from our ordinary way of speaking or writing. Corbett's system divides figures broadly into **schemes** and **tropes**. Study this list showing the definitions, categories, and subdivisions of tropes and schemes:

Scheme: Artful variation from the common pattern or arrangement of words[3]

- ◆ Words
- ◆ Construction
    - ▪ Balance
    - ▪ Word Order
    - ▪ Omission
    - ▪ Repetition

Trope: Artful variation from the ordinary and principal meaning of a word[4]

- ◆ Comparison
- ◆ Wordplay
- ◆ Substitution
- ◆ Overstatement & Understatement
- ◆ Semantic Inversion

In the three levels of *Poetics & Progym*, you will learn almost fifty figures of speech slowly and steadily. *Bards & Poets* students will recognize about the first dozen or so, and then we will be adding a few new ones here in *Poetics & Progym I*.

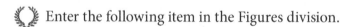 Enter the following item in the Figures division.

- ◆ Figures of Speech, P&P 70: Title FIGURES OF SPEECH, then copy Quintilian's definition. Add subtitle CLASSIFICATION OF FIGURES with the attribution information. Copy the subdivisions of Figures, definitions of scheme and trope, and then the chart showing categories and subcategories of each.

Prose & Poetry Handbook

FIGURE OF SPEECH – SIMILE

A **simile** is an explicit comparison between two things of unlike nature by using the words *like*, *as*, or *than*. For a writer, choosing an appropriate and engaging comparison is the "artful" part; expressing that comparison with the words *like*, *as*, or *than* is the "variation" part. We will classify **simile** as a **trope of comparison**.

3. Corbett, *Classical Rhetoric*, 424-458.
4. *Ibid*, 426.

My luve (love) is like a red, red rose. — Robert Burns

As the hart (deer) panteth after the water brooks, so panteth my soul after thee, O God.
— Psalm 42:1

. . . my soul waits for the Lord

more than watchmen for the morning,

more than watchmen for the morning. — Psalm 130:6

Pay attention to the context, though. Not every use of *like*, *as*, or *than* indicates a simile. Consider these non-similes: The girl likes her new shoes. (*Like* expresses action here, not a comparison.) The boy is as tall as his father. (*Boy* and *father* have a like nature— they both are people.) My dog runs faster than a cheetah. (*Dog* and *cheetah* have a like nature—they both are animals.)

Enter the following item in the Figures division of your Prose & Poetry Handbook.

Prose & Poetry Handbook

◆ Simile, P&P 83: Add category TROPES OF COMPARISON.
Add <u>Simile</u> with the definition and one example.

Lesson 2.4

Classical Composition

THE WRITING SEQUENCE

Composition is rarely a "one and done" thing. A three-step sequence is fairly standard practice for most compositions: plan, write, revise. Writing begins, before you put pen to paper for the actual composition, with a plan or outline for what you are going to say. After your composition is complete, you must revise. Your first draft will almost never be your final draft.

Follow this sequence, whether you are writing an academic essay, a personal letter, or a blog post. Aside from personal journaling and some electronic correspondence, there are few times when we should simply dash off some words on paper and be done with it.

WRITING SEQUENCE FOR POETICS & PROGYM

- ◆ Plan: Outline
- ◆ Write: First Draft
- ◆ Revise with your Editor's Pen
  - ✓ Big Picture
  - ✓ Zoom 5x: Paragraphs
  - ✓ Zoom 10x: Sentences
  - ✓ Fine Focus: Words

Notice that the Revise step is broken into smaller sequential steps. The photography theme here should help you "picture" the sequence. First, read over your composition, making sure you have said all that you mean to say; you are looking at the Big Picture. Next, zoom in a bit closer to look at paragraphs. Zoom in again to look at sentences. Finally, focus in on the fine details of spelling, grammar, and word choice. Following these steps in sequence will yield the best results with the least frustration (i.e., the sentence for which you just painstakingly chose the perfect word is completely dropped from the final composition).

PROGYMNASMA FABLE

A **fable** (also called **mythos** or **logos**) is a short fictional story illustrating a moral point. In the ancient Fable exercise, the student's task was to retell or paraphrase the fable in other words and to **amplify**, or expand, it. To amplify a fable, add **dialogue** (see Lesson 1.3) and **figures of description** (we studied five figures of description in *Bards & Poets*; we will be reviewing these in Lesson 6). Some teachers of rhetoric also required their students to **slant** the narrative in favor of one of the characters in the fable, and/or **abbreviate** the fable.

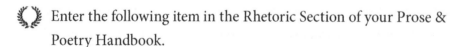

Prose & Poetry Handbook

Enter the following item in the Rhetoric Section of your Prose & Poetry Handbook.

- ◆ Invention/Arrangement, The Progymnasmata – Fable, P&P 10:
  Title CANONS OF INVENTION AND ARRANGEMENT.
  Add subtitle THE PROGYMNASMATA, and add FABLE
  (MYTHOS, LOGOS) with the definition of the Fable exercise,
  the three ways to retell the fable (amplify, slant, and abbreviate), with the subpoints for amplification.

PROGYMNASMA FABLE – AMPLIFY

🏵 Retell and amplify "The Dog and His Master's Dinner." Your final
version should be about one third to one half longer than the original
(Lesson 1).

A. Use the copia devices from Lesson 1.3 Eloquent Expression to
paraphrase the original fable. You may also refer to Eloquent
Expression Through Copia in the Appendix. These devices were
covered in *Bards & Poets*. Feel free to use any of these also.

B. Amplify by adding more dialogue and description in your retelling. You may review
the figures of description from *Bards & Poets* in Lesson 6.3 and use those, or simply add
appropriate descriptive detail.

C. Save and print your amplified fable.

EDITOR'S PEN: AMPLIFIED FABLE

🏵 Revise your fable using the checklist below. Work through the checklist once on your own,
and then a second time with your writing mentor, making notes on the print copy of your
fable. Transfer all additions and corrections from your print copy to the computer file. Save
and print the document.

Editor's Pen – The Big Picture

- ✓ All important plot elements included
- ✓ All characters represented correctly
- ✓ Sequence: *linear from the beginning*
- ✓ Length: *one-third to one-half times longer than original*

Editor's Pen – Zoom 5x: Paragraphs

- ✓ Formatting: *proper indentation*
- ✓ Length: *neither too wordy nor too short*
- ✓ Sentence class by use: *effective use*
- ✓ Sentence openers: *varied*
- ✓ Dialogue: *effective use*
- ✓ Verb Tense: *consistent*

✓ Pronouns clear: *easily identified antecedents*
✓ Person for Nouns & Pronouns: *3rd person except within dialogue*

Editor's Pen – Zoom 10x: Sentences

✓ Complete thought expressed
✓ Subject and predicate agree in number
✓ Correct capitalization and punctuation
  ◆ No comma splices!

Editor's Pen – Fine Focus: Words

✓ Word choices varied; word meanings clear; consider denotation AND connotation
  ◆ Verbs: *strong, fitting; appropriate adverbs if needed*
  ◆ Nouns: *clear, descriptive; appropriate adjectives if needed*
  ◆ Dialogue: *dialogue tags varied if appropriate*
  ✓ Correct spelling
✓ Final read-through

PROGYMNASMA FABLE – SLANT

Rewrite your amplified version of "The Dog and His Master's Dinner," slanting it from the Dog's perspective.

  ◆ Put yourself in the place of the Dog. Consider how he might defend his thoughts and actions as perfectly reasonable.
  ◆ Rewrite your amplified fable in the first person (as if the Dog is speaking, using pronouns *I, me,* etc.) with these considerations in mind.
  ◆ Save and print your revised fable.

EDITOR'S PEN: SLANT FABLE

Revise your fable using the checklist below. Work through the checklist once on your own, and then a second time with your writing mentor, making notes on the print copy of your fable. Transfer all additions and corrections from your print copy to the computer file. Save and print the document.

Editor's Pen – The Big Picture

✓ All important plot elements included

✓ All characters represented correctly from the perspective of the Dog

✓ Sequence: *linear from the beginning*

✓ Length: *one-third to one-half times longer than original*

✓ Figures of Description (or other appropriate description): *anemographia, chronographia, hydrographia, astrothesia, topographia*

Editor's Pen – Zoom 5x: Paragraphs

✓ Formatting: *proper indentation*

✓ Length: *neither too wordy nor too short*

✓ Sentence class by use: *effective use*

✓ Sentence openers: *varied*

✓ Dialogue: *effective use*

✓ Verb Tense: *consistent*

✓ Pronouns clear: *easily identified antecedents*

✓ Person for Nouns & Pronouns: *appropriate to 3rd person point of view*

Editor's Pen – Zoom 10x: Sentences

✓ Complete thought expressed

✓ Subject and predicate agree in number

✓ Correct capitalization and punctuation

  ◆ No comma splices!

Editor's Pen – Fine Focus: Words

✓ Word choices varied; word meanings clear; consider denotation AND connotation

  ◆ Verbs: *strong, fitting; appropriate adverbs if needed*

  ◆ Nouns: *clear, descriptive; appropriate adjectives if needed*

  ◆ Dialogue: *dialogue tags varied if appropriate*

  ✓ Correct spelling

✓ Final read-through

Lesson 2.5

Reflection & Review

COMMONPLACE BOOK

Commonplace
Book

Enter in your Commonplace Book:

- ◆ a favorite passage or two from the reading assigned in this lesson in *The Age of Fable*
- ◆ at least two examples of simile from your reading in history or literature

BOOK OF CENTURIES

Record in your Book of Centuries:

- ◆ Trojan War, Homer, *The Odyssey*, *The Iliad*

MEMORY WORK

GRAMMAR
FLASHCARDS

Review to mastery:

- ◆ Parts of Speech – *Bards & Poets* Review
- ◆ Sentence Terms – *Bards & Poets* Review

Lesson 3

☙

THE COUNSEL OF ATHENE
from THE STORY OF THE ODYSSEY, by Alfred Church

When the great city of Troy had been taken, all the chiefs who had fought against it set sail for their homes. But there was wrath in heaven against them, so that they did not find a safe and happy return. For one was shipwrecked, and another was shamefully slain by his false wife in his palace, and others found all things at home troubled and changed, and were driven to seek new dwellings elsewhere; and some were driven far and wide about the world before they saw their native land again. Of all, the wise Ulysses was he that wandered farthest and suffered most, for when ten years had well-nigh passed, he was still far away from Ithaca, his kingdom.

The gods were gathered in council in the hall of Olympus, all but Poseidon, the god of the sea, for he had gone to feast with the Ethiopians. Now Poseidon was he who most hated Ulysses, and kept him from his home.

Then spake Athene among the immortal gods: "My heart is rent for Ulysses. Sore affliction doth he suffer in an island of the sea, where the daughter of Atlas keepeth him, seeking to make him forget his native land. And he yearns to see even the smoke rising up from the land of his birth, and is fain [wishes to] to die. And thou regardest it not at all. Did he not offer thee many sacrifices in the land of Troy? Wherefore hast thou such wrath against him?" To her Zeus, the father of the gods, made reply: "What is this that thou sayest, my daughter? It is Poseidon that hath great wrath against Ulysses, because he blinded his son Polyphemus the Cyclops. But come, let us take counsel together that he may return to his home, for Poseidon will not be able to contend against us all."

Then said Athene: "If this be thy will, then let us speed Hermes the messenger to the island of Calypso, and let him declare to the goddess our purpose that Ulysses shall return to his home. And I will go to Ithaca, and stir up the spirit of his son Telemachos, that first he speak out his mind to the suitors of his mother who waste his substance, and next that he go to Sparta and to Pylos, seeking tidings of his father. So shall the youth win good report among men."

So she went to Ithaca, and there she took upon her the form of Mentes, who was chief of the Taphians.

Now there were gathered in the house of Ulysses many princes from the islands, suitors of the Queen Penelope, for they said that Ulysses was dead, and that she should choose another husband. These were gathered together, and were sitting playing draughts and feasting. And Telemachus sat among them, vexed at heart, for they wasted his substance; neither was he master in his house. But when he saw the guest at the door, he rose from his place, and welcomed him, and made him sit down, and commanded that they should give him food and wine. And when he had ended his meal, Telemachus asked him his business.

Thereupon the false Mentes said: "My name is Mentes, and I am King of the Taphians, and I am sailing to Cyprus for copper, taking iron in exchange. Now I have been long time the friend of this house, of thy father and thy father's father, and I came trusting to see thy father, for they told me that he was here. But now I see that some god hath hindered his return, for that he is yet alive I know full well. But tell me, who are these that I see? Is this the gathering of a clan, or a wedding feast?"

Telemachus made answer: "O sir, while my father was yet alive, our house was rich and honoured; but now that he is gone, things are not well with me. I would not grieve so much had he fallen in battle before Troy; for then the Greeks would have builded a great burial mound for him, and he would thus have won great renown, even for his son. But now the storms of the sea have swept him away, and I am left in sore distress. For these whom thou seest are the princes of the islands that come here to woo my mother. She neither refuseth nor accepteth; and meanwhile they sit here, and waste my substance."

Then said the false Mentes: "Now may the gods help thee! Thou art indeed in sore need of Ulysses. But now hearken to my counsel. First call an assembly of the people. Bid the suitors go back, each man to his home; and as for thy mother, if she be moved to wed, let her return to her father's house, that her kinsfolk may furnish a wedding feast, and prepare gifts such as a well-beloved daughter should have. Afterwards do thou fit up a ship with twenty oars, and go, inquire concerning thy father; perhaps some man may give thee tidings of him; or, may be, thou wilt hear a voice from Zeus concerning him. Go to Pylos first, and afterwards to Sparta, where Menelaus dwelleth, who of all the Greeks came back the last to his home. If thou shouldest hear that he is dead, then come back hither, and raise a mound for him, and give thy mother to a husband. And when thou hast made an end of all these things, then plan how thou mayest slay the suitors by force or craft, for it is time for thee to have the thoughts of a man."

Then said Telemachus: "Thou speakest these things out of a friendly heart, as a father might speak to his son, nor will I ever forget them. But now, I pray thee, abide here for a space, that I may give thee a goodly gift, such as friends give to friends, to be an heirloom in thy house."

But the false Mentes said, "Keep me no longer, for I am eager to depart; give me thy gift when I shall return."

So the goddess departed; like to an eagle of the sea was she as she flew. And Telemachus knew her to be a goddess as she went.

Meanwhile Phemius the minstrel sang to the suitors, and his song was of the unhappy return of the Greeks from Troy.

When Penelope heard the song, she came down from the upper chamber where she sat, and two handmaids bare her company. And when she came to where the suitors sat, she stood by the gate of the hall, holding her shining veil before her face. Then spake she to the minstrel, weeping, and said: "Phemius, thou knowest many songs concerning the deeds of gods and men; sing, therefore, one of these, and let the guests drink the wine in silence. But stay this pitiful strain, for it breaketh my heart to hear it. Surely, of all women I am the most unhappy, so famous was the husband for whom I mourn."

But Telemachus made reply: "Why dost thou grudge the minstrel, my mother, to make us glad in such fashion as his spirit biddeth him? It is no blame to him that he singeth of the unhappy return of the Greeks, for men most prize the song that soundeth newest in their ears. Endure, therefore, to listen, for not Ulysses only missed his return, but many a famous chief besides. Go, then, to thy chamber, and mind thy household affairs, and bid thy handmaids ply their tasks. Speech belongeth unto men, and chiefly to me that am the master in this house."

Then went she back to her chamber, for she was amazed at her son, with such authority did he speak. Then she bewailed her lord, till Athene sent down sleep upon her eyes.

When she was gone, Telemachus spake to the suitors, saying: "Let us now feast and be merry, and let there be no brawling among us. It is a good thing to listen to a minstrel that hath a voice as the voice of a god. But in the morning let us go to the assembly, that I may declare my purpose, to wit, that ye leave this hall, and eat your own substance. But if ye deem it a better thing that ye should waste another man's goods, and make no recompense, then work your will. But certainly Zeus shall repay you."

So he spake, and they all marvelled that he used such boldness.

And Antinous answered: "Surely, Telemachus, it is by the bidding of the gods that thou speakest so boldly. Therefore I pray that Zeus may never make thee King in Ithaca."

Then said Telemachus: "It is no ill thing to be a king, for his house groweth rich, and he himself is honoured. But there are others in Ithaca, young and old, who may have the kingship, now that Ulysses is dead. Yet know that I will be lord of my own house and of the slaves which Ulysses won for himself with his own spear."

Thereupon spake Eurymachus, saying: "It is with the gods to say who shall be King in Ithaca; but no man can deny that thou shouldest keep thine own goods and be lord in thine own house. Tell me, who is this stranger that came but just now to thy house? Did he bring tidings of thy father? Or came he on some matter of his own? In strange fashion did he depart, nor did he tarry that we might know him."

Telemachus made answer: "Verily, Eurymachus, the day of my father's return hath gone by forever. As for this stranger, he said that he was Mentes, King of the Taphians."

So spake Telemachus, but in his heart he knew that the stranger was Athene. Then the suitors turned them to the dance and to the song, making merry till the darkness fell. Then went they each to his own house to sleep.

But Telemachus went to his chamber, pondering many things in his heart. And Eurycleia, who had nursed him when he was little, went with him, bearing torches in her hands. He opened the door of the chamber, and took off his doublet, and put it in the wise woman's hands. She folded it, and smoothed it, and hung it on a pin, and went forth from the room, and pulled to the door, and made it fast. And all the night Telemachus thought in his heart of the journey which Athene had showed him.

☙

Lesson 3.1

Prose & Poetry

THE EPIC

In Lesson 2.1, you read about (or researched) the characteristics of an epic. You should have found at least these:

- Invention
  - epic hero, "who embodies (despite imperfections) the ideals of the author's culture" – Ryken, *Homer's The Odyssey*
  - epic feat or quest: action of great historic or mythical importance
  - epic sweep: cosmic scope/setting "encompasses the whole earth, a supernatural world, and the afterlife." – Ryken, *Homer's The Odyssey*
  - often concerned with foundings or re-foundings of a civilization or culture
  - supernatural intervention
  - invocation of the Muse and a statement of purpose
  - "An epic sums up what an entire age wants to say." – Ryken, *Literary Forms in the Bible*

- ◆ Arrangement
  - ◆ *in medias res*
- ◆ Style: epic style
  - ◆ exalted, formal or "high" language
  - ◆ epic simile: extended simile over several (or many!) lines
  - ◆ epithets: repeated titles or descriptive phrases for persons, places, or things
  - ◆ periphasis or circumlocution: indirect or roundabout way of expressing something

As you read Homer's *Odyssey*, you should take notice when you see these epic conventions employed. As you learn to recognize these literary devices in epic poetry, you will begin to see them in literature through the ages. This is one way that you can "see" The Great Conversation (see Introduction for Teachers & Students).

Prose & Poetry Handbook

Enter the following item in the Literature Section.

- ◆ The Epic, P&P 53: Title LITERARY FORMS, then copy the definition of epic, along with the list of its features.

THE ODYSSEY

In this lesson, you embark on a slow and careful reading of Homer's *Odyssey* in an English poetic translation of the original Greek. Epic poetry, like all poetry, is meant to be *heard*, so we heartily recommend that you read the *Odyssey* aloud. If at all possible, read it aloud with others in your family or classroom, with each fluent reader taking a turn. It should take about 45 minutes to an hour to complete the assigned reading for each lesson. Alternately, find a good recording of the poetic translation and listen as you follow along in your own copy of the book.

You will also read the selection at the beginning of this lesson, taken from *The Story of the Odyssey*, by Alfred Church. This is Church's retelling from the original Greek of Homer's *Odyssey* Book One. Because epic poetry and all the names and places may be new to you, reading a well-written retelling like this can be a valuable help for both students and teachers who are new to this classic. When you are learning to ride a bike, regardless of your age, training wheels make the job easier. Think of these short retellings as training wheels. We will use them only for the first four books of Homer's *Odyssey*, which tell the story of Telemachos as he searches for news about his father.

Beginning in Lesson 3.4, you will also complete a brief plot observation and narrative summary of each book of the Odyssey as well. This will enhance your reading comprehension as well as provide the raw material for your final papers in this course.

 Read

• *The Odyssey of Homer*, Book One

• "The Counsel of Athene" (at the beginning of this lesson)

NOTA BENE: Alfred Church uses the Roman names for characters in his retelling, while Lattimore uses Greek names. So, Church has Ulysses, while Lattimore has Odysseus. This is the most striking difference; most of the other differences are just variation in spelling like Telemachus (Roman) vs. Telemachos (Greek).

As you read, mark the text and make notes in your Writer's Journal[1] as as follows:

• Any literary concepts and terms you recognize in the narrative from the notes you have made (and will make) in the Literature section of your Prose & Poetry Handbook. Discuss what you observe with your teacher. Of course, as you continue reading, you will gain additional insights, and may amend some of your earlier thoughts.

• Instances of **epic simile**, like this one from Virgil's *Aeneid*:

> Souls of a thousand nations filled the air,
>
> As bees in meadows at the height of summer
>
> Hover and hone on flowers and thickly swarm
>
> On snow-white lilies, and the countryside
>
> Is loud with humming. — Book VI

• A running list of the **epithets** that Homer uses for each character, such as "gray-eyed Athene" or "rosy-fingered Dawn." It will also help you to keep a list of alternate names for each character. For example, Athene is referred to as Mentor on the journey.

• Passages reflecting on the value of **hearth and home**. Passages related to these will also make great Commonplace Book entries for your Reflection & Review lesson (along with the examples of epic similes that you mark).

Discuss this week's reading with your teacher, along with all your notes and observations. Narrate the main action of the book, and discuss any parts you did not understand. How was this reading **delightful**? What **wisdom** does this reading furnish?

---

1 You may wish to keep a separate Reading Journal for these types of entries.

NARRATIVE INVENTION: THEON'S SIX

Bards & Poets students will remember these well. Theon, who gives us our definition of narrative, also gives us six elements that will be found in every narrative: **Person**, **Action**, **Place**, **Time**, **Manner**, and **Cause**. These are similar to the "**Five W's and an H**" that newspaper reporters must answer for a good story: **Who?**, **What?**, **Where?**, **When?**, **Why?**, and **How?** Theon's Six and the "Five W's and an H" line up perfectly:

Person	Who?
Action	What?
Place	Where?
Time	When?
Cause	Why?
Manner	How?

For each of these six elements, Theon developed questions to thoroughly investigate a narrative.

Turn to the Appendix and review Theon's Six Narrative Elements. Although there are several questions for each component, they will not all apply to every narrative. The list of questions is simply meant to stimulate your thinking and to remind you of all the possibilities for that component.

Enter the following item in the Literature Section.

Prose & Poetry Handbook

◆ Narrative Elements, Six By Theon, P&P 44: Title NARRATIVE ELEMENTS: SIX BY THEON, then list each of the six elements with brief descriptions of each of the subpoints under the elements. It is probably best just to copy this directly from the P&P Handbook page image in the Appendix.

NARRATIVE ARRANGEMENT: STORY STRUCTURE

Each of Theon's Six elements is important, but Action is particularly so because the entire narrative "is a clarification of an action."[2] Under Person, we name the story's characters. The Action in a narrative forms its **plot**, or storyline. Theon's other elements will add detail about those actions and the overall plot. Very often the action in a narrative is **physical**. But narrative action will also frequently depict **dialogue,** including **thoughts** related as dialogue inside of a character's mind.

2 George A. Kennedy, *Progymnasmata*, 184.

Often an author will include some additional details between actions or even in the middle of an action. These are often an integral part of the overall narrative, but they are not actually part of the action. At the beginning of the narrative, the author may provide a **prologue** to give historical or background context to the main storyline. At the end, the author may provide an **epilogue** to give details about what comes after, sometimes even far into the future.

In addition to these, the author may give **background**, **explanation**, or **description** to help the reader understand or visualize an action or a character or a setting better. The author may provide a **summary** of a time period that is not otherwise detailed, or supply some other kind of **transition** between actions. Sometimes the **author comments** on some aspect of the story to help the reader fully understand the importance of what has happened.

Most of these elements will be **essential** to the plot of a particular narrative—if these were removed, the story would make no sense or some important part of the message would be obscured. Usually the author will also include **non-essential** details that give us more information, and help us picture an action more vividly, but the storyline would still make sense and the message would still be conveyed if they were not included. Elements that you have classified in your observation of Theon's Six will often be essential elements.

() Enter the following item in the Literature division.

- ◆ Narrative Arrangement, Story Structure, P&P 49: Subtitle STORY STRUCTURE, then add Action and the information as indicated in the Appendix, with the three types of action (physical, dialogue, thoughts). Skip a line and add the Other Elements. Write subtitle ESSENTIAL ELEMENTS OF A NARRATIVE, with the definitions for both essential and non-essential elements.

Prose & Poetry Handbook

NARRATIVE STYLE: POINT OF VIEW

Every narrative account has a **narrator** (from the Latin verb *narrare*, to tell), literally, *one who tells*. The **point of view** refers to the "voice" that the narrator uses to tell the story (**person** – usually first or third), along with how much he or she knows (**level of omniscience**). In the last chapter, you worked with this a bit as you retold a fable from the point of view of one of the characters. This chart shows the terms that are used to describe point of view in a story:

- ◆ Person
  - ■ First Person – "I" and/or "we"
  - ■ Third Person – "he," "she," "it," "they"

- ◆ Level of Omniscience
  - ▪ Omniscient – "all knowing" about the story and its characters, including all thoughts, feelings, and motives
  - ▪ Limited – knows only the thoughts, feelings, and motives of one (or only a very few) character(s)
  - ▪ Objective or Dramatic – reports only actions and dialogue, does not have access to (or does not relate) character's thoughts, feelings, or motives

To name the point of view of a particular narrative, combine the **person** in which the narrator speaks with the **level of omniscience**, such as 1st person limited, or 3rd person omniscient. Some stories will have multiple narrators speaking in different persons and with varying levels of omniscience.

❦ Enter the following item in the Literature division.

Prose & Poetry Handbook

- ◆ Narrative Invention: Point of View, P&P 50: Subtitle POINT OF VIEW, and write the definition of narrator, plus the process of naming Point of View.

❦ With your teacher, discuss the point of view (person and omniscience) of *Odyssey*, Book One.

Lesson 3.2

Language Logic

SENTENCE DIAGRAMMING: REVIEW PATTERNS & MODIFIERS

These beginning sentence diagramming lessons will also be review for *Bards & Poets* students. This is a quick review, and besides providing a refresher course on sentence diagramming, this review will also familiarize you thoroughly with the contents of *Sentence Sense*. Throughout *Poetics & Progym*, you will diagram sentences taken from literary works. *Sentence Sense* is your diagramming how-to reference book.

❦ Review the following sections in *Sentence Sense* with your teacher.

III. Sentence Diagramming – Sentence Patterns

- ◆ 12.1 Basic Pattern: Subject – Predicate
- ◆ 12.2 Subject – Verb
- ◆ 12.3 Subject – Verb – Direct Object
- ◆ 12.4 Subject – Verb – Subject Complement

III. Sentence Diagramming – Modifiers

- ◆ 13.1 Adjectives
- ◆ 13.2 Adverbs Which Modify Verbs
- ◆ 13.3 Adverbs Which Modify Adjectives
- ◆ 13.4 Adverbs Which Modify Adverbs
- ◆ 13.5 Prepositional Phrases
- ◆ 13.7 Adverbial Nouns

In your Writer's Journal, copy these sentences.[3] Mark the prepositional phrases, subjects, and verbs. Then diagram each one. Refer to *Sentence Sense* as needed.

1. She saw a glory in each cloud.

2. Still waters are commonly deepest.

3. Few days pass without some clouds.

4. One chief was shamefully slain by his false wife in his palace.

5. The storms of the sea have swept him away.

6. Penelope came down from the upper chamber with two handmaids.

7. He singeth of the unhappy return of the Greeks.

8. All night Telemachus thought in his heart of the journey.

SENTENCE PARSING

Orally parse these words taken from the sentences above with your teacher. Use the charts in *Sentence Sense*, Chapter IV to guide you. Skip the information in the gray boxes for now.

3 These sentences are taken from exercises in *Harvey's Elementary Grammar.*

(1) in each cloud; (2) waters; (2) are; (3) some; (4) shamefully; (5) him; (6) Penelope; (7) singeth; (8) his

---

Lesson 3.3

Eloquent Expression

COPIA OF CONSTRUCTION

Copia of Construction devices change the grammatical pattern or structure of a sentence, also while preserving the original meaning. *Bards & Poets* students learned a number of devices. For now, you will just make a list of the devices, and then we will review just the most basic ones. Do not worry if you cannot remember or have not yet learned all of these, as we will review all of these in upcoming lessons. But do feel free to use this list as a prompt for revising sentences in your writing.

In the *Poetics & Progym I* Appendix, study Copia of Construction on the Eloquent Expression Through Copia chart.

Enter the following item in the Rhetoric Section:

Prose & Poetry Handbook

◆ Copia of Construction, P&P 27: Subtitle COPIA OF CONSTRUCTION, then copy the chart from the Appendix from the top to Verb Tense. Do not copy the Lesson #s where we will review or learn each device.

COPIA OF CONSTRUCTION: SENTENCE CLASS BY USE

Review the four classes of sentences by use: **Declarative**, **Interrogative**, **Exclamatory**, and **Imperative**. Any one of these can be rewritten as any of the other three classes.

Your letter pleased me greatly.
Your letter pleased me greatly!
Did not your letter please me greatly?
Dear friend, please me greatly with your letter.

Sometimes the word order will have to be altered or the verb will have to be changed in order for the sentence to remain grammatically correct. Imperative sentences will probably have to change the most.

COPIA OF CONSTRUCTION: SENTENCE OPENING WORD

Most English sentences begin with a subject, as should most of the sentences in your writing. But it is very tedious to read an entire paragraph, let alone an entire essay, in which every sentence begins with a subject.

There are some very specific grammatical methods for varying your **sentence opening words** that we will cover in this book. But here is one quick and easy way to get started immediately: just choose another word from the sentence and move it to the beginning. Adjust the rest of the sentence as needed so that it makes complete sense.

> I received your letter, which pleased me greatly, yesterday.
>
> Your letter, which pleased me greatly, I received yesterday.
>
> Yesterday I received your letter, which pleased me greatly.

COPIA OF WORDS: DIALOGUE

Dialogue adds interest to a story by allowing the narrator to show the reader what the characters say or think. The exact words of the speaker are repeated in **direct quotations**.

> "Your letter pleased me greatly," said Erasmus.
>
> Erasmus said, "Your letter pleased me greatly."
>
> "Your letter," said Erasmus, "pleased me greatly."

In the sentences above, the words *said Erasmus* are called **dialogue tags**. They can be placed at different points in the direct quotation – beginning, middle, or end. Use correct comma and quotation mark placement when writing dialogue. Rules for this are reviewed in *Sentence Sense* 11.3C, Rem. 5.

There are times when using direct quotations is not appropriate or expedient, such as when you empasizing the action, or when you are writing a summary of the action. Direct quotations can easily be switched to **indirect quotations**, which do not repeat the exact words of the speaker.

> Erasmus said, "Thank you for your letter."
>
> Erasmus thanked him for his letter.

> Erasmus cried, "This letter brings me great joy!"
>
> Erasmus expressed great joy on reading the letter.
>
>   OR Erasmus read the letter with joy.

Use the dialogue tag *said* sparingly when you write indirect quotations. In the back of your Writer's Journal, title a page DIALOGUE TAGS and make a list of all the synonyms for *said* that you can think of. Keep adding to this list as you come across examples in your reading. Check this list when you need to find appropriate substitutes, or paraphrase the sentence entirely as in the last example above.

COPIA OF CONSTRUCTION: POINT OF VIEW

A sentence written in **third person** may be changed to **first person** or **second person** and vice versa by changing the pronoun used. You will probably need to adjust the rest of the sentence.

> Erasmus was pleased by your letter. (3rd person)
>
> I was pleased by your letter. (1st person)
>
> You pleased me by your letter. (2nd person)

The noun property of person is used most often to create dialogue, but it can also be used to change the **point of view** (speaker) of an entire paragraph or narrative.

COPIA OF CONSTRUCTION: VERB TENSE

You can also work with a verb's property of **tense** (Harvey's Lessons 101-102). For example, a sentence written in present may be changed to past or future tense. This may or may not require some adjustment to the rest of the sentence. **Nota Bene**: *For a complete explanation of each tense, see* Sentence Sense, *3.7 Verb Property – Tense. We will review these in a later lesson as well.*

> Your letter pleases Erasmus. (present)
>
> Your letter pleased Erasums. (past)
>
> Your letter will please Erasmus. (future)
>
> Your letter has pleased Erasmus. (present perfect)
>
> Your letter had pleased Erasmus. (past perfect)
>
> Your letter will have pleased Erasmus. (future perfect)

Copy each sentence below in your Writer's Journal. Paraphrase each sentence using the Copia of Construction devices listed above. Try to use more than one device in each sentence, and be sure to use each device at least once. For the final sentence, use both Copia of Constuction and Copia of Words.

Writer's Journal

1. Paris decided in favor of Venus and gave her the golden apple, thus making the two other goddesses his enemies.

2. Achilles submitted, but declared that he would take no further part in the war.

3. Laocoön, the priest of Neptune, exclaims, "For my part, I fear the Greeks even when they offer gifts."

4. After visiting his father's tomb and sacrificing upon it, according to the rites of the ancients, he made himself known to his sister Electra, and soon after slew both Aegisthus and Clytemnestra.

Lesson 3.4

Classical Composition

PROGYMNASMA NARRATIVE

A **narrative** is an account of something that has happened, or as though it has happened. In other words, a narrative is a story. In the ancient Narrative exercise, the student retold the narrative with a **clear articulation of the details**, according to Theon's Six. Often, the student was instructed to rewrite the narrative in a different **sequence**—*ab ovo, in medias res,* etc. We practiced this quite a bit in *Bards & Poets II.* As with the fable, the narrative might also be **amplified**, particularly with description, or it might be **slanted**, or it might be **abbreviated**. Abbreviation will be our focus throughout the remaining lessons of *Poetics & Progym I.*

Prose & Poetry Handbook

⬙ Enter the following item in the Rhetoric Section.

◆ Invention/Arrangement, The Progymnasmata – Narrative, P&P 10: Subtitle NARRATIVE, then copy the definition of the Narrative exercise. Below that, list the two ways to retell the fable (clear articulation of details, sequence).

PROGYMNASMA NARRATIVE: PLOT OBSERVATION – THEON'S SIX

As you read each book of the *Odyssey* to accompany the lessons in *Poetics & Progym I,* you will complete a plot observation and summary of each book, as you learned to do in *Bards & Poets.* In Lesson 6.4, you will use this observation work to summarize (abbreviate) the first four books of the *Odyssey.* In the final lessons of this book, you will use these to create a hierarchical outline and summary of the entire epic. Complete details on this project and examples of each step are included in the Appendix. You will be directed to read through these sections here and at the appropriate time in upcoming lessons.

Work in your Writer's Journal, and follow these steps to complete a plot observsation with Theon's Six for Book One of Homer's *Odyssey*. Before you begin your own observation of *Odyssey* Book One, read completely through the instructions below, and then study the Example Narrative and the Example Plot Observation – Theon's Six in the Appendix under "Example Narrative Plot Observation."

A. First, take a look at the big picture, following these steps:

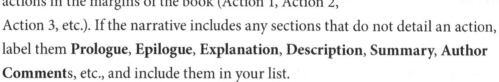

- ◆ Person: List all the important characters, with a brief description of each.

- ◆ Action: List the major actions of the plot in the order they occur in the story. Your list should have no less than two, and no more than five. If possible, first number the actions in the margins of the book (Action 1, Action 2, Action 3, etc.). If the narrative includes any sections that do not detail an action, label them **Prologue**, **Epilogue**, **Explanation**, **Description**, **Summary**, **Author Comment**s, etc., and include them in your list.

- ◆ Place: Name and briefly describe the main place(s) where the action took place. Consult the questions listed for Theon's Six Elements in the Appendix and make notes about as many of the questions as the narrative answers.

- ◆ Time: Briefly describe the time period in which the action took place (this may be relative: before *x* or after *y*, or it may be more specific: one year later). Consult the questions listed for Theon's Six Elements in the Appendix and make notes about as many of the questions as the narrative answers.

B. Use Theon's Six to observe the narrative plot. Consult the questions listed for Theon's Six Elements in the Appendix to complete this part of the assignment.

- ◆ Person: First, make notes on what you learn about Odysseus, Telemachos, Penelope, and Athene in this book. Also note what you learn about the suitors (as a group). For each character, answer as many of Theon's Six questions about Person as you are able to answer directly from the narrative itself.

- ◆ Action: Create a numbered list with each of the actions you identified in order. If there are any sections of the narrative that do not detail an action, include these as well, and label them **Prologue**, **Epilogue**, **Explanation**, **Description**, **Summary**, **Author Comments**, etc.

- ◆ Under each action, answer Theon's Six questions about Time and Place if there are specifics attached to the action that you have not already detailed in Step A.

- ◆ Under each action, also answer as many of Theon's Six questions about Cause and Manner that the narrative answered.
- ◆ If you identified any sections that do not detail an action, add a brief note indicating the content of the section.

PROGYMNASMA NARRATIVE: PLOT OBSERVATION – SUMMARY

A written summary is essentially a brief narration, or retelling, of the plot. The process of writing a summary is an aid to reading comprehension and retention. By limiting the length of the retelling, we are asking you to discriminate, or choose, only the most important details. You are responding to and even interacting with the author as you compose your summary. This is an important first step in entering the Great Conversation for yourself!

A. Review your notes and compose a one paragraph summary of Book One that captures the main action, characters, and any other details from Theon's Six that are needful. You may either write this on the computer in a running file that you use for the entire *Odyssey*, or write each summary out by hand in your Writer's Journal, then transfer it to the running computer file.

B. Read over your summary to make sure you have not left out any **essentials** or included too many **non-essentials**. Revise as needed, and edit so that you have a smooth and eloquent summary paragraph.

Lesson 3.5

Reflection & Review

COMMONPLACE BOOK

 Enter in your Commonplace Book:

Commonplace Book

- ◆ a favorite passage or two from Homer's *Odyssey*
- ◆ an example or two of epithet and/or epic simile

MEMORY WORK

Review to mastery:

- Parts of Speech – *Bards & Poets* Review
- Sentence Terms – *Bards & Poets* Review

Lesson 4

ॐ

THE ASSEMBLY

from THE STORY OF THE ODYSSEY, **by Alfred Church**

When the morning came, Telemachus bade the heralds call the people to the assembly. So the heralds called them, and they came in haste. And when they were gathered together, he went his way to the place of meeting, holding in his hand a spear, and two dogs followed him. Then did Athene shed a marvellous grace upon him, so that all men wondered at him, as he sat him down in his father's place.

First spake Aegyptus, who was bowed with many years, and was very wise. Four sons he had. One had gone with Ulysses to Troy, and one was among the suitors of the Queen, and two abode with their father in the field. He said: "Hearken to me, men of Ithaca! Never hath an assembly been called in Ithaca since Ulysses departed. Who now hath called us together? If it be Telemachus, what doth he want? Hath he heard any tidings of the coming back of the host? He, methinks, is a true man. May Zeus be with him and grant him his heart's desire!"

So spake the old man, and Telemachus was glad at his speech. Then he rose up and said:—

"I have great trouble in my heart, men of Ithaca, for first my father, whom ye all loved, is dead; and next the princes of the islands come hither, making suit to my mother, but she waits ever for the return of her husband. And they devour all our substance; nor is Ulysses here to defend it, and I, in truth, am not able. And this is a grievous wrong, and not to be borne."

Then he dashed his sceptre on the ground, and sat down weeping.

And Antinous, who was one of the suitors, rose up and said:—

"Nay, Telemachus, blame not us, but blame thy mother, who indeed is crafty above all women. For now this is the fourth year that we have come suing for her hand, and she has cheated us with hopes. Hear now this that she did. She set up a great web for weaving, and said to us: 'Listen, ye that are my suitors. Hasten not my marriage till I finish this web to be a burial cloth for Laertes, the father of Ulysses, for indeed it would be foul shame if he who has won great possessions should lack this honour.' So she spake, and for three years she cheated us, for what she wove in the day she unravelled at night. But when the fourth year was come, one of her maidens told us of the matter, and we came upon her by night and found her unravelling what she had woven in the day. Then did she finish it, much against her will. Send away, therefore, thy mother, and bid her marry whom she will. But till this be done we will not depart."

Then answered Telemachus: "How can I send away against her will her who bare me and brought me up? I cannot do this thing."

So he spake; and there came two eagles, which flew abreast till they came over the assembly. Then did they wheel in the air, and shook out from each many feathers, and tare each other, and so departed.

Then cried Alitherses, the prophet: "Beware, ye suitors, for great trouble is coming to you, and to others also. And as for Ulysses, I said when he went to Troy that he should return after twenty years; and so it shall be."

And when the suitors would not listen, Telemachus said: "Give me a ship and twenty rowers, that I may go to Pylos and to Sparta; perhaps I may hear news of my father. And if I hear that he is dead, then will I come back hither and raise up a mound for him and give my mother to a husband."

Having thus spoken, he sat down, and Mentor, whom Ulysses, when he departed, set over his household, rose up in the midst, and spake, saying: "Now henceforth never let any king be kind and gentle in his heart or minded to work righteousness. Let him rather be a hard man and unrighteous. For now no man of all the people whose lord he was remembereth Ulysses. Yet he was gentle as a father. If the suitors are minded to do evil deeds, I hinder them not. They do them at the peril of their own heads. It is with the people that I am wroth, to see how they sit speechless, and cry not shame upon the suitors; and yet they are many in number, and the suitors are few."

Then Leocritus, who was one of the suitors, answered: "Surely thy wits wander, O Mentor, that thou biddest the people put us down. Of a truth, if Ulysses himself should come back, and should seek to drive the suitors from the hall, it would fare ill with him. An evil fate would he meet, if he fought with them. As for the people, let them go to their own houses. Let Mentor speed the young man's voyage, for he is a friend of his house. Yet I doubt whether he will ever accomplish it."

So he spake, and the assembly was dismissed.

But Telemachus went apart to the shore of the sea, and he washed his hands in the water of the sea, and prayed to Athene, saying: "Hear me, thou who didst come yesterday to the house, and bid me take a ship, and sail across the sea, seeking tidings of my father! The people delay my purpose, and the suitors stir them up in the wickedness of their hearts."

And while he prayed, Athene stood by him, like to Mentor in shape and speech. She spake, saying: "Thou art not without spirit, and art like to be a true son of Ulysses and Penelope. Therefore, I have good hopes that this journey of which thou speakest will not be in vain. But as for the suitors, think not of them, for they talk folly, and know not of the doom that is even now close upon them. Go, therefore, and talk with the suitors as before, and get ready food for a journey, wine and meal. And I will gather men who will offer themselves freely for the journey, and I will find a ship also, the best in Ithaca."

Then Telemachus returned to the house, and the suitors were flaying goats and singeing swine in the court. And Antinous caught him by the hand and said, "Eat and drink, Telemachus, and we will find a ship and rowers for thee, that thou mayest go where thou wilt, to inquire for thy father."

But Telemachus answered: "Think ye that I will eat and drink with you, who so shamefully waste my substance? Be sure of this, that I will seek vengeance against you, and if ye deny me a ship, I will even go in another man's."

So he spake, and dragged his hand from the hand of Antinous.

And another of the suitors said, "Now will Telemachus go and seek help against us from Pylos or from Sparta, or may be he will put poison in our cups, and so destroy us."

And another said: "Perchance he also will perish, as his father has perished. Then we should divide all his substance, but the house we should give to his mother and to her husband."

So they spake, mocking him. But he went to the chamber of his father, in which were ranged many casks of old wine, and gold and bronze, and clothing and olive oil; and of these things the prudent Eurycleia, who was the keeper of the house, had care. To her he spake: "Mother, make ready for me twelve jars of wine, not of the best, but of that which is next to it, and twenty measures of barley-meal. At even will I take them, when my mother sleeps, for I go to Pylos and Sparta; perchance I may hear news of my father."

But the old woman said, weeping: "What meanest thou, being an only son, thus to travel abroad? Wilt thou perish, as thy father has perished? For this evil brood of suitors will plot to slay thee and divide thy goods. Thou hadst better sit peaceably at home."

Then Telemachus said: "'Tis at the bidding of the gods I go. Only swear that thou wilt say naught to my mother till eleven or twelve days be past, unless, perchance, she should ask concerning me."

And the old woman sware that it should be so. And Telemachus went again among the suitors. But Athene, meanwhile, taking his shape, had gathered together a crew, and also had borrowed a ship for the voyage. And, lest the suitors should hinder the thing, she caused a deep sleep to fall upon them, so that they slept where they sat. Then she came in the shape of Mentor to the palace, and called Telemachus forth, saying:

"The rowers are ready; let us go."

Then Athene led the way, and they found the ship's crew upon the shore. To them spake Telemachus, saying, "Come now, my friends, let us carry the food on board, for it is all in the chamber, and no one knoweth of the matter; neither my mother, nor any of the maidens, but one woman only."

POETICS & PROGYM I

Lesson 41 ♦ 69

So they went to the house with him, and carried all the provision, and stowed it in the ship. Then Telemachus climbed the ship and sat down on the stern, and Athene sat by him.

And when he called to the crew, they made ready to depart. They raised the pine tree mast, and set it in the hole that was made for it, and they made it fast with stays. Then they hauled up the white sails with ropes of ox-hide. And the wind filled out the sail, and the water seethed about the stem of the ship, as she hasted through the water. And when all was made fast in the ship, then they mixed wine in the bowl, and poured out drink offerings to the gods, especially to Zeus.

So all the night, and till the dawn, the ship sped through the sea.

ॐ

Lesson 4.1

Prose & Poetry

NARRATIVE INVENTION: PLOT

As you learned in Lesson 3.1, the **plot** of a narrative is its storyline. It is the structure or scheme into which the author has arranged each action and event making up the complete story. (The plot structure may or may not correspond to the temporal or chronological order of the actions and events. See Narrative Arrangement: Sequence in Lesson 4).

The basic structure of every plot is simple: **beginning**, **middle**, and **end**. There are certain elements that make up each of these three divisions.

Prose & Poetry
Handbook

Enter the following item in the Literature division.

♦ Narrative Invention, Plot, P&P 41: Subtitle PLOT, write the definition of plot.

NARRATIVE INVENTION: PLOT STRUCTURE – BEGINNING

The beginning of a narrative plot is called the **exposition** or **introduction**. Here the author must include three elements: the **characters**, the **conflict**, and the **catalyst**.

In the exposition, we begin to meet the characters, particularly the **protagonist**. This is the central character. It does not matter very much whether we actually *like* the protagonist, but the author's task in the exposition is to *make us care about what happens* to him or her. We also become aware that there is an **antagonist** working in opposition to the protagonist. This may be a person or persons, or it may be some circumstance or social convention, or it may even a character trait within the protagonist himself or herself, such as a fatal flaw or besetting sin.

Conflict is also made evident in the exposition. Without conflict, there is no story. If the conflict comes from within the character himself or herself, it is **internal conflict**. If it comes from another person or from something outside the character, it is **external conflict**. Sometimes the conflict will be a larger **thematic conflict** between virtue and vice or even between competing ideals like duty vs. friendship or love.

Finally in the exposition, some **catalyst** must occur. This is the action or event that sets off the action.

🏵 Enter the following item in the Literature division.

Prose & Poetry Handbook

♦ Narrative Invention, Plot Structure – Beginning, P&P 41: Subtitle PLOT STRUCTURE: BEGINNING (EXPOSITION, INTRODUCTION), then list the three elements with their definition and components (Characters, including protagonist and antagonist, Conflict, including internal, external, and thematic, and Catalyst). Include definitions of each component as well.

NARRATIVE INVENTION: PLOT STRUCTURE – MIDDLE

In the middle of the narrative, the author turns his attention to the **rising action** as the conflict continues to grow and situations begin to develop. Then a **climax**, or turning point is reached. Now, the decision is made, the "die is cast," and in the **falling action**, the consequences become evident.

Prose & Poetry Handbook

🏵 Enter the following item in the Literature division.

♦ Narrative Invention, Plot Structure – Middle, P&P 42: Subtitle PLOT STRUCTURE: MIDDLE, then list the three elements with their definitions.

NARRATIVE INVENTION: PLOT STRUCTURE – END

Finally, the **denouement** or **resolution** of the story comes. *Denouement* is a French word, literally meaning *unknotting* or *unraveling*. This may be some final **consequence**. It may be a **reversal** in fortune or situation for the protagonist. It may be an **epiphany**—an aha! moment—for one of the main characters. Or it may be a combination of some or all of these.

We generally classify the ending of a story as **happy** or **unhappy**. An ending may also be **indeterminate**, where no definite conclusion or complete resolution is reached. Most of us find that unsatisfying, and therefore, unhappy. There is no doubt that the ending of a story is very important in discerning the author's purpose or message, and even in discerning the framework through which he or she views the world.

Sometimes, the ending is prescribed by the genre. For example, a classical tragedy like *Antigone* or *Hamlet* demands what we would consider an unhappy ending, usually with most of the main characters dead or at least exiled. A classical comedy like *A Midsummer Night's Dream* demands a happy (or happier) ending, usually involving a wedding or a reunion/restoration of loved ones or a feast of some kind. Why do we love happy endings so? Why do you think our happy endings usually involve weddings or reunions or restoration or feasts?

One other kind of ending must be mentioned here, largely thanks to the modern film industry. This is the **sequel set-up**. Here, the ending may be happy or sad, but there is at least some small detail that is left without closure, leaving the possiblity of another story for another day.

Enter the following item in the Literature division.

Prose & Poetry Handbook

◆ Narrative Invention, Plot Structure – End, P&P 43: Subtitle PLOT STRUCTURE: END (DENOUEMENT, RESOLUTION), then list the three elements with their definitions. Add Types of Endings – Often Determined By the Author's Purpose or Messsage, then list the four types with definitions as needed.

NARRATIVE ARRANGEMENT: SEQUENCE

Narrative sequence is the order in which the events and actions are told within the narrative account. A story may be told in a linear fashion, moving through the events from A to Z in **chronological** order. A narrative that starts from the very earliest point of the action and proceeds through to the end is said to be told **ab ovo** – Latin for *from the egg*, referring to the fabled birth of Helen from a swan's egg. As Helen is considered the cause of the Trojan War (all roads do eventually lead to Troy!), a story told *ab ovo* begins at its earliest beginning or cause (often the birth of the main character) and ends at the end (often the death, or at least ripe old age of the main character), with all the events recounted in the sequence in which they happened. *David Copperfield*, the classic novel by Charles Dickens, is an example of *ab ovo* narrative. Dickens tells the life story of David, modeled loosely on his own life, beginning at his birth.

Horace, the ancient Roman poet who coined the phrase *ab ovo*, commended Homer for NOT using an *ab ovo* sequence in his epic poetry. Instead, Homer's tales begin **in medias res** – Latin for *in the middle of things*. Technically, any narrative that begins somewhere in the "middle" is considered *in medias res*, even if it is told chronologically from there on out. For example, *A Christmas Carol* by Dickens is *in medias res*, according to Horace's definition, since Scrooge is already a grown man when we meet him.

The *Odyssey* begins in the midst of the action and then, through the journey of Telemachus, fills in the story of the intervening years since the fall of Troy. A tale told *in medias res* may begin at some point close to the main action, or sometimes even very near the end of the story, as Homer's *Iliad* does. Or it may begin at the most exciting and suspenseful point. The author then goes back to an earlier point in the story and proceeds through in generally chronological sequence to a point in time on the other side of the main action, sometimes with an epilogue at the end.

Another way an author may fill in the details of previous events or actions is with a **flashback** (or series of flashbacks) in the form of a character's reminiscence or the author's commentary. The story of King Arthur, for example, may be told by one of his knights as a very old man reminiscing about days gone by.

Authors through the ages have heeded the advice of Horace and the example of Homer. Most of our timeless tales are told *in medias res*. Sometimes this comes from the expectation that the audience already knows what has come before, as is the case in most ancient stories. Sometimes, the author plans to weave in the necessary details of the back-story as the narrative proceeds.

An **episodic** arrangement presents a series of mosly unrelated stories or scenes instead of a single unified plot. In a **frame narrative**, these episodes are connected to each other in the context of a larger, overarching story, as in *The Canterbury Tales* or *1001 Arabian Nights*.

When you study modern literature, you will find few other arrangements, such as **stream of consciousness** and **reverse order**. As these are not characteristic of classical literature, we will not detail them here, but you should at least recognize these terms as describing narrative sequence.

Because literature is an art and not an exact science, a story may not fit perfectly into one of these categories of arrangements. These terms used to describe narrative arrangement are not mutually exclusive; more than one may apply to a particular narrative.

◯ Enter the following item in the Literature division.

Prose & Poetry Handbook

♦ Narrative Arrangement, Sequence, P&P 48: Title NARRATIVE ARRANGEMENT, then add SEQUENCE and its definition. Add the terms used to describe narrative arrangement, then list the terms detailed in the paragraphs above with a short description of each. Include stream of consciousness and reverse order at the end of the list, but do not add a description for these now.

◯ With your teacher, discuss the sequence of *The Odyssey*.

THE ODYSSEY

THE ODYSSEY OF HOMER

◯ Read

♦ *The Odyssey of Homer,* Book Two

◯ As you read, continue to mark the text and make notes:

♦ Literary concepts and terms you observe in the narrative. Do any of your earlier thoughts need revision?

♦ Instances of **epic simile**.

♦ **Epithets** to add to your running list.

♦ Passages reflecting on the value of **hearth and home**.

Writer's Journal

◯ Discuss this week's reading with your teacher, along with all your notes and observations. Narrate the main action of the book, and discuss any parts you did not understand. How was this reading **delightful**? What **wisdom** does this reading furnish?

Lesson 4.2

Language Logic

SENTENCE DIAGRAMMING: REVIEW COMPOUNDS

These lessons will also be review for *Bards & Poets* students.

 Review the following sections in *Sentence Sense* with your teacher.

III. Sentence Diagramming – Compounds

- ◆ 19.1 Compound Subjects
- ◆ 19.2 Compound Verbs
- ◆ 19.3 Compound Direct Objects
- ◆ 19.4 Compound Adjectives
- ◆ 19.5 Compound Adverbs
- ◆ 19.6 Compound Objects of Prepositions
- ◆ 19.7 Compound Sentences

III. Sentence Diagramming – Independent Elements

- ◆24.1 Conjunctions Introducing Sentences

Writer's Journal

 In your Writer's Journal, copy these sentences. Mark the prepositional phrases, subjects, and verbs. Bracket the clauses. Then diagram each one. Refer to *Sentence Sense* as needed.

1. So the heralds called them, and they came in haste.

2. Then did they wheel in the air, and shook out from each many feathers, and tare each other, and so departed.

3. Athene stood by him, like Mentor in shape and speech.

4. We will find a ship and rowers for thee.

5. Telemachus and the crew raised the pine tree mast, and set it in its place, and they made it fast with stays.

6. So all night, and till the dawn, the ship sped through the sea.

Orally parse these words with your teacher. Use the charts in *Sentence Sense* to guide you, skipping the information in the gray boxes for now.

(1) the, they; (2) did wheel, many; (3) Mentor; (4) ship, and; (5) pine, it, its, fast; (6) all, night, till the dawn

Lesson 4.3

Eloquent Expression

COPIA OF CONSTRUCTION

Copia of Construction devices change the grammatical pattern or structure of a sentence, also while preserving the original meaning. Here you will finish copying the chart into your *Poetics & Progym* Handbook. Return to this page often for reminders when you are revising sentences!

 Enter the following item in the Rhetoric Section.

Prose & Poetry Handbook

◆ Copia of Construction, P&P 27: Add Sentence Combination, Sentence Structure, and Figures of Speech, along with all the devices listed under each, to your Copia of Construction chart.

LITERARY IMITATION

In this exercise, which will be familiar to *Bards & Poets* students, we imitate the structure of a well-written sentence from literature. First, diagram the original sentence. Next, make a copy of just the **diagram skeleton** (the lines of the diagram without the words—the bones without the flesh!) and construct a new sentence on a new topic to fit the diagram.

Your letter greatly pleased me.

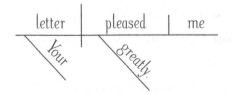

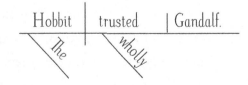

The Hobbit wholly trusted Gandalf.

Work with the sentences below that you diagrammed in Language Logic. Copy each sentence's **diagram skeleton**. On those skeletons, construct new sentences based on a different part of *The Odyssey*. Finally, write the new sentences below each diagram.

1. Then did they wheel in the air, and shook out from each many feathers, and tare each other, and so departed.

2. So all the night, and till the dawn, the ship sped through the sea.

Lesson 4.4

Classical Composition

PROGYMNASMA NARRATIVE: PLOT OBSERVATION – THEON'S SIX.

Work in your Writer's Journal, and follow these steps to complete a plot observsation with Theon's Six for Book Two of Homer's *Odyssey*. If you need reminders on how to do this, refer to the Example Narrative and the Example Plot Observation – Theon's Six in the Appendix under "Example Narrative Plot Observation."

A. First, take a look at the big picture, following these steps:

- Person: List all the important characters, with a brief description of each.
- Action: List the major actions of the plot in the order they occur in the story. Your list should have no less than two, and no more than five. If possible, first number the actions in the margins of the book (Action 1, Action 2, Action 3, etc.). If the narrative includes any sections that do not detail an action, label them **Prologue, Epilogue, Explanation, Description, Summary, Author Comment**s, etc., and include them in your list.
- Place: Name and briefly describe the main place(s) where the action took place. Consult the questions listed for Theon's Six Elements in the Appendix and make notes about as many of the questions as the narrative answers.
- Time: Briefly describe the time period in which the action took place (this may be

relative: before *x* or after *y*, or it may be more specific: one year later). Consult the questions listed for Theon's Six Elements in the Appendix and make notes about as many of the questions as the narrative answers.

B. Use Theon's Six to observe the narrative plot. Consult the questions listed for Theon's Six Elements in the Appendix to complete this part of the assignment.

- ◆ Person: First, make notes on what you learn about the main characters in this book. For each character, answer as many of Theon's Six questions about Person as you are able to answer directly from the narrative itself.
- ◆ Action: Create a numbered list with each of the actions you identified in order. If there are any sections of the narrative that do not detail an action, include these as well, and label them **Prologue**, **Epilogue**, **Explanation**, **Description**, **Summary**, **Author Comments**, etc.
- ◆ Under each action, answer Theon's Six questions about Time and Place if there are specifics attached to the action that you have not already detailed in Step A.
- ◆ Under each action, also answer as many of Theon's Six questions about Cause and Manner that the narrative answered.
- ◆ If you identified any sections that do not detail an action, add a brief note indicating the content of the section.

PROGYMNASMA NARRATIVE: PLOT OBSERVATION – SUMMARY

Work on the computer, or write your summary by hand in your Writer's Journal, and then transfer to your running file with *Odyssey* summaries.

A. Review your notes and compose a one paragraph summary of Book One that captures the main action, characters, and any other details from Theon's Six that are needful. You may either write this on the computer in a running file that you use for the entire course, or write each summary out by hand in your Writer's Journal, then transfer it to the running computer file.

B. Read over your summary to make sure you have not left out any **essentials** or included too many **non-essentials**. Revise as needed, and edit so that you have a smooth and eloquent summary paragraph.

Lesson 4.5

Reflection & Review

Commonplace Book

COMMONPLACE BOOK

 Enter in your Commonplace Book:

- a favorite passage or two from your reading in Homer's *Odyssey*
- an example or two of epithet and/or epic simile

MEMORY WORK

GRAMMAR FLASHCARDS

 Review to mastery:

- Parts of Speech – *Bards & Poets* Review
- Sentence Terms – *Bards & Poets* Review

Use the combine sets and test features at Quizlet for an online or printed quiz over these two sets.

Lesson 5

❧

NESTOR

from THE STORY OF THE ODYSSEY, by Alfred Church

At sunrise the ship came to Pylos, where Nestor dwelt. Now it so chanced that the people were offering a great sacrifice upon the shore to Poseidon. Nine companies there were, and in each company five hundred men, and for the five hundred there were nine bulls. And they had tasted of the inner parts and were burning the slices of flesh on the thigh-bones to the god, when Telemachus's company moored the ship and came forth from it to the shore. Athene spake to Telemachus, saying: "Now thou hast no need to be ashamed. Thou hast sailed across the sea to hear tidings of thy father. Go, therefore, to Nestor, and learn what counsel he hath in the deep of his heart."

But Telemachus answered, "How shall I speak to him, being so untried and young?"

"Nay," said the goddess; "but thou shalt think of something thyself, and something the gods will put into thy mouth."

So saying she led the way, and they came to where Nestor sat, with his sons, and a great company round him, making ready the feast. When these saw the strangers, they clasped their hands, and made them sit down on soft fleeces of wool. And Nestor's son Peisistratus brought to them food, and wine in a cup of gold. To Athene first he gave the wine, for he judged her to be the elder of the two, saying, "Pray now to the Lord Poseidon, and make thy drink offering, and when thou hast so done, give the cup to thy friend that he may do likewise."

Then Athene took the cup and prayed to Poseidon, saying: "Grant renown to Nestor and his son, and reward the men of Pylos for this great sacrifice. And grant that we may accomplish that for which we have come hither."

And the son of Ulysses prayed in like manner.

When they had eaten and drunk their fill, Nestor said: "Strangers, who are ye? Sail ye over the seas for trade, or as pirates that wander at hazard of their lives?"

To him Telemachus made reply, Athene putting courage into his heart: "We come from Ithaca, and our errand concerns ourselves. I seek for tidings of my father, who in old time fought by thy side, and sacked the city of Troy. Of all the others who did battle with the men of Troy, we have heard, whether they have returned, or where they died; but even the death of this man remains untold. Therefore am I come hither to thee; perchance thou mayest be willing to tell me of him, whether thou sawest his death with thine own eyes, or hast heard it from another. Speak me no soft words for pity's sake, but tell me plainly what thou hast seen."

Nestor made answer: "Thou bringest to my mind all that we endured, warring round Priam's mighty town. There the best of us were slain. Valiant Ajax lies there, and there Achilles, and there Patroclus, and there my own dear son. Who could tell the tale of all that we endured? Truly, no one, not though thou shouldst abide here five years or six to listen. For nine whole years we were busy, devising the ruin of the enemy, which yet Zeus brought not to pass. And always Ulysses passed the rest in craft, thy father Ulysses, if indeed thou art his son, and verily thy speech is like to his; one would not think that a younger man could be so like to an elder. But listen to my tale. When we had sacked the town, I returned across the sea without delay, leaving behind the others, so that I know not of my own knowledge which of the Greeks was saved and which was lost. But wander not thou, my son, far from home, while strangers devour thy substance. Go to Menelaus, for he hath but lately come back from a far country; go and ask him to tell thee all that he knoweth. If thou wilt, go with thy ships, or, if it please thee better, I will send thee with a chariot and horses, and my sons shall be thy guides."

Then said Athene: "Let us cut up the tongues of the beasts, and mix the wine, and pour offerings to Poseidon and the other gods, and so bethink us of sleep, for it is the time."

So she spake, and they hearkened to her words. And when they had finished, Athene and Telemachus would have gone back to their ship. But Nestor stayed them, saying: "Now Zeus and all the gods forbid that ye should depart to your ships from my house, as though it were the dwelling of a needy man that hath not rugs and blankets in his house, whereon his guests may sleep! Not so; I have rugs and blankets enough. Never shall the son of my friend Ulysses lay him down on his ship's deck, while I am alive, or my children after me, to entertain strangers in my hall."

Thereupon said the false Mentor: "This is good, dear father. Let Telemachus abide with thee; but I will go back to the ship, and cheer the company, and tell them all. There I will sleep this night, and to-morrow I go to the Cauconians, where there is owing to me a debt neither small nor of yesterday. But do thou send this man on his way in thy chariot."

Then the goddess departed in the semblance of a sea-eagle, and all that saw it were amazed.

Then the old man took Telemachus by the hand, and said: "No coward or weakling art thou like to be, whom the gods attend even now in thy youth. This is none other than Athene, daughter of Zeus, the same that stood by thy father in the land of Troy."

After this the old man led the company to his house. Here he mixed for them a bowl of wine eleven years old; and they prayed to Athene, and then lay down to sleep. Telemachus slept on a bedstead beneath the gallery, and Peisistratus slept by him.

The next day, as soon as it was morning, Nestor and his sons arose. And the old man said: "Let one man go to the plain for a heifer, and let another go to the ship of Telemachus, and bid all the company come hither, leaving two only behind. And a third shall command the goldsmith to gild the horns of the heifer, and let the handmaids prepare all things for a feast."

They did as the old man commanded; and after they had offered sacrifice, and had eaten and drunk, old Nester said, "Put now the horses in the chariot, that Telemachus may go his way."

So they yoked the horses, and the dame that kept the stores put into the chariot food and wine and dainties, such as princes eat. And Peisistratus took the reins, and Telemachus rode with him. And all that day they journeyed; and when the land grew dark they came to the city of Pherae, and there they rested; and the next day, travelling again, came to Lacedaemon, to the palace of King Menelaus.

ᕦᕤ

Lesson 5.1

Prose & Poetry

NARRATIVE INVENTION: SETTING

The **setting** of a narrative is the time and place in which the action happens. This may be an **historical** (actual) time and place, as Dickens gave us in *A Tale of Two Cities*, set during the French Revolution in London and Paris. Or the author may create his own time and place, as Tolkien does with Middle Earth in *The Lord of the Rings*. Or it may be some **combination** of an historical setting and a created setting, as Lewis gives us in *The Lion, The Witch, and The Wardrobe*, set in both London during World War II and in Narnia during the reign and fall of the White Witch.

❧ Enter the following item in the Literature division.

Prose & Poetry Handbook

◆ Narrative Invention, Setting, P&P 40: Title NARRATIVE INVENTION, subtitle SETTING, then copy the definition and categories.

◆ With your teacher, discuss the setting of *The Odyssey*, Book One. On a map of ancient Greece, find the places mentioned in Book One.

NARRATIVE INVENTION: CHARACTERS

Human life began, we are told, when God breathed life into a handful of dust and created Adam. Fictional life begins when an author breathes life into his characters and convinces us of their reality. — Laurence Perrine, *Literature: Structure, Sound, and Sense*

An author may straightforwardly *tell* us everything we need to know about a particular character, either through the words of the narrator or through the words of another character in the story. This is **direct characterization**. Often, though, an author instead *shows* us what we need to know by the character's own actions and words. This is **indirect characterization**. Within a particular narrative, an author may use both of these ways of drawing characters for the reader.

There will also usually be a variety of **character types** in a narrative. A **flat** or **static** character does not change throughout the story, and we generally do not learn much about him or her. In Dickens's *A Christmas Carol*, Scrooge's nephew Fred is such a character. A **stock** (or **stereotypical**) character is a flat character that we immediately recognize. He or she acts according to our expectations in every situation. This is the "bad guy" who always does the evil or selfish thing, or the "good guy" who always does the right thing. Although these may sound boring, almost every story needs a few of these. In *A Christmas Carol*, the unscrupulous pawn-broker is such a character.

But the most intriguing characters are generally **rounded** or **complex** characters. They are multi-faceted (literally, *many faces*). A rounded character does not always act according to expectations, formulas, or sterotypes. This may be the "good guy" who gives in to temptation or makes a tragic error in judgment. Or this may be the "bad guy" who betrays some tiny inkling of kindness or tenderness. Very often, a rounded character is one who undergoes a significant change as the story progresses, as we see in the case of Mr. Scrooge. This is the **dynamic** character, one who changes in some aspect of his personality or perspective through the course of the narrative. Perhaps this is even a flat character at the beginning of a book who becomes a complex character by the end.

An entire story devoted to the moral, emotional, or spiritual development of a particular character has a nifty German name: **bildungsroman** (bil dungs RO män). The more prosaical name is *coming-of-age* story. The first four books of Homer's *Odyssey*, collectively called the *Telemachia*, is considered by many to be the world's first bildungsroman.

❀ Enter the following item in the Literature division.

Prose & Poetry Handbook

- ◆ Narrative Invention: Characters, P&P 39: Title NARRATIVE INVENTION, then subtitle CHARACTERS. Add the Perrine quote, then list direct and indirect characterization with their definitions. Below this, list the character types detailed above, with a short description of each.

❀ Can you think of any characters in books you have read that might be classified as any of the types listed here? Discuss this with your teacher.

THE ODYSSEY

◯ Read

◆ *The Odyssey of Homer,* Book Three

◯ As you read, continue to mark the text and make notes:

◆ Literary concepts and terms you observe in the narrative. Do any of your earlier thoughts need revision?

◆ Instances of **epic simile**.

◆ **Epithets** to add to your running list.

◆ Passages reflecting on the value of **hearth and home**.

Writer's Journal

◯ Discuss this week's reading with your teacher, along with all your notes and observations. Narrate the main action of the book, and discuss any parts you did not understand. How was this reading **delightful**? What **wisdom** does this reading furnish?

Lesson 5.2

Language Logic

SENTENCE DIAGRAMMING: REVIEW

These lessons continue the review from *Bards & Poets.*

◯ Review the following sections in *Sentence Sense* with your teacher.

III. Sentence Diagramming – Verbals As Modifiers

◆ 17.1 Participles

◆ 17.2 Participial Phrases

◆ 17.3 Infinitive Phrases Used as Modifiers

◆ 17.4 The Complementary Infinitive

III. Sentence Diagramming – Verbals As Nouns

◆ 18.1 Participial Nouns (Gerunds)

◆ 18.2 Gerund Phrases

◆ 18.3 Infinitives Used as Nouns

◆ 18.4 Infinitive Phrases Used as Nouns

In your Writer's Journal, copy these sentences. Mark the prepositional phrases, subjects, and verbs. Bracket the clauses. Then diagram each one. Refer to *Sentence Sense* as needed.

1. At length the sun departed, setting in a sea of gold.

2. Few are qualified to shine in company, but it is in the power of most men to be agreeable.

3. I heard the ripple washing in the reeds,
   And the wild water lapping on the crags. — Tennyson

4. Our duty is to try, and our determination is to succeed.

5. Thou hast sailed across the sea to hear tidings of thy father.

Orally parse these words with your teacher. Use the charts in *Sentence Sense* to guide you, skipping the information in the gray boxes for now.

(1) setting; (2) to shine, most; (3) I, heard; (4) determination; (5) to hear, tidings, of thy father

<hr>

Lesson 5.3

Eloquent Expression

COPIA OF WORDS: NOUNS – VERB/VERBAL SWITCH

If the sentence has a **participle** or **participle phrase**, you can often exchange it for the **main verb**:

Receiving your letter, Erasmus was pleased.

Erasmus, pleased, received your letter.

COPIA OF WORDS: NOUNS – GERUND/INFINITIVE SWITCH

If the sentence has an **infinitive** used as a noun, you can often exchange it for a **gerund**, and vice versa:

The receiving of your letter brought me great joy.

To receive your letter brought me great joy.

Note that while this may not yield the best sentences in the world, the practice is beneficial. And there are times when it may turn up a gem in your own writing.

Writer's Journal

⚜ Copy each sentence below in your Writer's Journal. Paraphrase each using the Copia of Words devices listed above.

1. The company came hither, leaving two only behind.

2. Few are qualified to shine in company, but it is in the power of most men to be agreeable.

LITERARY IMITATION

⚜ Work with the sentences below that you diagrammed in Language Logic. For each sentence, copy the **diagram skeleton**, construct a new sentence, and write the new sentence below the diagram. Your new sentence should be based on a different part of *The Odyssey*; make it one that you can use in your retelling.

1. I heard the ripple washing in the reeds,

   And the wild water lapping on the crags. — Tennyson

2. Our duty is to try, and our determination is to succeed.

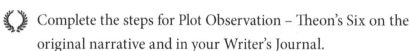

Lesson 5.4

Classical Composition

PROGYMNASMA NARRATIVE: PLOT OBSERVATION – THEON'S SIX AND SUMMARY

Observe and summarize Homer's *Odyssey*, Book Three. Refer to the instructions and example in the Appendix under "Narrative Plot Observation" and "Example Narrative Plot Observation."

Writer's Journal

⚜ Complete the steps for Plot Observation – Theon's Six on the original narrative and in your Writer's Journal.

Write a one paragraph summary of this book, following the steps for Plot Observation – Summary. Work either in your Writer's Journal or on the computer. Add this summary to your running file of *Odyssey* summaries, and save the file.

Lesson 5.5

Reflection & Review

COMMONPLACE BOOK

 Enter in your Commonplace Book:

Commonplace Book

- ◆ a favorite passage or two from your reading in Homer's *Odyssey*
- ◆ an example or two of epithet and/or epic simile

MEMORY WORK

GRAMMAR FLASHCARDS

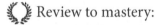 Review to mastery:

- ◆ Figures – Set #1 – *Poetics & Progym I*

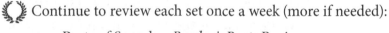 Continue to review each set once a week (more if needed):

- ◆ Parts of Speech – *Bards & Poets* Review
- ◆ Sentence Terms – *Bards & Poets* Review

Lesson 6

☙

IN SPARTA

from THE STORY OF THE ODYSSEY, **by Alfred Church**

Now it chanced that Menelaus had made a great feast that day, for his daughter, the child of the fair Helen, was married to the son of Achilles, to whom she had been promised at Troy; and his son had also taken a wife. And the two wayfarers stayed their chariot at the door, and the steward spied them, and said to Menelaus:—

"Lo! here are two strangers who are like the children of kings.

Shall we keep them here, or send them to another?"

But Menelaus was wroth, and said: "Shall we, who have eaten so often of the bread of hospitality, send these strangers to another? Nay, unyoke their horses and bid them sit down to meat." So the squires loosed the horses from the yoke, and fastened them in the stall, and gave them grain to eat and led the men into the hall. Much did they marvel at the sight, for there was a gleam as of the sun or moon in the palace of Menelaus. And when they had gazed their fill, they bathed them in the polished baths. After that they sat them down by the side of Menelaus. Then a handmaid bare water in a pitcher of gold, and poured it over a basin of silver that they might wash their hands. Afterwards she drew a polished table to their side, and a dame brought food, and set it by them, laying many dainties on the board, and a carver placed by them platters of flesh, and set near them golden bowls.

Then said Menelaus: "Eat and be glad; afterwards I will ask you who ye are, for ye seem like to the sons of kings."

And when they had ended the meal, Telemachus, looking round at the hall, said to his companion:—

"See the gold and the amber, and the silver and the ivory. This is like the hall of Zeus."

This he spake with his face close to his comrade's ear, but

Menelaus heard him and said:—

"With the halls of the gods nothing mortal may compare. And among men also there may be the match of these things. Yet I have wandered far, and got many possessions in many lands. But woe is me! Would that I had but the third part of this wealth of mine, and that they who perished at Troy were alive again! And most of all I mourn for the great Ulysses, for whether he be alive or dead no man knows."

But Telemachus wept to hear mention of his father, holding up his purple cloak before his eyes. This Menelaus saw, and knew who he was, and pondered whether he should wait till he should himself speak of his father, or should rather ask him of his errand. But while he pondered there came in the fair Helen, and three maidens with her, of whom one set a couch for her to sit, and one spread a carpet for her feet, and one bare a basket of purple wool; but she herself had a distaff of gold in her hand. And when she saw the strangers she said:—

"Who are these, Menelaus? Never have I seen such likeness in man or woman as this one bears to Ulysses. Surely 'tis his son Telemachus, whom he left an infant at home when ye went to Troy for my sake!"

Then said Menelaus: "It must indeed be so, lady. For these are the hands and feet of Ulysses, and the look of his eyes and his hair. And but now, when I made mention of his name, he wept, holding his mantle before his face."

Then said Peisistratus: "King Menelaus, thou speakest truth. This is indeed the son of Ulysses who is come to thee; perchance thou canst help him by word or deed."

And Menelaus answered: "Then is he the son of a man whom I loved right well. I thought to give him a city in this land, bringing him from Ithaca with all his goods. Then should naught have divided us but death itself. But these things the gods have ordered otherwise."

At these words they all wept—the fair Helen and Telemachus and Menelaus; nor could Peisistratus refrain himself, for he thought of his dear brother who was slain at Troy.

Then said Menelaus: "Now we will cease from weeping; and to-morrow there is much that Telemachus and I must say one to the other."

Then the fair Helen put a mighty medicine in the wine whereof they drank—nepenthe, men call it. So mighty is it that whoever drinks of it, weeps not that day, though father and mother die, and though men slay brother or son before his eyes.

And after this she said: "It would take long to tell all the wise and valiant deeds of Ulysses. One thing, however, ye shall hear, and it is this: while the Greeks were before Troy he came into the city, having disguised himself as a beggar-man, yea, and he had laid many blows upon himself, so that he seemed to have been shamefully treated. I alone knew who he was, and questioned him, but he answered craftily. And I swore that I would not betray him. So he slew many Trojans with the sword, and learnt many things. And while other women in Troy lamented, I was glad, for my heart was turned again to my home."

Then Menelaus said: "Thou speakest truly, lady. Many men have I seen, and travelled over many lands, but never have I seen one who might be matched with Ulysses. Well do I remember how, when I and other chiefs of the Greeks sat in the horse of wood, thou didst come. Some god who loved the sons of Troy put the thing into thy heart. Thrice didst thou walk round our hiding-place and call by name to each one of the chiefs, speaking marvellously like his wife. Then would we have risen from our place or answered thee straightway. But Ulysses hindered us, and thus saved all the Greeks."

But Telemachus said: "Yet all these things have not kept him, for he has perished."

And after that they slept.

CR

Lesson 6.1

Prose & Poetry

PROGYMNASMA ANECDOTE AND PROGYMNASMA PROVERB

As we prepare to move to these next two exercises in the Progymnasmata, we must first lay some groundwork in identifying and understanding anecdotes and proverbs themselves.

WHAT IS AN ANECDOTE?

When Alexander, the king of the Macedonians, was asked by someone where he kept his treasures, he pointed to his friends.

Cornelia, daughter of Scipio Africanus, and mother of famous Roman reformers Tiberias and Gaius Gracchus, once received a visit from a wealthy Roman lady. The lady proudly displayed her jewelry before Cornelia, and then insisted on seeing Cornelia's jewels. Calling her sons to her side, Cornelia replied, "These are my jewels."

Theodore Roosevelt used to say, "Speak softly and carry a big stick."

The twentieth century martyr, Jim Eliot, said, "He is no fool who gives what he cannot keep to gain that which he cannot lose."[1]

An **anecdote** is "a recollection of a noteworthy statement, action, or combination of statement and action."[2] It is a little story about a person, usually well-known, who has exhibited wit and/or wisdom. Anecdotes may be classified as **verbal** if the person speaks in a witty or wise way, **action** if the person acts in a witty or wise way, or **mixed** if it involves both speech and action. Sometimes an anecdote includes a **circumstance**—a question or a situation to which the person is responding. **Chreia** (plural **chreiai**) is another name for an anecdote.

 Read through the anecdotes above once more and discuss them with your teacher. Classify each one as verbal, action, or mixed. Also note whether or not each has a circumstance.

WHAT IS A PROVERB?

A slack hand causes poverty, but the hand of the diligent makes rich. — Proverbs 10:4

---

1 Eliot, who was a prolific journaler and commonplacer, may have been paraphrasing theologian Matthew Henry, who attributed a very similar saying to his own father, Philp. Visit the Archives at Wheaton College to learn more: http://www2.wheaton.edu/bgc/archives/faq/20.htm

2 Gibson, *Libanius' Progymnasmata*, 43.

Wise men speak because they have something to say; fools because they have to say something. – Plato

If you are patient in one moment of anger, you will escape a hundred days of sorrow. – Chinese Proverb

The true soldier fights not because he hates what is in front of him, but because he loves what is behind him. – G.K. Chesterton

A **proverb** is a "pithy, universal statement"[3] that often seeks to persuade or dissuade the hearer from some course of action or thought. Some proverbs, though, simply seek to explain how things are or ought to be. Also known as *maxims* or *morals*, these "words to live by" are found in virtually every culture. Many are drawn from Scripture, from literary works, or from the words of historical figures. Some are anonymous, and a few are attributed to an entire people group.

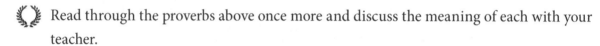 Read through the proverbs above once more and discuss the meaning of each with your teacher.

AN ANCEDOTE OR PROVERB?

There are four main differences between anecdotes and proverbs, according to Theon and other ancient writers:[4]

1. An anecdote is always **attributed** to a specific person or group of persons. This means that the person or group of persons is named as either saying or doing the wise or witty thing. A proverb may or may not be attributed to a specific person.

2. An anecdote may be a **universal statement**, applying at all times and in all places, or it may be more particularly related to the circumstance at hand. A proverb is always a universal statement.

3. An anecdote may be "useful" or it may be simply amusing. A proverb is always meant to be useful.

4. An anecdote may be a saying or it may be an action. A proverb is always a saying.

A proverb can always be converted to an anecdote:

Plato once said, "Wise men speak because they have something to say; fools because they have to say something."

Plato once said that wise men speak because they have something to say; fools because they have to say something.

---

3 *Ibid*, 87.
4 Kennedy, *Progymnasmata*, 15-16.

A verbal anecdote may sometimes be converted to a proverb if its wit or wisdom is universal, and not limited to a particular circumstance.

> He is no fool who gives what he cannot keep to gain that which he cannot lose. – Jim Eliot

Writer's Journal

Copy each saying below in your Writer's Journal. Note whether each is an anecdote or a proverb. If it is an anecdote, classify it as verbal, action, or mixed. Also note whether or not it has a circumstance. Finally, if possible, rewrite the anecdotes as proverbs and proverbs as anecdotes.

> A Laconian, when someone asked him where the Lacedaemonians consider the boundaries of their land to be, showed his spear.

> A liar will not be believed even when he speaks the truth. – Aesop

> General Stonewall Jackson, when asked by a young officer how he could be so fearless in battle, replied, "Captain, my religious belief teaches me to feel as safe in battle as in bed. God has fixed the time for my death. I do not concern myself about that, but to be always ready, no matter when it may overtake me." He added, after a pause, looking (him) full in the face: "That is the way all men should live, and then all would be equally brave."

> As vinegar to the teeth, and as smoke to the eyes, so is the sluggard to them that send him. – Proverbs 10:26

> Early to bed and early to rise, makes a man healthy, wealthy, and wise. – Ben Franklin, *Poor Richard's Almanac*

THE ODYSSEY

We are taking the training wheels off halfway through Book Four, and you will no longer be assigned reading in *The Story of the Odyssey* after this lesson. In fact, Church breaks Homer's Book Four into two chapters, and we are only assigning the first one. If you find the reading in *The Story of the Odyssey* is a needed help in understanding Homer's *Odyssey*, feel free to continue. You can find it on gutenberg.org.

⟨⟩ Read

- *The Odyssey of Homer,* Book Four

⟨⟩ As you read, continue to mark the text and make notes:

- Literary concepts and terms you observe in the narrative. Do any of your earlier thoughts need revision?
- Instances of **epic simile**.
- **Epithets** to add to your running list.
- Passages reflecting on the value of **hearth and home**.

Writer's Journal

⟨⟩ Discuss this week's reading with your teacher, along with all your notes and observations. Narrate the main action of the book, and discuss any parts you did not understand. How was this reading **delightful**? What **wisdom** does this reading furnish?

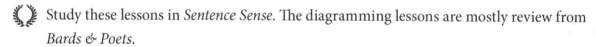

Lesson 6.2

Language Logic

NOUN PROPERTY – CASE

These lessons complete the concepts needed to fully parse a noun.

⟨⟩ Study these lessons in *Sentence Sense*. The diagramming lessons are mostly review from *Bards & Poets*.

I. Etymology – The Noun

- 1.7A Property – Case
- 1.7B The Nominative Case
- 1.7C The Possessive Case
- 1.7D The Objective Case
- 1.7E The Absolute Case

III. Sentence Diagramming – Objects and Complements

- 16.1 Indirect Objects
- 16.2 Objective Complements
- 16.3 Objective Complements Introduced by "As"

GRAMMAR TERMS & DEFINITIONS: NOUN TERMS

🏅 Grammar Terms to Master: Noun. In the Quizlet classroom, review or print flashcards from Noun Terms – *Poetics & Progym I*.

GRAMMAR FLASHCARDS

- ◆ Property – Case
- ◆ Nominative Case
- ◆ Possessive Case
- ◆ Objective Case
- ◆ Absolute Case

🏅 In your Writer's Journal, copy these sentences. Mark the prepositional phrases, subjects, and verbs. Bracket the clauses. Then diagram each one. Refer to *Sentence Sense* as needed.

Writer's Journal

1. So the squires loosed the horses from the yoke, and fastened them in the stall, and gave them grain to eat, and led the men into the hall.

2. I have wandered far, and got(ten) many possessions in many lands.

3. Telemachus wept to hear mention of his father, holding up his purple cloak before his eyes.

4. Menelaus made Helen his queen.

5. Now thou hast no need to be ashamed.

🏅 Orally parse these words with your teacher. Use the charts in *Sentence Sense* to guide you. Add Property – Case to your noun and pronoun parsing.

(1) squires, grain, (2) lands, (3) Telemachus, cloak, (4) made, Helen, queen; (5) need, to be ashamed

Lesson 6.3

Eloquent Expression

FIGURES OF DESCRIPTION

A figure of description is a vivid portayal – "a bringing to life" in the mind's eye of the reader. Figures of description are classified by the thing they describe: a person's face, a tree, the wind, the stars, etc. *Bards & Poets* students learned the first five of these figures of description that the ancient Greeks identified and that are used very often in narrative writing:

Anemographia: vivid description of the wind; <Greek *anemos* – wind

> On stormy nights, when the wind shook the four corners of the house, and the surf roared along the cove and up the cliffs . . . — Robert Louis Stevenson, *Treasure Island*

Chronographia: vivid description of a particular time; an historical time period, or a recurring time period, such as a season or a particular time of day; <Greek *chronos* – time

> It was one of those March days when the sun shines hot and the wind blows cold: when it is summer in the light and winter in the shade. — Charles Dickens, *Great Expectations*

Astrothesia: vivid description of the stars or the night sky <Greek *astron* – star

> Silently, one by one, in the infinite meadows of heaven,
> Blossomed the lovely stars, the forget-me-nots of the angels."
> — Henry Wadsworth Longfellow, "Evangeline: A Tale of Acadie"

Topographia: the vivid description of a place; <Greek *topos* – place

> A damp mist rose from the river, and the marshy ground about; and spread itself over the dreary fields. It was piercing cold, too; all was gloomy and black. — Charles Dickens, *Oliver Twist*

Hydrographia: vivid description of water; <Greek *hydro* – water

> Never in his life had he seen a river before—this sleek, sinuous, full-bodied animal, chasing and chuckling, gripping things with a gurgle and leaving them with a laugh, to fling itself on fresh playmates that shook themselves free, and were caught and held again. All was a-shake and a-shiver—glints and gleams and sparkles, rustle and swirl, chatter and bubble. — Kenneth Grahame, *The Wind in the Willows*

◯ Enter the following item in the Figures division of your Prose & Poetry Handbook.

Prose & Poetry Handbook

- ◆ Figures of Description P&P 94: Title FIGURES OF DESCRIPTION, then copy the definitions and examples of anemographia, chronographia, astrothesia, topographia, and hydrographia.

LITERARY IMITATION

◯ Work with the sentence below that you diagrammed in Language Logic. Copy the **diagram skeleton**, construct a new sentence, and write the new sentence below the diagram. Your new sentence should be based on a different part of *The Odyssey*; make it one that you can use in your summary.

Writer's Journal

Telemachus wept to hear mention of his father, holding up his purple cloak before his eyes.

Lesson 6.4

Classical Comoposition

PROGYMNASMA NARRATIVE: PLOT OBSERVATION – THEON'S SIX AND SUMMARY
Observe and summarize Homer's *Odyssey*, Book Four. Refer to the instructions and example in the Appendix under "Narrative Plot Observation" and "Example Narrative Plot Observation."

◯ Complete the steps for Plot Observation – Theon's Six on the original narrative and in your Writer's Journal.

Writer's Journal

◯ Write a one paragraph summary of this book, following the steps for Plot Observation – Summary. Work either in your Writer's Journal or on the computer. Add this summary to your running file of *Odyssey* summaries, and save the file.

PROGYMNASMA NARRATIVE: TELEMACHIA SUMMARY

The first four books of the *Odyssey* are commonly referred to as the *Telemachia*. In this lesson, you will use your plot observations from the last few lessons to create a summary of the *Telemachia*. A summary of the entire *Telemachia* may seem like a daunting task, but happily you have already done most of the work by writing narrative summaries as you read each book. All you need to do now is assemble them into a complete narrative, and add a few descriptive details for interest.

🏅 Write a narrative summary of the Telemachia. Your summary should be about two to three pages of type, double-spaced.

A. Review your Plot Observations for each of the first four books of the *Odyssey*.

B. Open the running computer file with your one-paragraph summaries of the *Telemachia*. Cut and paste these into a new document, and save as a new file. You will need the original file for all future lessons, so make sure you keep track of it!

C. Revise and rework your summaries into a smoothly flowing narrative. Pay attention to transitions. Consider the narrative chronology. Would your summary benefit from choosing a new *in medias res* starting point? If so, rearrange your paragraphs to fit your preferred arrangement. If you choose to do this, make sure that characters and important details are adequately introduced in your revised order, and that you do not re-introduce them later on in the retelling.

D. Add details as needed for interest and to connect summaries. Aim to have one longer or two briefer paragraphs for each book. Remember to indent each paragraph. Include in this summary:

   ◆ a heading, properly formatted
   ◆ figures of description (at least two): *anemographia, chronographia, hydrographia, astrothesia, topographia*

E. Ask your writing mentor to check that the assignment is complete. Print and file.

EDITOR'S PEN: SUMMARY OF THE TELEMACHIA

🏅 Revise your summary using the checklist below. Work through the checklist once on your own, and then a second time with your writing mentor, making notes on the print copy of your narrative. Transfer all additions and corrections from your print copy to the computer file. Save and print the document.

Editor's Pen – The Big Picture

✓ All important plot elements included

✓ All characters represented correctly

✓ Sequence: *linear from the beginning, or a new* in medias res *arrangement*

✓ Length: *3-5 pages, typed and double-spaced*

✓ Point of View: *3rd person*

✓ Figures of Description (at least three): *anemographia, chronographia, hydrographia, astrothesia, topographia*

Editor's Pen – Zoom 5x: Paragraphs

✓ Formatting: *proper indentation*

✓ Length: *neither too wordy nor too short*

✓ Sentence class by use: *effective use*

✓ Sentence openers: *varied*

✓ Dialogue: *none or very limited*

✓ Verb Tense: *consistent (may use historical present)*

✓ Pronouns clear: *easily identified antecedents*

✓ Person for Nouns & Pronouns: *appropriate to 1st person point of view*

Editor's Pen – Zoom 10x: Sentences

✓ Complete thought expressed

✓ Subject and predicate agree in number

✓ Correct capitalization and punctuation

  ◆ No comma splices!

Editor's Pen – Fine Focus: Words

✓ Word choices varied; word meanings clear; consider denotation AND connotation

  ◆ Verbs: *strong, fitting; appropriate adverbs if needed*

  ◆ Nouns: *clear, descriptive; appropriate adjectives if needed*

  ◆ Dialogue: *dialogue tags varied if appropriate*

  ✓ Correct spelling

✓ Final read-through

Lesson 6.5

Reflection & Review

COMMONPLACE BOOK

 Enter in your Commonplace Book:

Commonplace Book

- ◆ a favorite passage or two from your reading in Homer's *Odyssey*
- ◆ an example or two of epithet and/or epic simile
- ◆ examples from your reading of other figures you have learned (see Figures list in *Poetics & Progym I* Appendix)
- ◆ several anecdotes and several proverbs from this lesson
- ◆ one additional anecdote and one additional proverb from your own reading or from research

Nota Bene: As you research proverbs and anecdotes, you will find that not every proverb or anecdote embodies a noble or true idea. You will be likely to come across more than a few with which you do not agree, such as:

He who flees poverty . . . should cast himself into the sea, and from steep cliffs. – Theognis

Cleanliness is next to godliness. – Ancient Near Eastern Proverb

In the study of proverbs and anecdotes, as in all things, carefully evaluate the ideas being put forth. Always read and study with discernment. Even if a particular proverb or anecdote expresses a view in conflict with your own beliefs, it may be a valuable help in understanding the priorities and practices of people in other times, places, or situations. Do not discount proverbs, anecdotes, or quotes with which you disgree as possible additions to your Commonplace Book. They may make excellent topics for you to explore in an essay someday.

MEMORY WORK

GRAMMAR FLASHCARDS

 Review to mastery:

- ◆ Noun Terms – *Poetics & Progym I*
- ◆ Figures – Set #1 – *Poetics & Progym I*

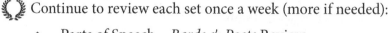 Continue to review each set once a week (more if needed):

- ◆ Parts of Speech – *Bards & Poets* Review
- ◆ Sentence Terms – *Bards & Poets* Review

Lesson 7

❦

THE ATHENIAN SCHOOLBOY
THE BOOK OF THE ANCIENT GREEKS by Dorothy Mills

The chief aim of Athenian education was the building of character. The Athenians were more concerned that their sons should grow up to be good citizens, loving what was beautiful and hating all that was ugly, than that they should know any great number of facts . . . they believed it was a glory to live for their city, and to this end, they trained the mind and the imagination as well as the body. To an Athenian, a good man was a good citizen, one who, being physically perfect, would be able to defend his city in time of war, who being able to think, would be capable of governing, and loving all that was beautiful, would set high standards of taste in art, in letters, and in conduct.

. . . The Athenian boy went to school when he was seven years old. At this age, he was placed in the charge of a pedagogue, a trusted slave who accompanied him to school, carried his books for him, and helped him, when necessary, with his lessons. The pedagogue was also expected to keep him in good order, to teach him good manners, to answer his many questions, and to punish him whenever he thought fit, which was probably very often.

. . . Arrived at school, the pedagogue remained in an ante-room, where he waited with all the other pedagogues until morning school was over. The boy entered a larger room beyond, where he settled down to his lessons . . . Athenian boys were taught three main subjects: letters, music, and gymnastics . . . Athenian boys had no books for children—they began by reading great poetry and literature. Much of the literature they learned by heart, standing in front of the master who recited it to them, and they learnt it by repeating it after him line by line. In this way they mastered passages from the *Iliad* and the *Odyssey* . . . "My father," said one man speaking on his school days, "in his pains to make me a good man, compelled me to learn the whole of Homer's poems, and even now I can repeat the *Iliad* and the *Odyssey* by heart." (Xenophon, *Banquet*)

. . . According to Plato, this education turned the Athenian boy from being "the most unmanageable of animals" into "the most amiable and divine of living beings." This change had not taken place without many a punishment of the boy, and it was a proverb that "he who is not flogged cannot be taught."

ॐ

Lesson 7.1

Prose & Poetry

EDUCATION IN ANCIENT GREECE

In upcoming lessons, we will study several ancient progymnasma Anecdote elaborations written by ancient Greek teachers of rhetoric as examples for their students to follow.

 For background on the subjects of these essays, read the short excerpt from *The Book of the Ancient Greeks* by Dorothy Mills at the beginning of this lesson. (If you have this book at home, read the entire chapter.)

UNDERSTANDING AN ANECDOTE OR PROVERB

In order to write about an anecdote or a proverb, as you will do in upcoming lessons, you must first fully comprehend its meaning. This can be accomplished first by careful analysis. Consider the syntax (grammatical structure) of the anecdote or proverb by diagramming it. Consider the meaning of the words used in the anecdote or proverb itself, and work with synonyms to express the same meaning in different words. Next, explicate the anecdote or proverb by inflection—paraphrasing with different grammatical structure.

 Study the example analysis and inflection below.

Pride goeth before destruction. — Proverbs 16:18, KJV

Analysis

◆ **Diagram** the sentence:

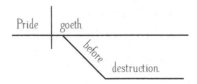

◆ **Definitions**: Look up any words you do not understand in the dictionary. Do a complete Vocabulary Study on a few **key words.** (See Appendix for Vocabularly Study instructions.)

pride: (noun) an excessively high opinion of oneself; conceit, arrogance; <ME pride, prude, prute <OE pryte, pryde, from prüt, prüd. SYN: conceit, arrogance, haughtiness, vainglory, self-importance; ANT: meekness, modesty, humility; "It was pride that changed angels into devils; it is humility that makes men as angels." — St. Augustine

destruction: the act of destroying (to ruin completely, spoil so that restoration is impossible, consume), <ME destruccioun, <OF destruction <L destructio, destroy. SYN: eradication, annihilation, extermination, carnage, loss, ruin; ANT: creation, construction, reparation, restoration. "...they were his counsellors after the death of his father to his destruction." — II Chronicles 22:4

◆ **Copia of Words**: Rewrite at least two times, replacing all the important words or phrases with synonyms each time. Refer to Copia of Words in the Appendix.

Vainglory precedes ruin. A lack of humility leads to annihilation.

Inflection

◆ **Number**: Rewrite, changing the number of nouns and pronouns from singular to plural or vice versa. Change other words in the sentence as necessary.

Prides go before destructions.

Declension: (Refer to *Sentence Sense*, 1.7 Noun Property – Case.) Rewrite four times, changing the case of the underlined noun or pronoun to each of the other cases. For the objective case, write two sentences changing the case each time to indicate different types of objects.

1. Nominative – noun or pronoun as subject of sentence or clause.

2. Possessive – possessive noun formed with 's; possessive pronoun form, noun or pronoun as the object of the preposition *of*.

3. Objective – noun or pronoun as an object – direct, indirect, object of preposition (besides *of*), objective complement, object of a verbal, etc.

4. Absolute – noun or pronoun as an independent element such as a vocative.

1. Pride goeth before destruction. [Nominative – original]
2. Pride's consequence is destruction. [Possessive]
3a. Where you find destruction, you will find pride. [Objective – direct object]
3b. Destruction is a consequence of pride. [Objective – object of the preposition]
4. O Pride, you are the cause of so much destruction! [Absolute]

◆ **Copia of Construction**: Paraphrase two more times with copia of construction. You may also employ copia of words. Refer to Copia of Construction in the Appendix.

Does not pride go before destruction? Pride went before his fall. Haughty and arrogant pride surely lead to utter and complete destruction.

As you work through these exercises, keep in mind that they are designed to promote understanding of the proverb by applying the lessons you have learned in Language Logic and Eloquent Expression. They will not always result in sentences that are elegant. This is particularly true for declining anecdotes and proverbs. Some of the sentences may be quite wordy or awkward. Do your best make them as eloquent as possible, but do not worry too much if they sound wooden.

In your Writer's Journal, write the proverb below, then analyze and inflect it, following the listed steps. Refer to the examples above and to diagramming helps in *Sentence Sense* as needed.

Writer's Journal

Courage is going from failure to failure without losing enthusiasm. — Winston Churchill

Analysis	**Inflection**
◆ Diagram	◆ Number
◆ Definitions	◆ Declension
◆ Copia of Words	◆ Copia of Construction

🏅 Read

- *The Odyssey of Homer,* Book Five

🏅 As you read, continue to mark the text and make notes:

- Literary concepts and terms you observe in the narrative. Do any of your earlier thoughts need revision?
- Instances of **epic simile**.
- **Epithets** to add to your running list.
- Passages reflecting on the value of **hearth and home**.

Writer's Journal

🏅 Discuss this week's reading with your teacher, along with all your notes and observations. Narrate the main action of the book, and discuss any parts you did not understand. How was this reading **delightful**? What **wisdom** does this reading furnish?

Lesson 7.2

Language Logic

🏅 Study these sections in *Sentence Sense*. The diagramming lessons are mostly review from *Bards & Poets*.

I. Etymology – The Noun

- 1.7F Case and Nouns in Apposition
- 1.7G Noun Declension

III. Sentence Diagramming – Appositives

- 15.1 Appositives and Their Modifiers
- 15.2 Appositives Introduced by Emphatic Words

III. Sentence Diagramming – Modifiers

- 13.6 Adjectives as Substantives

In your Writer's Journal, copy these sentences. Mark the prepositional phrases, subjects, and verbs. Bracket the clauses. Then diagram each one. Refer to *Sentence Sense* as needed.

Writer's Journal

1. The poet Homer was blind.

2. Telemachus went to Pylos the sacrosanct in quest of his father.

3. He shall see his people and come back to his house with the high roof and to the land of his fathers.

4. Kalypso, shining among goddesses, questioned Hermes.

5. So she spoke to him, but long-suffering great Odysseus shuddered to hear, and spoke again in turn and addressed her.

Orally parse these words with your teacher, using the charts in *Sentence Sense* to guide you.

(1) poet, Homer; (2) quest, Pylos, sacrosanct; (3) shall see, and (second use), land; (4) Hermes; (5) again, but, her

---

Lesson 7.3

Eloquent Expression

COPIA OF WORDS: NOUNS – APPOSITIVE MODIFIERS

Appositive nouns (Harvey's Lesson 34) are also adjective elements. Titles, professions, or ranks are often appositive nouns. Compound pronouns like himself, herself, itself, myself, etc. may also be used as appositives. Recall the comma rule about appositives which are modified by any words other than the. Review the lesson from Harvey's if you need to.

Erasmus was pleased by your letter.

Erasmus the rhetorician was pleased by your letter.

Erasmus, the great rhetorician, was pleased by your letter.

Erasmus himself was pleased by your letter.

Copy each sentence below in your Writer's Journal. Paraphrase these sentences adding an appositive noun for each underlined noun.

1. The <u>pedagogue</u> was also expected to keep him in good order.

2. The wanderings of Odysseus are recorded in the <u>Odyssey</u>.

LITERARY IMITATION

Work with the sentence below which you diagrammed in Language Logic. Copy the **diagram skeleton**, construct a new sentence, and write the new sentence below the diagram. Your new sentence should be based on a different part of *The Odyssey*; make it one that you can use in your summary of the entire book (see Lesson 7.4).

Kalypso, shining among goddesses, questioned Hermes.

Lesson 7.4

Classical Composition

PROGYMNASMA NARRATIVE: PLOT OBSERVATION – THEON'S SIX AND SUMMARY

As you read through the rest of *The Odyssey* in upcoming lessons, you will continue to observe the plot and write summaries for each book, which you will then use beginning in Lesson 26 to create an outline, a summary, and a précis of the entire book. You will definitely want to keep track of these summaries so you do not have to recreate them later.

Observe and summarize Homer's *Odyssey*, Book Five. Refer to the instructions and example in the Appendix under "Narrative Plot Observation" and "Example Narrative Plot Observation."

Complete the steps for Plot Observation – Theon's Six on the original narrative and in your Writer's Journal.

✦ Write a one paragraph summary of this book, following the steps for for Plot Observation – Summary. Work either in your Writer's Journal or on the computer. Add this summary to your running file of *Odyssey* summaries, and save the file.

PROGYMNASMA NARRATIVE: THE TELEMACHIA PRÉCIS #1

A **précis** (*pray-see*) is a concise summary of a text. The original text may be an entire book or just a chapter, an article, an essay, a speech, a sermon, etc. Other names for a brief summary of this kind include **abstract**, **summa**, and **synopsis**. A précis may be single sentence, or it may be up to a paragraph or two if the original text is very long. Your assignment now is to write a one-paragraph précis of *The Telemachia*.

The root word for *précis* is the same as the root word for *precise*. This is a good way to think about a précis. In order to convey the essence of the story, you must be very precise with the words you use. Take every opportunity to hone this skill—it will serve you well in your academic career and beyond.

✦ Write a one-paragraph précis of *The Telemachia*.

A. Begin with the summary that you completed in Lesson 6.4. Save it as a separate file.

B. Condense the summary to a one-paragraph précis. Though this paragraph will be concise, make sure the narrative flows smoothly and eloquently, using these tips for condensing a narrative:

   ◆ Remove any dialogue, description, and repetition.
   ◆ Whittle down the remaining sentences using the sentence combination devices you have learned.
   ◆ Wherever possible, substitute single words for phrases or clauses.
   ◆ If you have items in a series joined by a conjunction, look for a way to express the same idea with a single word or phrase.

EDITOR'S PEN: THE TELEMACHIA PRÉCIS #1

✦ Revise your précis using the checklist below. Work through the checklist once on your own, and then a second time with your writing mentor, making notes on the print copy of your narrative. Transfer all additions and corrections from your print copy to the computer file. Save and print the document. Be sure to keep this file; you will need it for your summary of the entire book in Lesson 26.4.

Editor's Pen – The Big Picture

✓ All major plot elements accounted for

✓ All characters represented correctly

✓ Sequence: *linear from the beginning*

✓ Length: *one paragraph*

✓ Point of View: *3rd person*

Editor's Pen – Zoom 5x: Paragraphs

✓ Formatting: *proper indentation*

✓ Length: *neither too wordy nor too short*

✓ Sentence class by use: *effective use*

✓ Sentence openers: *varied*

✓ Dialogue: *none*

✓ Verb Tense: *consistent (may use historical present)*

✓ Pronouns clear: *easily identified antecedents*

✓ Person for Nouns & Pronouns: *consistent and appropriate*

Editor's Pen – Zoom 10x: Sentences

✓ Complete thought expressed

✓ Subject and predicate agree in number

✓ Correct capitalization and punctuation

   ◆ No comma splices!

Editor's Pen – Fine Focus: Words

✓ Word choices varied; word meanings clear; consider denotation AND connotation

   ◆ Verbs: *strong, fitting; appropriate adverbs if needed*

   ◆ Nouns: *clear, descriptive; appropriate adjectives if needed*

   ✓ Correct spelling

✓ Final read-through

Lesson 7.5

Reflection & Review

Commonplace
Book

COMMONPLACE BOOK

Enter in your Commonplace Book:

- a favorite passage or two from your reading in Homer's *Odyssey*
- an example or two of epithet and/or epic simile
- examples from your reading of other figures and literary devices you have learned (see Figures and Literary Devices lists in *Poetics & Progym I* Appendix)

MEMORY WORK

GRAMMAR
FLASHCARDS

Review to mastery:
- Noun Terms – *Poetics & Progym I*
- Figures – Set #1 – *Poetics & Progym I*

Continue to review each set once a week (more if needed):
- Parts of Speech – *Bards & Poets* Review
- Sentence Terms – *Bards & Poets* Review

Use the test features at Quizlet for an online or printed quiz over Figures Set #1.

○⅋

Diogenes and the Pedagogus
Ancient Anecdote elaboration By Pseudo-Nicolaus

Diogenes, on seeing a youth misbehaving, beat the pedagogus, adding,
"Why do you teach such things?"

It is proper to praise every philosophy but especially that which
Diogenes practised. For he left to others the investigation of the paths of
the stars and the examination of the circuit of the sun, whereas he himself
applied his knowledge to the correction of character.

This is why, when he had entered the marketplace and chanced upon a
boy who was showing a lack of self-control although his paedagogus was
in attendance, he disregarded the boy, went after the paedagogus, and
chastised the guardian instead of the boy. Nor did he conceal the reason
for his blow: "This much at least," he said, "anyone who is not a good
paedagogus will understand." And so this is what he has done, but it is
possible from what follows to understand that he has acted properly.

Diogenes understood that youth is an irrational sort of being, whereas
old men have acquired, if nothing else, the experience of old age. He also
knew that parents pay a high price for old men and set them as guardians
over their young men, so that they correct the thoughtless nature of youth
by the thoughtfulness of their elders. Knowing these things, he ignored
the young man and went after the paedagogus, on whom the parents were
relying to discipline their boy, and deliberately chose the man instead of
the boy.

Indeed, if he had inflicted the blow, not on the paedagogus, but on the
boy, who would not fault Diogenes's discipline? For youth understands
nothing but is always impressed by what has happened in matters where
he lacks judgement.

Just as the mistakes of sailors are attributed to pilots, and a chorus, when it hits a false note, allows the trainer to be blamed, and an army, when it is disorderly, causes the general to be blamed, so a boy, when he makes a mistake, causes his paedagogus to be accused.

Consider, if you will, the city of the Athenians which, when its soldiers died in the Hellespont, passed judgment on the generals, rather than on the Hellespont, because they had not retrieved the soldiers who had died. And so what occurred because of other factors was alleged to be the faults of the generals. The Athenians also credited Themistocles with the victory at Salamis, even though the people and the city fought, too. Thus, in either case, the Athenians held responsible those in charge, both when they succeeded and when they blundered.

For this reason, it is necessary to admire Sophocles, who said that every city is under the influence of its leaders, and people who are unruly become wicked through the character of their teachers.

After looking at all these points, we have to admire Diogenes as the best disciplinarian.

—translated by RONALD HOCK AND EDWARD O'NEIL

℞

Lesson 8.1

Prose & Poetry

PROGYMNASMA ANECDOTE AND PROGYMNASMA PROVERB

Now we are ready to consider the actual exercises of Progymnasma Anecdote and Progymnasma Proverb. In this essay, the student composed an **elaboration** of a well-known anecdote or proverb in order to examine and consider its wisdom or wit. First we will take a look at an ancient elaboration of this kind.

ANCIENT ANECDOTE ELABORATION BY PSEUDO-NICOLAUS

Read the ancient elaboration by Pseudo-Nicolaus at the beginning of this lesson. If possible, read it aloud with your teacher.

A. In your Writer's Journal, research and answer (in writing) these questions about the anecdote.

Writer's
Journal

- ◆ Who was Diogenes of Sinope (the Cynic)?
- ◆ The author refers to "Athenian soldiers [who] died in the Hellespont." This occurred after the Battle of Arginusae during the Peloponnesian War. Research this. Briefly describe what happened there, and how the Athenians responded.
- ◆ Research and briefly tell about the Battle at Salamis, and the role of Themistocles in that battle.
- ◆ Who was Sophocles?

B. In your Writer's Journal, write the anecdote from the essay, then analyze and inflect it, following these steps. Refer to Lesson 7 for complete instructions and to diagramming helps in *Sentence Sense* as needed.

Diogenes, on seeing a youth misbehaving, beat the paedagogus.

Analysis	Inflection
◆ Diagram	◆ Number
◆ Definitions	◆ Declension
◆ Copia of Words	◆ Copia of Construction

ANCIENT ANECDOTE & PROVERB ELABORATION HEADERS

The ancients listed eight topics (or headers) to elaborate in the Anecdote exercise. The Proverb exercise elaborates the same eight topics.

1. **Encomion** is a brief praise of the person represented as speaking or acting

2. **Paraphrase** is a restatement of the anecdote (proverb) in your own words

3. **Cause** is a discussion of the rationale behind the words and/or action in the anecdote (proverb)

4. **Contrast** is a consideration contrasting words or action

5. **Comparison** is a consideration of an analogous situation

6. **Example** is a discussion of relevant illustration(s) from history or literature

7. **Authority** is a credible testimony supporting the wisdom or wit behind the anecdote or proverb

8. **Exhortation** is a brief epilogue exhorting the reader to admire the wit and/or emulate the wisdom

Notice the progression of these topics. The Encomion and Paraphrase paragraphs are "big picture" kind of paragraphs, setting the stage for what is to come. The Cause and Contrast paragraphs are more specific, and focus the elaboration on the author's understanding of the importance of the witty or wise words and/or action. The Comparison, Example, and Authority paragraphs progressively and more specifically support the author's reasoning in the Cause and Contrast paragraphs. The Exhortation is the most specific of all, persuading or dissuading the particular person(s) reading the elaboration to act or think in a certain way.

⟨❀⟩ On the Ancient Essay Elaboration by Pseudo-Nicolaus at the beginning of this lesson, mark the eight topics (headers).

THE ODYSSEY

⟨❀⟩ Read

◆ *The Odyssey of Homer*, Book Six

⟨❀⟩ As you read, continue to mark the text and make notes:

◆ Literary concepts and terms you observe in the narrative. Do any of your earlier thoughts need revision?

◆ Instances of **epic simile**.
◆ **Epithets** to add to your running list.
◆ Passages reflecting on the value of **hearth and home**.

Writer's Journal

⟨❀⟩ Discuss this week's reading with your teacher, along with all your notes and observations. Narrate the main action of the book, and discuss any parts you did not understand. How was this reading **delightful**? What **wisdom** does this reading furnish?

Lesson 8.2

Language Logic

DIAGRAMMING & PARSING

 Study these sections in *Sentence Sense*. They are mostly review from *Bards & Poets*.

III. Sentence Diagramming – Sentence Classes by Form

- ◆ 20.1 Simple Sentences
- ◆ 20.2 Compound Sentences
- ◆ 20.3 Complex Sentences
- ◆ 20.4 Compound-Complex Sentence

III. Sentence Diagramming – Clauses

- ◆ 21.1 Adjective Clauses
- ◆ 21.2 Adverb Clauses
- ◆ 21.3 Noun Clauses

III. Sentence Diagramming – Quotations

- ◆ 23.1 Direct Quotations
- ◆ 23.2 Indirect Quotations

Writer's Journal

In your Writer's Journal, copy these sentences. Mark the prepositional phrases, subjects, and verbs. Bracket the clauses. Classify the sentence as simple, compound, complex, or compound-complex. Then diagram each one. Refer to *Sentence Sense* as needed. Note in Sentence #3, *train* is a noun, metaphorically referring to the line or procession of workers returning home in the evening.

1. She made acquaintance with the birds that fluttered by.

2. How long didst thou think that his silence was slumber?

3. How often have I blessed the coming day.

   When toil remitting lent its turn to play,

   And all the village train, from labor free,

   Led up their sports beneath the spreading tree. — Goldsmith

4. For he left to others the investigation of the paths of the stars and the examination of the circuit of the sun, whereas he himself applied his knowledge to the correction of character.

🏅 Orally parse these words with your teacher, using the charts in *Sentence Sense* to guide you.

(1) acquaintance, fluttered; (2) his, slumber; (3) How, free, beneath the spreading tree; (4) left, the (sun), himself

---

Lesson 8.3

Eloquent Expression

FIGURES OF SPEECH – METAPHOR AND PERSONIFICATION

A **metaphor** is an implied comparison between two things of unlike nature. Instead of boldly announcing itself like a simile does, the metaphor quietly hints at the comparison:

How frugal is the chariot that bears the human soul! – Emily Dickinson, "A Book"

This kind of metaphor is the most straightforward—a simple statement of x = y, where x and y are nouns, and the = represents a linking verb.

Another kind of metaphor that is fairly easy to spot uses the preposition of or a possessive form: *Father has a heart of gold* or *Her heart's treasure was revealed*. Relative clauses, adjectives, or verbals are sometimes used to create a metaphor: . . . *his hair, which was a red mop* or *She learned a bitter lesson* or *His tangled thoughts confused him*.

There are many other kinds of metaphor, some of which are not so easy to spot. The more you practice (and the more widely you read!) the easier it will be to recognize and comprehend metaphor. Creating a meaningful metaphor certainly requires a good bit of "art" on the part of the writer. It requires imagination and the ability to "see" relevant connections. Metaphor paints pictures in our mind's eye, making abstract or complex ideas take on shape and form, as we see in these literary metaphors:

All the world's a stage, and all the men and women merely players. — Shakespeare

Necessity is the mother of invention. — Aesop

No man is an island. — John Donne

Personification is found very often in prose, poetry, and everyday speech. In essence, it is a type of metaphor. Living characteristics are attributed to an abstract idea or inanimate thing; or human characteristics are attributed to a non-human thing. There are three degrees of personification.

First-degree personification deals with qualities. Those that belong only to living beings only may be ascribed to inanimate objects, for example, a *majestic tree*. Qualities or properties of human beings may be ascribed to non-human creatures: *crafty fox*. Gender that does not ordinarily or naturally belong to the object may be attributed to it: *The ship's sailors heaved up her anchor.*

Second-degree personification deals with actions. Actions, thoughts, or feelings properly belonging to a living creature are ascribed to an inanimate object: *The river rages* or even an abstract idea: *Fortune smiled on him.* A literary example:

Lands intersected by a narrow frith abhor each other. — William Cowper

Third-degree personification directly addresses an inanimate object as if it were a human creature:

Roll on, thou dark and deep blue ocean, roll! — Byron

After simile, personification is probably the most prevalent figure of speech, so much so that we hardly notice it. Apt personification, a kissing-cousin to metaphor, also requires the "art" of seeing and expressing relevant connections.

🌿 Discuss the examples of metaphor and personification with your teacher. Can you identify any additional figures? Scan selections from earlier lessons in this book to see if they contain this figure.

🌿 Enter the following items in the Figures division.

◆ Metaphor and personfication, P&P 83: Add <u>Metaphor</u> and line <u>Personification</u>, including the three degrees. Include definitions and one literary example of each.

Prose & Poetry
Handbook

LITERARY IMITATION

🏵 Work with the sentence below that you diagrammed in Language Logic. Copy the **diagram skeleton**, construct a new sentence, and write the new sentence below the diagram. The topic of your new sentence is Diogenes's wise action concerning the pedagogue.

Writer's Journal

For he left to others the investigation of the paths of the stars and the examination of the circuit of the sun, whereas he himself applied his knowledge to the correction of character.

Lesson 8.4

Classical Composition

PROGYMNASMA NARRATIVE: PLOT OBSERVATION – THEON'S SIX AND SUMMARY

Observe and summarize Homer's *Odyssey*, Book Six. Refer to the instructions and example in the Appendix under "Narrative Plot Observation" and "Example Narrative Plot Observation."

🏵 Complete the steps for Plot Observation – Theon's Six on the original narrative and in your Writer's Journal.

Writer's Journal

🏵 Write a one paragraph summary of this book, following the steps for Plot Observation – Summary. Work either in your Writer's Journal or on the computer. Add this summary to your running file of *Odyssey* summaries, and save the file.

PROGYMNASMA NARRATIVE: THE TELEMACHIA PRÉCIS #2

Refine your précis even further to express the central essence of *The Telemachia* in a single sentence. Take the time to make this a perfect sentence that gets at the heart of the story. Your one sentence précis must capture just the essence of the story, with little to no detail.

🏵 Write a one sentence precis of *The Telemachia*.

EDITOR'S PEN: THE TELEMACHIA PRÉCIS #2

🏵 Revise your précis using the checklist below. Obviously, there is no need for Big Picture and Paragraph editing since your précis is only one sentence. Work through the checklist once on your own, and then a second time with your writing mentor, making notes on the print copy of your narrative. Transfer all additions and corrections from your print copy to the computer file. Save and print the document.

Editor's Pen – Zoom 10x: Sentences

✓ Complete thought expressed

✓ Subject and predicate agree in number

✓ Correct capitalization and punctuation

   ◆ No comma splices!

Editor's Pen – Fine Focus: Words

✓ Word choices varied; word meanings clear; consider denotation AND connotation

   ◆ Verbs: *strong, fitting; appropriate adverbs if needed*

   ◆ Nouns: *clear, descriptive; appropriate adjectives if needed*

   ✓ Correct spelling

✓ Final read-through

PROGYMNASMA ANECDOTE AND PROGYMNASMA PROVERB

In the progymnasma Anecdote (also called *chreia*) and progymnasma Proverb (also called *maxim*) exercise, you will compose an **elaboration** of a well-known anecdote or proverb in order to examine and consider its wisdom or wit. The eight elaboration topics (headers) you studied in Lesson 8.1 will provide the outline for this essay.

Prose & Poetry Handbook

⬕ Enter the following item in the Rhetoric Section.

   ◆ Invention/Arrangement, The Progymnasmata – Anecdote and Proverb, P&P 10-11: Title CANONS OF INVENTION AND ARRANGEMENT, subtitle ANECDOTE (CHREIA) AND PROVERB (MAXIM). Write the definitions of an anecdote from and a proverb from Lesson 6.1. Below that, write "Elaborate a proverb or anecdote, in this order:" and then list the eight topics (headers) from Lesson 8.1 along with a brief description of each one.

⬕ Memorize the eight topics (headers) for an anecdote or Proverb elaboration from Lesson 8.1.

Lesson 8.5

Reflection & Review

COMMONPLACE BOOK

Commonplace Book

Enter in your Commonplace Book:

- a favorite passage or two from your reading in Homer's *Odyssey*
- an example or two of epithet and/or epic simile
- an example of metaphor and an example of personification from your reading
- examples from your reading of other figures and literary devices you have learned (see Figures and Literary Devices lists in *Poetics & Progym I* Appendix)

BOOK OF CENTURIES

Record in your Book of Centuries:

- Diogenes of Sinope (the Cynic), Themistocles, Sophocles

MEMORY WORK

GRAMMAR FLASHCARDS

Review to mastery:

- Noun Terms – *Poetics & Progym I*

Continue to review each set once a week (more if needed):

- Parts of Speech – *Bards & Poets* Review
- Sentence Terms – *Bards & Poets* Review
- Figures – Set #1 – *Poetics & Progym I*

☙

ISOCRATES ON EDUCATION
Ancient Anecdote Elaboration by Aphthonius

Isocrates said that the root of education is bitter, its fruit sweet.

It is right to admire Isocrates for his art; he made its name most illustrious, and in his practice he showed how great the art was and proclaims its greatness, rather than having been himself proclaimed by it. Now it would take a long time to go through all the benefits he has brought to human life, whether in proposing laws to kings or in advising private individuals, but [we can note] his wise teaching about education.

One who longs for education, he is saying, begins with toils, but yet the toils end in an advantage. The wisdom of these words we shall admire in what follows.

Those who long for education attach themselves to educational leaders, whom it is frightening to approach and very stupid to abandon. Fear comes on boys both when they are there and when they are about to go to school. Next after the teachers come the pedagogues, fearful to see and more dreadful when they beat the boys. Fright anticipates discovery, and punishment follows fright; they go looking for the boys' mistakes but regard the boys' successes as their own doing. Fathers are more strict than pedagogues, dictating the routes to be followed, demanding boys go straight to school, and showing suspicion of the market place. And if there is need to punish, fathers ignore their natural feelings. But the boy who has experienced these things, when he comes to manhood wears a crown of virtue.

If, on the other hand, out of fear of these things someone were to flee from teachers, run away from parents, and shun pedagogues, he is completely deprived of training in speech and has lost ability in speech with his loss of fear. All these considerations influenced Isocrates' thought in calling the root of education bitter.

Just as those who work the earth cast the seeds in the ground with toil but reap the fruits with greater pleasure, in the same way those exchanging toil for education have by toil acquired future renown.

Look, I ask you, at the life of Demosthenes, which was the most filled with labor of any orator but became the most glorious of all. He showed such an abundance of zeal that he took the ornament from his head, because he thought the ornament that comes from virtue was the best; and he expended in toils what others lavished on pleasures.

Thus, one should admire Hesiod's saying (cf. *Works and Days* 289-92) that the road of virtue is rough, but the height is easy, the same philosophy as found in the maxim of Isocrates; for what Hesiod indicated by a "road" is what Isocrates called a "root," both expressing one thought, but with different words.

Looking at all this, one should admire Isocrates for his wise and beautiful speculation about education.

—translated by GEORGE KENNEDY

⌘

Lesson 9.1

Prose & Poetry

ANCIENT ANECDOTE ELABORATION BY APHTHONIUS

Read the ancient elaboration by Aphthonius at the beginning of this lesson. If possible, read it aloud with your teacher.

A. In your Writer's Journal, research and answer (in writing) these questions about the anecdote.

   ◆ Who was Isocrates?
   ◆ Who was Demosthenes? The incident alluded to in the elaboration is taken from Plutarch's *Morals*, which includes *Lives of the Ten Orators*. This work is in the

public domain. Look it up and read the story of Demosthenes so you will understand the allusion.

◆ Who was Hesiod? What is *Works and Days*?

B. In your Writer's Journal, write the anecdote from the essay, then analyze and inflect it, following these steps. Refer to Lesson 7 for complete instructions and to diagramming helps in *Sentence Sense* as needed. This proverb, like many proverbs, uses the figure of ellipsis that we will study later in this book. See *Sentence Sense* 25.1 Ellipsis, for a sneak preview and help with diagramming this.

The root of <u>education</u> is bitter, its fruit sweet.

Analysis	Inflection
◆ Diagram	◆ Number
◆ Definitions	◆ Declension
◆ Copia of Words	◆ Copia of Construction

C. On the Ancient Essay Elaboration by Aphthonius at the beginning of this lesson, mark the eight topics (headers). Refer to Lesson 8.1 if you have not yet fully memorized the eight headers.

THE ODYSSEY

○ Read

◆ *The Odyssey of Homer,* Book Seven

○ As you read, continue to mark the text and make notes:

◆ Literary concepts and terms you observe in the narrative. Do any of your earlier thoughts need revision?

◆ Instances of **epic simile**.
◆ **Epithets** to add to your running list.
◆ Passages reflecting on the value of **hearth and home**.

Writer's Journal

○ Discuss this week's reading with your teacher, along with all your notes and observations. Narrate the main action of the book, and discuss any parts you did not understand. How was this reading **delightful**? What **wisdom** does this reading furnish?

Lesson 9.2

Language Logic

DIAGRAMMING & PARSING

 Study these sections in *Sentence Sense*. This completes our review of diagramming from *Bards & Poets*. Now, use it frequently as a reference when you have sentences to diagram! We will be introducing some additional sections in upcoming lessons.

> III. Sentence Diagramming – Possessives
> - ◆ 14.1 Nouns and Pronouns Showing Possession
> - ◆ 14.2 Possessive Pronouns
>
> III. Sentence Diagramming -Sentence Classes by Use
> - ◆ 22.1 Declarative Sentence
> - ◆ 22.2 Interrogative Sentence
> - ◆ 22.3 Exclamatory Sentences
> - ◆ 22.4 Imperative Sentences
>
> III. Sentence Diagramming – Independent Elements
> - ◆ 24.2 Interjections
> - ◆ 24.3 Expletives

Writer's Journal

In your Writer's Journal, copy these sentences. Mark the prepositional phrases, subjects, and verbs. Bracket the clauses. Classify the sentence as simple, compound, complex, or compound-complex. Then diagram each one. Refer to *Sentence Sense* as needed. Notice the use of simile, metaphor, and personification in #2.

1. How dreadful is this place, for God is here! — based on Genesis 28:16-17

2. The night, methinks, is but the daylight sick.

3. Young man, do not flee from your teachers, abscond from your parents, or avoid your attendants.

4. My child, would you show me the way to the house of a certain man, Alkinoös, who is lord over all these people?

5. For there is no good intelligence that she herself lacks.

6. For this reason, it is necessary to admire Sophocles, who said that every city is under the influence of its leaders.

Orally parse these words with your teacher. Use the charts in *Sentence Sense,* Chapter IV to guide you.

(1) dreadful, for, is (second use); (2) but; (3) do flee; (4) Alkinoös; (5) no, that (6) is, necessary, to admire

Lesson 9.3

Eloquent Expression

FIGURES OF SPEECH – ALLITERATION, ONOMATOPOEIA, AND ANASTROPHE

These are three figures often associated with poetry, but are found just as often in prose.

Alliteration is the repetition of beginning sounds in words that are adjacent or very close to each other. Alliteration is a scheme of construction (subcategory: repetition).

No guest on God's earth would he gladlier greet. — *Sir Gawain and the Green Knight*

Signs are small measurable things, but interpretations are illimitable . . . — George Eliot, *Middlemarch*

She opened the window and looked out. Dark, dull, dingy, and desolate house-tops. — Charles Dickens, *Martin Chuzzlewit*

In **onomatopoeia**, the sound of the word "echoes the sense."[1] The easiest form of onomatopoeia to recognize is in the words we use to indicate animal sounds such as *bark, oink, cock-a-doodle-do,* etc. Other examples of onomatopoeia are words that sound like the sound they are describing: *ring, babble, crash, boom, bang, whoosh,* etc. Onomatopoeia is a trope of wordplay.

1. Corbett, *Classical Rhetoric.,* 455.

That buzzing noise means something. Now, the only reason for making a buzzing noise that I know of is because you are a bee! — A. A. Milne, *Winnie-the-Pooh*

But all the leaves of the New Testament are rustling with the rumour that it will not always be so. — C. S. Lewis, *The Weight of Glory* (marvelous juxtaposition of onomatopoeia and alliteration!)

Anastrophe inverts the usual or natural word order of a phrase, clause, or sentence.[2] Anastrophe is a scheme of construction (subcategory: word order).

(Of) Arms and the man I sing. — Virgil, *Aeneid*

Talent, Mr. Micawber has; capital, Mr. Micawber has not. — Charles Dickens, *David Copperfield*

The normal sentence pattern of Subject – Verb – Object (or Complement) may be inverted by putting the object or the verb first. Or a noun may precede its adjective, instead of the expected adjective – noun order. Any "artful deviation" from the usual or expected word order may be classified as anastrophe. Full of anastrophe is poetry!

Discuss the examples of alliteration, onomatopoeia, and anastrophe with your teacher. Can you identify any additional figures? Scan selections from earlier lessons in this book to see if they contain this figure.

Enter the following items in the Figures division.

◆ Alliteration, P&P 73. Title SCHEMES OF CONSTRUCTION. Subtitle REPETITION, then add Alliteration, with its definition and one literary example.

◆ Onomatopoeia, P&P 86: Title TROPES OF WORDPLAY, then add Onomatopoeia, with its definition and one literary example.

◆ Anastrophe, P&P 79: Title WORD ORDER, then add Anastrophe, with its definition and one literary example.

Prose & Poetry Handbook

---

2 Some sources use the term **hyperbaton** for inversions of the natural order of a sentence, reserving the term **anastrophe** only for reversal of noun and adjective order. Our terminology follows that of *Silva Rhetoricae*.

LITERARY IMITATION

Writer's Journal

🏵 Work with the sentence below that you diagrammed in Lesson
9.1. Copy the **diagram skeleton**, construct a new sentence,
and write the new sentence below the diagram. The topic of
your new sentence is the toils and rewards of education.

The root of education is bitter, its fruit sweet.

Lesson 9.4

Classical Composition

Observe and summarize Homer's *Odyssey*, Book Seven. Refer to the instructions and example in
the Appendix under "Narrative Plot Observation" and "Example Narrative Plot Observation."

🏵 Complete the steps for Plot Observation – Theon's Six on the
original narrative and in your Writer's Journal.

Writer's Journal

🏵 Write a one paragraph summary of this
book, following the steps for Plot
Observation – Summary. Work either in
your Writer's Journal or on the computer.
Add this summary to your running file of
Odyssey summaries, and save the file.

ANCIENT ANECDOTE/PROVERB ELABORATION PARAPHRASE

A paraphrase is a restatement of the original. If you are able to restate the main idea of a
paragraph in your own words, you are likely to have a good understanding of what the author
is trying to say. This is one more area where copia is so helpful. Study the two paragraphs below.
The first is taken from the Cause paragraph of another ancient elaboration of the anecdote about
Diogenes and the pedagogue. The second is a paraphrase of the first.

Nota Bene: In this lesson, we are just practicing the general composition skill of paraphrasing
(lowercase). In a future lesson, you will write a Paraphrase (uppercase) paragraph for a
progymnasmata Anecdote/Proverb elaboration. This will become more clear as we progress
through the Anecdote/Proverb essay instructions.

I praise the man for both reasons: that he did not hesitate to use his hands to bring someone to his senses, and that he stated the reason for which he did it. For he thought it proper to take action to educate those who were doing great harm, and not passing over in silence the reason for which he had been provoked to blows was the act of one who reveals to the victim why he had suffered; for if after beating him Diogenes had gone away in silence, nothing would have prevented the pedagogue from remaining ignorant of what he had done wrong and, because of his ignorance, becoming in no way better. Moreover, the punishing of the pedagogue for the mistakes of the youth we will find to be characteristic of intelligent individuals.[3]

Diogenes is to be lauded on two counts. First, he immediately employed his fists in the elevation of virtue. Second, he set forth his reasoning. Did he not judge rightly that he should instruct the one who was causing great damage? Would it not have been unjust to withhold the cause for which obliged him to correct the man? Was it not proper for him to inform him why he had been beaten? Instead, if Diogenes had departed with no explanation, would not the pedagogue have remained oblivious concerning his fault? Without understanding how could he mend his fault? Chastising the pedagogue for the foibles of the schoolboy, upon reflection, is the only reasonable response of the sage man.

❦ Choose one of the ancient Anecdote elaborations from Lesson 8 or 9 to paraphrase. Work paragraph by pargraph, restating each one in your own words. Your final paraphrase of the elaboration should be very close in length to the original. You will probably find it easiest to do this in a word-processing program.

A. Read the first paragraph carefully two or three times. Look up any words or references that you do not understand. If you wish, type the paragraph in your word-processing program, then copy and paste for your working copy. Keep the original in case you decide to start over at any point. (This is advice based on sad experience!)

B. Underline key words in the paragraph. Choose synonyms (words, phrases, or clauses) for each one.

C. First rewrite each sentence using copia of words. (Refer to the Copia in Your Writing in the Appendix.) When you are done, use copia of construction techniques. Keep the meaning intact, but completely restate each sentence and paragraph in your own words.

3 Gibson, *Libanius' Progymnasmata*, 57.

D. Repeat the three steps above for each paragraph.

E. Save and print your paraphrase.

Lesson 9.5

Reflection & Review

Commonplace
Book

COMMONPLACE BOOK

❀ Enter in your Commonplace Book:

- ◆ a favorite passage or two from your reading in Homer's *Odyssey*
- ◆ an example or two of epithet and/or epic simile
- ◆ examples from your reading of alliteration, onomatopoeia, and anastrophe
- ◆ examples from your reading of other figures you have learned (see Figures and Literary Devices list in *Poetics & Progym I* Appendix)

BOOK OF CENTURIES

❀ Record in your Book of Centuries:

- ◆ Isocrates, Demosthenes, Hesiod

MEMORY WORK

GRAMMAR
FLASHCARDS

❀ Review to mastery:

- ◆ Noun Terms – *Poetics & Progym I*

❀ Use the test features at Quizlet for an online or printed quiz over this set. If you wish, use combine set features to include previous sets.

❀ Continue to review each set once a week (more if needed):

- ◆ Parts of Speech – *Bards & Poets* Review
- ◆ Sentence Terms – *Bards & Poets* Review
- ◆ Figures – Set #1 – *Poetics & Progym I*

Lesson 10

☙

DEMODOCUS THE BARD OF FAME
HOMER'S ODYSSEY

Be there Demodocus the bard of fame,
Taught by the gods to please, when high he sings
The vocal lay, responsive to the strings."

. . . The herald now arrives, and guides along
The sacred master of celestial song;
Dear to the Muse! who gave his days to flow
With mighty blessings, mix'd with mighty woe;
With clouds of darkness quench'd his visual ray,
But gave him skill to raise the lofty lay.
High on a radiant throne sublime in state,
Encircled by huge multitudes, he sate;
With silver shone the throne; his lyre, well strung
To rapturous sounds, at hand Poutonous[1] hung.

. . . Then, fired by all the Muse, aloud he sings
The mighty deeds of demigods and kings.

". . . Lives there a man beneath the spacious skies
Who sacred honours to the bard denies?
The Muse the bard inspires, exalts his mind;
The muse indulgent loves the harmonious kind."

— BOOK VIII, TRANSLATED BY ALEXANDER POPE

☙

1 Lattimore's rendering of this name is *Pontonoös* (lines 62-65).

Lesson 10.1

Prose & Poetry

WHAT IS POETRY?

Professor Harvey tells us, "A poem is a metrical composition. Its aim is to please by addressing the imagination and the sensibilities."[2] A rather un-poetical definition of poetry, yet its three points will serve us well.

1. **Poetry is metrical**. The poetry of western civilization is traditionally metrical, which means it has some kind of patterned or rhythmic sound. In classical Greek and Latin poetry (like Homer's *Odyssey*), this was produced by alternating the length of syllables in each verse; in Old English poetry, by a pattern of regular stresses in each. Most English poetry from the Renaissance into the modern age relies on a pattern of accents coupled with a prescribed number of syllables in each verse.

2. **Poetry seeks to please**. Rhythmic sound, rhyming words, poetic expression, and figures of speech delight readers of all ages. Poets aim to charm and delight their readers by making them see ordinary things in extraordinary ways. Remember the words of Horace and Shelley from Lesson 1. Poetry is a source of both delight and wisdom.

3. **Poetry addresses the imagination and sensibilities**. Poetry captivates our imaginations, very often by engaging our senses—making us see, feel, hear, touch, and taste things in new and memorable ways. In the words of Shelley, it "makes familiar objects...as if they were not familiar."

LITERARY ELEMENTS IN THE POEM: POPE'S TRANSLATION OF THE ODYSSEY

This selection is Alexander Pope's poetic rendering of the same lines that Richmond Lattimore translates in Book VIII, lines 44-45, 62-65, 73-75, and 477-482. Many think Homer is describing himself in this section of the poem, and is one reason scholars believe that he was blind.

1 **Read**
◆ Follow along and listen carefully as the poem is read aloud, OR read it aloud yourself. Read it at least two or three times. **Delight** in the meter, the rhyme, and the images.

2 **Inquire**
◆ Are there any unfamiliar persons, places, or things mentioned in the poem? Discuss these with your teacher.

2 Harvey, *A Practical Grammar of the English Language*, 253.

◆ Look up the meaning of any words in the work that are not familiar to you; conduct a complete Vocabulary Study for **key words.**

◆ Was there any part of the poem you did not understand? If so, discuss this with your teacher and classmates.

3 Observe the Invention, Arrangement, and Style

◆ **Lyrical Elements**

  ▪ What does the poet describe?

  ▪ Does the poet make you see, hear, smell, taste, or touch anything?

  ▪ Does the poet compare something in the poem to some other thing? Notice the beautiful metaphorical description of the bard's blindness contrasted with his storytelling gift.

◆ **Narrative Elements** Does this poem tell a story? If so, observe the

  ▪ **Setting** When and where does this story take place?

  ▪ **Characters** Who is (are) the main character(s) in this story?

  ▪ **Conflict** What is the main problem or crisis for the character(s)?

  ▪ **Resolution** Is the problem solved? If so, how? If not, why not?

  ▪ **Sequence** Is this story told *ab ovo*, or *in medias res*, or some other way?

  ▪ **Point of View** Identify the **person** (and **level of omniscience** if applicable).

◆ **Figures** Look for figures of speech and figures of description. (See Appendix for the list of figures taught in *Poetics & Progym*.) Why did the poet choose these particular figures?

4 Investigate the Context

◆ Research a bit about the **poet**. Make notes in your Writer's Journal about Alexander Pope's

Writer's Journal

  ▪ **Origin** Who were the poet's parents/ancestors? Where was his homeland?

  ▪ **Historical Time Period** When did the poet live? What events happened around the time that the poet lived?

  ▪ **Influences** What education, training, books, ideas, and other people or events shaped the poet's thinking?

◆ **Identify the poem's Literary Genre**

  ▪ **Genre by literary period** In which century (time period) and country was this work written?

  ▪ **Genre by poetic/narrative category** Is this poem chiefly **lyrical** (describes an event, or a person, or a feeling, or a time and place, etc., but it does not tell a particular story) or **narrative** (tells a story)? If narrative, is it primarily **non-fiction** (a story that really happened) or **fiction** (a story told as if it really happened)?

5 **Connect the Thoughts**

◆ Does this poem remind you of other poems, or of stories with similar plots, messages, or characters?

◆ Does this poem remind you of any proverbs or other well-known quotations? If so, enter these in your Commonplace Book.

Commonplace Book

6 **Profit and Delight**

◆ **Delight** What are the sources of delight in this poem?

◆ **Wisdom** What wisdom does this poem furnish?

◆ **Read** the poem to your teacher with expression and proper pauses. Pause ONLY where you see punctuation marks, not necessarily at the end of each line. Commas get a short pause; end punctuation gets a longer pause. This may take some practice, as the tempation to pause at the end of each line is great!

◆ **Read** other works by this poet.

◆ **Memorize** this poem and recite it before an audience.

POETRY TERMS AND DEFINITIONS

These are a few terms and definitions you should be familiar with as we begin our study of poetry.

Prosody: the study of meter, rhyme, and stanza forms in poetry.

Versification: "the art of metrical composition."[3]

Verse: a line of poetry – often incorrectly used in place of the term **stanza**, which refers to a grouping of verses (lines).

Prose: the ordinary form of speaking or writing, without meter or rhyme, "having reference, mainly, to a clear and distinct meaning of the author's meaning."[4] Herodotus, the ancient Greek historian, coined the phrase *pedzos logos* to describe prose—language that walks on feet, where poetry rides in a winged chariot.

Make the entries indicated below in the Poetry division.

Prose & Poetry Handbook

◆ Poetry Definition and Etymology, P&P 55: Use the definition from Harvey's *Practical Grammar*. Look up and add the etymology of the word (see Vocabulary Study Step 5 in the Appendix).

3. Harvey, *A Practical Grammar of the English Language*, 253.
4 *Ibid*, 253.

◆ Poetry Terms & Definitions, P&P 55: Subtitle TERMS AND DEFINITIONS. Add the terms Prosody, Versification, Verse, and Prose with their definitions. Include Herodotus's name for prose in your definition.

THE ODYSSEY

(laurel icon) Read

  ◆ *The Odyssey of Homer*, Book Eight

(laurel icon) As you read, continue to mark the text and make notes:

  ◆ Literary concepts and terms you observe in the narrative. Do any of your earlier thoughts need revision?
  ◆ Instances of **epic simile**.
  ◆ **Epithets** to add to your running list.
  ◆ Passages reflecting on the value of **hearth and home**.

Writer's Journal

(laurel icon) Discuss this week's reading with your teacher, along with all your notes and observations. Narrate the main action of the book, and discuss any parts you did not understand. How was this reading **delightful**? What **wisdom** does this reading furnish?

Lesson 10.2

Language Logic

VERB PROPERTY – VOICE

 Study these sections in *Sentence Sense*.

I. Etymology – Verbs

  ◆ 3.8 A, 3.8B, and 3.8C Property – Voice

V. Exercises

  ◆ Harvey's 86 *Complete this exercise orally with your teacher.*

GRAMMAR TERMS & DEFINITIONS: VERB TERMS

 Grammar Terms to Master: In the Quizlet classroom, review or print flashcards from Verb Terms – *Poetics & Progym I.*

- ◆ Property – Voice
- ◆ Active Voice
- ◆ Passive Voice

DIAGRAMMING & PARSING

 In your Writer's Journal, copy these sentences. Mark the prepositional phrases, subjects, and verbs. Bracket the clauses. Classify the sentence as simple, compound, complex, or compound-complex. Then diagram each one. Refer to *Sentence Sense* as needed. Treat *Dear to the Muse!* and following as a relative clause with the relative pronoun understood instead of stated. Think about who is being described here, and diagram accordingly. Note that there is only one subject in this long clause, but there are three verbs. Also, note that *to flow* is a complementary infinitive for the verb *gave*.

Writer's Journal

The herald now arrives, and guides along

The sacred master of celestial song;

Dear to the Muse! who gave his days to flow

With mighty blessings, mix'd with mighty woe;

With clouds of darkness quench'd his visual ray,

But gave him skill to raise the lofty lay.

 Orally parse these words with your teacher. Use the charts in *Sentence Sense,* Chapter IV to guide you. Add Verb Property – Voice to your parsing.

now, arrives, to the Muse, gave, quench'd, him, skill, lofty

Lesson 10.3

Eloquent Expression

COPIA OF WORDS: ACTIVE AND PASSIVE VERB SWITCH

The verbs in many sentences can be switched between **active voice** and **passive voice**.

Your letter pleased Erasmus.

Erasmus was pleased by your letter.

In general, active verbs give your writing a livelier, more vigorous tone. For that reason, you may often be advised, or even required, to avoid the passive voice in your academic writing. Although this is a good general rule, there are times when the passive voice is a better choice, as Professor Harvey mentions in his lesson on the verb property of voice (*Sentence Sense* 3.8C). For now, work on honing your skill in converting passive voice verbs to active. We will revisit this topic in *Poetics & Progym II*, looking more closely at sentences where the passive voice should be used.

Notice in the first sentence above, *Erasmus* is the direct object of the active verb *pleased*. In the second sentence, who is pleased? It is still Erasmus, but he has now become the subject, and the letter becomes the object of the preposition *by*. Latin students will recognize this as the **agent of means** construction. Converting this construction to active is simple: the subject becomes the direct object, the agent of means becomes the subject, and the verb is switched from passive to active. Some are a little trickier.

Your letter was received.

This is not quite as straightforward, because the person who is doing the action *receiving* is actually not mentioned. To convert this sentence to active voice, you will need to supply a subject. In this case, you could use *Erasmus*, or *he*, or even *I*, depending on the context of the rest of the paragraph:

Erasmus received your letter. He received your letter. I received your letter.

There are other passive constructions, but these are the most common, so be on the lookout for these in your writing and convert active to passive where it makes sense.

Copy each sentence below in your Writer's Journal. Rewrite the passive voice verbs in these sentences as active voice, and the active voice verbs as passive. Adjust any other words in the sentences as needed. You will find it easiest to do this by first identifying clauses, and then the verb within each clause.

1. The mistakes of sailors are attributed to pilots.

2. And so what occurred because of other factors was alleged to be the faults of the generals.

3. He is utterly deprived of eloquence; along with his fear he has set aside eloquence.

4. But by these experiences the boy, when he reaches adulthood, is crowned with virtue.

LITERARY IMITATION

Work with lines from *The Odyssey* that you diagrammed in Language Logic. Copy the **diagram skeleton**, construct a new sentence, and write the new sentence below the diagram. The topic of your new sentence is a famous or revered person from history or literature. Do not worry about keeping the meter or rhyme; you will work with that in a later lesson.

The herald now arrives, and guides along

The sacred master of celestial song;

Dear to the Muse! who gave his days to flow

With mighty blessings, mix'd with mighty woe;

With clouds of darkness quench'd his visual ray,

But gave him skill to raise the lofty lay.

Lesson 10.4

Classical Composition

PROGYMNASMA NARRATIVE: PLOT OBSERVATION – THEON'S SIX AND SUMMARY

Observe and summarize Homer's *Odyssey*, Book Eight. Refer to the instructions and example in the Appendix under "Narrative Plot Observation" and "Example Narrative Plot Observation."

Writer's Journal

- Complete the steps for Plot Observation – Theon's Six on the original narrative and in your Writer's Journal.

- Write a one paragraph summary of this book, following the steps for Plot Observation – Summary. Work either in your Writer's Journal or on the computer. Add this summary to your running file of *Odyssey* summaries, and save the file.

QUOTE FOR ELABORATION: PLUTARCH ON CHARACTER

In this and upcoming lessons, you will plan, write, and edit an elaboration of your own, based on this anecdote:

> Character is habit long continued. — Plutarch

- Copy the quote into your Writer's Journal. Is it a proverb or an anecdote?

- Analyze and inflect the saying, following these steps. Refer to Lesson 7 for complete instructions, and to diagramming helps in *Sentence Sense* as needed.

Writer's Journal

Analysis	Inflection
◆ Diagram	◆ Number
◆ Definitions	◆ Declension
◆ Copia of Words	◆ Copia of Construction

ANECDOTE/PROVERB ELABORATION: ENCOMION

As you have already learned, the **Encomion** is a brief praise of the person who is represented as speaking or acting. In the ancient elaboration Encomion paragraphs, this is not a biographical sketch of the person. Instead, it is clear that the author of the elaboration is familiar with the person's life and legacy. The Encomion should also mention the essential wisdom behind the wise or witty words and/or action. In some cases, this could vary, according to what the author of the elaboration wishes to emphasize. For example, in the proverb from Jim Eliot, the most obvious understanding would be a focus on earthly vs. eternal possessions. But one could also focus on the virtue of zealously advancing the Great Commission, as Jim Eliot gave his life to do. Of course these are related and overlapping, but they would each require slightly different choices in the rest of the elaboration.

To write an Encomion, you first must gather some basic information about the person. The **5 W's and an H** (refer back to Lesson 3.1) are a good place to start. Here are some ways you may use them:

- **Who** is the person represented as speaking or acting?
- **What** is he or she known for? **What** was this person's vocation/profession? **What** is this person's legacy?
- **Where** did he or she live? **Where** did this person work?
- **When** did he or she live?
- **Why** is he or she credible in this matter? **Why** is his or her advice worth listening to?
- **How** did the person acquire his or her wisdom? **How** did the person benefit or influence others?

The answers to these kinds of questions are revealed in encomia paragraphs of the ancient Anecdote elaborations we have already studied:

It is right to admire Isocrates (who?) for his art (what is he known for?), for he gave it a most glorious name and proved its greatness by his practice of it (why is he credible?); he made the art famous, he did not owe his fame to it. To go through the benefits he conferred on human life by giving laws to kings and advice to individuals (what is his legacy? how did he benefit others?) would be too long; I will speak only of his wise saying on education.[5]

It is proper to praise every philosophy (what is he known for?) but especially that which Diogenes practiced. For he left to others the investigation of the paths of the stars and the examination of the circuit of the sun, whereas he himself applied his knowledge to the correction of character (why is he credible?).[6]

5 "Aphthonius' Progymnasmata," translated by Malcolm Heath.
6 Hock & O'Neil, *The Chreia and Ancient Rhetoric*, 213.

Note that you do not find the answer to every single one of the reporter's questions in each Encomion. For example, there is no reference to **where?** or **when?** in these encomia. This is because the ancient authors trusted that their audiences knew exactly who Isocrates and Diogenes were, and so did not need to include this information. Instead, they focused on the men and their accomplishments.

Research Plutarch (Lucius Mestrius Plutarchus A.D. 46 – 120), the famous author of *Lives of the Noble Greeks and Romans* (also known as *Parallel Lives* or *Plutarch's Lives*).

Writer's Journal

A. Use the **Five W's an H**, and take notes in your Writer's Journal. Here are a few questions to get you started:

- **Who** was Plutarch?
- **What** is Plutarch best know for? **What** is *Lives of the Noble Grecians and Romans*? **What** were his other professions/vocations?
- **Where** did Plutarch live?
- **When** did Plutach live?
- **Why** is Plutarch credible in this matter? **Why** is his advice worth listening to?
- **How** did Plutarch acquire his wisdom? **How** did he benefit or influence others then and now?

B. Read the quote below from Plutarch's *Lives*. What does this tell you about Plutarch's purposes in writing his *Lives*, and particularly how he views the formation of character? Make additional notes for your Encomion and/or Paraphrase. Notice the comparison (or analogy) in the last sentence. To what does Plutarch compare his biographical sketches? How will this affect his selection of details to include in his work?

In writing the Lives of Alexander the Great and of Cæsar the conqueror of Pompeius, which are contained in this book, I have before me such an abundance of materials, that I shall make no other preface than to beg the reader, if he finds any of their famous exploits recorded imperfectly, and with large excisions, not to regard this as a fault. I am writing biography, not history; and often a man's most brilliant actions prove nothing as to his true character, while some trifling incident, some casual remark or jest, will throw more light upon what manner of man he was than the bloodiest battle, the greatest array of armies, or the most important siege. Therefore, just as portrait painters pay most attention to those peculiarities of the face and eyes, in which the likeness consists, and care but little for the rest of the figure, so it is my duty to dwell especially upon those actions which reveal

the workings of my heroes' minds, and from these to construct the portraits of
their respective lives, leaving their battles and their great deeds to be recorded by
others.—Plutarch's *Lives*, tr. Aubrey Stewart and George Long, 1908

C. Discuss your research with your teacher and classmates, your parents, siblings, or any
other interested and helpful parties. Make note of any additional ideas or questions to
pursue in your Writer's Journal.

IMITATING THE ANCIENT ELABORATION: ENCOMION

Imitation of a well-written paragraph with a new subject is a time-tested way to develop your own
writing skills. The original Encomion paragraph below is familiar—it comes from the elaboration
by Aphthonius of Isocrates's anecdote (Lesson 9). Below that, you will find a close paraphrase of
this paragraph for an elaboration of the proverb *Look Before You Leap*. Notice how the underlined
phrases in the original are replaced in the imitation with phrases appropriate to the new subject,
but the rest of the words are retained as much as possible.

> It is right to admire Isocrates for his art; he made its name most illustrious, and in
> his practice he showed how great the art was and proclaims its greatness, rather than
> having been himself proclaimed by it. Now it would take a long time to go through
> all the benefits he has brought to human life, whether in proposing laws to kings or in
> advising private individuals, but [we can note] his wise teaching about education. —
> Aphthonius[7]

> It is right to admire the ancient Greek slave* Aesop for his fables; he made their name a household
> word, and in his practice he showed how helpful it is to use a story to make a point about human be-
> havior. Now it would take a long time to go through all the wise sayings attributed to him, whether
> about avoiding temptation or telling the truth, but we can note his wise teaching about considering
> the consequences of our actions.

*In this Paraphrase, the **where?** and **when?** information is added since the modern audience may
not be as familiar with Aesop as the ancient audience was with Isocrates.

 Following the example above, write your Encomion paragraph for
the Plutarch proverb "Character is habit long continued" in close
imitation of an ancient Encomion paragraph. For the original to
imitate, you may choose either the ancient Encomion paragraph
from Pseudo-Nicolaus (Lesson 8) or from Aphthonius (Lesson 9).
Save and print the document.

7 "Aphthonius' Progymnasmata," translated by Malcolm Heath.

Lesson 10.5

Reflection & Review

Commonplace
Book

COMMONPLACE BOOK

◯ Enter in your Commonplace Book:

  ◆ a favorite passage or two from your reading in Homer's *Odyssey*
  ◆ an example or two of epithet and/or epic simile
  ◆ examples from your reading of other figures you have learned
    (see Figures and Literary Devices list in *Poetics & Progym I*
    Appendix)

BOOK OF CENTURIES

◯ Record in your Book of Centuries:

  ◆ Alexander Pope, Plutarch

MEMORY WORK

GRAMMAR
FLASHCARDS

◯ Review to mastery (go ahead and memorize all of these
cards, even though we will be covering this material over
the next several lessons):

  ◆ Verb Terms – *Poetics & Progym I*

◯ Continue to review each set once a week (more if needed):

  ◆ Parts of Speech – *Bards & Poets* Review
  ◆ Sentence Terms – *Bards & Poets* Review
  ◆ Noun Terms – *Poetics & Progym I*
  ◆ Figures – Set #1 – *Poetics & Progym I*

◯ Use the test features at Quizlet for an online or printed
quiz over this set. If you wish, use combine set features to
include previous sets.

☙

THE BUILDERS

All are architects of Fate,
Working in these walls of Time;
Some with massive deeds and great,
Some with ornaments of rhyme.

Nothing useless is, or low;
Each thing in its place is best;
And what seems but idle show
Strengthens and supports the rest.

For the structure that we raise,
Time is with materials filled;
Our to-days and yesterdays
Are the blocks with which we build.

Truly shape and fashion these;
Leave no yawning gaps between;
Think not, because no man sees,
Such things will remain unseen.

In the elder days of Art,
Builders wrought with greatest care
Each minute and unseen part;
For the gods see everywhere.

Let us do our work as well,
Both the unseen and the seen;
Make the house, where gods may dwell,
Beautiful, entire, and clean.

Else our lives are incomplete,
Standing in these walls of Time,
Broken stairways, where the feet
Stumble as they seek to climb.

Build to-day, then, strong and sure,
With a firm and ample base;
And ascending and secure
Shall to-morrow find its place.

Thus alone can we attain
To those turrets, where the eye
Sees the world as one vast plain,
And one boundless reach of sky.

— HENRY WADSWORTH
LONGFELLOW

☙

Lesson 11.1

Prose & Poetry

LITERARY ELEMENTS IN THE POEM: THE BUILDERS

1 Read

+ Follow along and listen carefully as the poem is read aloud, OR read it aloud yourself. Read it at least two or three times. **Delight** in the meter, the rhyme, and the images.

2 Inquire

+ Does the **title** give any hint as to the content or message of the poem? If this work was published by the poet in a larger book or anthology, does that title give any hint?

+ Are there any unfamiliar persons, places, or things mentioned in the poem? Discuss these with your teacher. What is meant by *the elder days of Art*?

+ Look up the meaning of any words in the work that are not familiar to you; conduct a complete Vocabulary Study for **key words.**

+ Was there any part of the poem you did not understand? If so, discuss this with your teacher and classmates.

3 Observe the Invention, Arrangement, and Style

+ **Lyrical Elements**
  ▪ What does the poet describe?
  ▪ Does the poet make you see, hear, smell, taste, or touch anything?
  ▪ Does the poet compare something in the poem to some other thing?

+ **Narrative Elements** Does this poem tell a story? If so, observe the
  ▪ **Setting** When and where does this story take place?
  ▪ **Characters** Who is (are) the main character(s) in this story?
  ▪ **Conflict** What is the main problem or crisis for the character(s)?
  ▪ **Resolution** Is the problem solved? If so, how? If not, why not?
  ▪ **Sequence** Is this story told *ab ovo*, or *in medias res*, or some other way?
  ▪ **Point of View** Identify the **person** (and **level of omniscience** if applicable).

+ **Figures** Look for figures of speech and figures of description. (See Appendix for the list of figures taught in *Poetics & Progym*.) Why did the poet choose these particular figures?

POETICS & PROGYM I

Investigate the Context

◆ Research a bit about the **poet**. Make notes in your Writer's Journal about Henry Wadsworth Longfellow's

  ■ **Origin** Who were the poet's parents/ancestors? Where was his homeland?

  ■ **Historical Time Period** When did the poet live? What events happened around the time that the poet lived?

  ■ **Influences** What education, training, books, ideas, and other people or events shaped the poet's thinking?

◆ **Identify the poem's Literary Genre**

  ■ **Genre by literary period** In which century (time period) and country was this work written?

  ■ **Genre by poetic/narrative category** Is this poem chiefly **lyrical** (describes an event, or a person, or a feeling, or a time and place, etc., but it does not tell a particular story) or **narrative** (tells a story)? If narrative, is it primarily **non-fiction** (a story that really happened) or **fiction** (a story told as if it really happened)?

5 **Connect the Thoughts**

◆ Does this poem remind you of other poems, or of stories with similar plots, messages, or characters?

◆ Does this poem remind you of any proverbs or other well-known quotations? If so, enter these in your Commonplace Book.

Commonplace Book

6 **Profit and Delight**

◆ **Delight** What are the sources of delight in this poem?

◆ **Wisdom** What wisdom does this poem furnish?

◆ **Read** the poem to your teacher with expression and proper pauses. (See Lesson 10.1)

◆ **Read** other works by this poet.

◆ **Memorize** this poem and recite it before an audience.

POETIC METER

Meter may be divided into two main categories: **qualitative** and **quantitative**. Quantitative meter relies on the length of syllables and consequently, the length of verses (lines). This is the meter of classical Greek and Latin poetry, including Homer's *Odyssey*. In contrast, qualitative meter relies on patterns of stressed and unstressed intervals. Qualitative meter may be further subdivided into two types. **Accentual** meter counts stresses in the verse; this is the meter of *Beowulf* and other Old

English poetry. **Accentual-Syllabic** counts accents and syllables, and is the predominant meter in post-Renaissance English poetry.

POETRY SCANSION

Scansion is analysis of a poem's meter. There are four basic steps to this process:[1]

1. Marking **stressed** (accented) and **unstressed** syllables in each verse

2. Dividing the lines into **feet**

3. Identifying the **metrical pattern**

4. Noting **significant variations** from the pattern

Make the entries indicated below in the Poetry division.

Prose & Poetry Handbook

◆ Poetic Meter P&P 57: Title POETIC METER, Subtitle DIVISIONS OF POETIC METER, then list the definitions of quantitative and qualitative, along with the 2 subdivisions of qualitative meter (accentual and accentual-syllabic). Note where each meter is commonly found.

◆ Poetry Scansion, P&P 57: Subtitle POETRY SCANSION, then add the definition of scansion and list the steps for scansion.

In the next few sections, we will cover a lot of ground, and you will make many entries in your P&P Handbook. *Bards & Poets* students will be familiar with much of this material. Making the notes in your P&P Handbook will help you to easily articulate this process, and provide a foundation for the poetry studies to come.

HOW TO SCAN A POEM

We have a few more technical terms to get through, and then we can actually try this out with a poem! First, the **foot** is basic unit used in scanning a verse. A foot usually is made up of one stressed and one or two unstressed syllables, but there are variations on this.

Now, let us take a look at each step in the process, using the first line from Emily Dickinson's poem, "A Book."

Step 1 Mark each syllable as either stressed (/) or unstressed (∪). The easiest way to do this is to say the line aloud several times to "get" the meter. Next, say the line aloud emphasizing the stressed syllables as you mark those only. Then go back and mark the unstressed syllables, saying the line aloud again to check your work.

1. Perrine, *Sound and Sense*, 380.

```
   ∪  /  ∪  /  ∪  /  ∪  /
There  is  no  frig ate  like  a  book
```

Step 2 Insert dividers (|) to mark off the feet. Look for a pattern of stresses. Here some patterns you will find in English poetry, with the first four being most common.

- ◆ **Iamb**: unstressed-stressed
- ◆ **Trochee**: stressed-unstressed
- ◆ **Anapest**: unstressed-unstressed-stressed
- ◆ **Dactyl**: stressed-unstressed-unstressed

- ◆ **Pyrrhee**: unstressed-unstressed
- ◆ **Spondee**: stressed-stressed
- ◆ **Amphibrach**: unstressed-stressed-unstressed
- ◆ **Molussus**: stressed-stressed-stressed

The pattern in the line from "A Book" is *unstressed-stressed);* the feet in this line are called **iambs**. We insert dividers between each iamb:

```
|  ∪  / |  ∪  / |  ∪  / | ∪  / |
There  is   no  frig ate  like  a  book
```

Step 3 Give the **metrical name** of the verse. You may have more than one type of foot in a verse, but the name should reflect the predominant feet in the verse.

   a. Make the predominant foot name (*iamb*) into an adjective ending in *-ic*: **iambic,
      trochaic, dactylic, anapestic**, etc.
   b. Count the number of feet: *four*. Take the Greek word for the number four, *tetra*, and add
      it to the word *meter*: **tetrameter**. The stress is on the second syllable: teTRAMeter.

And as easy as that, you have scanned this line of poetry and identified the meter as **iambic tetrameter**.

Here are the rest of the names for the number of feet in a verse.

NUMBER OF FEET	METER NAME	PRONUNCIATION
1	monometer	moNOMeter
2	dimeter	DIMeter
3	trimeter	TRIMeter
4	tetrameter	teTRAMeter
5	pentameter	penTAMeter
6	hexameter	hexAMeter
7	heptameter	hepTAMeter
8	octameter	ocTAMeter

Usually, a poem will have a predominant meter that we can name. Sometimes a poet will switch meter in the middle of a poem to create a certain effect. It is not at all unusual for a poem to have some stray syllables that do not fit the predominant pattern very well, particularly unstressed syllables at the beginning or end of a line. For now, when you scan a poem, you should look for and name the predominant meter. In *Poetics & Progym II,* we will add **Step 4** where we note and name intentional variations from the predominant pattern of a poem.

Prose & Poetry Handbook

🏵 Make the entry indicated below in the Poetry division.

- ◆ Poetic Meter P&P 58: Subtitle METRICAL PATTERNS, then write the definition of foot and list the eight types of feet. Subtitle LINE NAMES (NUMBER OF FEET PER VERSE), and list the number and the name of each. Subtitle NAMING VERSE, then list the two steps (a. and b.).

RHYME IN POETRY

Rhyme is actually a **figure of speech** in which "a correspondence of sound in the last syllables of two or more lines, succeeding each other immediately, or at no great distance."[2] It is certainly artful, requiring some thought and effort to do it well. And, unless you are a *Princess Bride* character, you probably do not make your words rhyme in everyday conversation. Rhyme is "artfully varied" from common speech.

Every poem does not need to rhyme, but **end-rhyme** is traditionally associated with poetry written in our English language. Rhyming words please the ear. They also aid the memory; think of how many things we learn by way of rhyme:

Thirty days hath September, April, June, and November...

In 1492 Columbus sailed the ocean blue...

I before E, except after C...

To mark end-rhyme, place corresponding capital letters at the end of each rhyming line. In the poem below (*The Swing,* by Robert Louis Stevenson) *swing* and *thing* rhyme, so we place an **A** at the end of those two lines; *blue* and *do* rhyme, so we place a **B** at the end of those two lines; and so on to the end of the poem.

How do you like to go up in a swing?   A
Up in the air so blue?   B

---

2   Harvey, *A Practical Grammar of the English Language,* 253.

Oh, I do think it the pleasantest thing	A
Ever a child can do!	B
Up in the air and over the wall	C
Till I can see so wide,	D
Rivers and trees and cattle and all	C
Over the countryside—	D
Till I look down on the garden green	E
Down on the roof so brown—	F
Up in the air I go flying again,	E
Up in the air and down!	F

For "The Swing," we denote the **rhyme scheme**, or pattern of rhyme within the stanzas, as ABAB. Notice that the spelling of these rhyming words may or may not be the same. It is the sound that matters. All of the rhymes in "The Swing" are **perfect rhymes**—the final syllable's stress, vowel sound, and ending consonant sound (if there is one) are the same in the rhyming words, with one exception. The rhyming pair *green* and *again* is an example of **imperfect rhyme**. The words have the impression of rhyme, in this case, using the figure of speech **consonance**, in which the consonant sounds of words are repeated. We will study this figure in *Poetics & Progym II*. For now, just be aware that you will come across many examples of imperfect rhyme.

Make the entry indicated below in the Poetry division.

Prose & Poetry Handbook

- ◆ Rhyme P&P 62: Title RHYME, then add the definitions of rhyme, perfect, imperfect (slant) rhyme, and rhyme scheme.

STANZA FORM

A poet chooses the form of a poem as well as the words in order to communicate the message. A **stanza** is a grouping of verses (lines) in a pattern, which is often repeated throughout the poem. Remember, the word **verse** correctly refers to a single line of the poem. Although many people commonly use stanza and verse interchangeably, this is not technically correct when you are analyzing a poem.

Stanza Forms are named according to the number of lines that are grouped together. For example, if the stanza has two lines, it is called a **couplet**.[3] Most of these are named using Latin derivatives for numbers:

---

3 The term **couplet** may also refer to any two successive lines of poetry that are rhymed, even if they are part of a larger stanza.

# OF LINES	STANZA FORM
2	Couplet
3	Tercet
4	Quatrain
5	Quintain (also called cinquain or quintet)
6	Sextet (also called sextain, sixain, sexain, sestet, or my favorite—hexastich!)
7	Septet
8	Octave (also called octet)

 Make the entry indicated below in the Poetry division.

Prose & Poetry Handbook

◆ Stanza Forms P&P 64: Title STANZA FORM, then add the definition of stanza and the list of stanza names according to the number of lines.

SCANSION AND ANALYSIS: THE BUILDERS
Finally, you get to put together the entire process!

A. Scan these stanzas, following the steps you have learned.

Step 1 Mark each syllable as either stressed (/) or unstressed (∪). Note that you will find a few metrical irregularities in this poem.
Step 2 Insert dividers (|) to mark off the feet.
Step 3 Name the poem's meter:

B. Mark the end rhyme on the poem above. Name the rhyme scheme:

C. Write the stanza name:

All are architects of Fate,

Working in these walls of Time;

Some with massive deeds and great,

Some with ornaments of rhyme.

Nothing useless is, or low;

Each thing in its place is best;

And what seems but idle show

Strengthens and supports the rest.

For the structure that we raise,

Time is with materials filled;

Our to-days and yesterdays

Are the blocks with which we build.

Truly shape and fashion these;

Leave no yawning gaps between;

Think not, because no man sees,

Such things will remain unseen.

In the elder days of Art,

Builders wrought with greatest care

Each minute and unseen part;

For the gods see everywhere.

THE ODYSSEY

- ⚜ Read

  - *The Odyssey of Homer,* Book Nine

- ⚜ As you read, continue to mark the text and make notes:

  - Literary concepts and terms you observe in the narrative. Do any of your earlier thoughts need revision?
  - Instances of **epic simile**.
  - **Epithets** to add to your running list.
  - Passages reflecting on the value of **hearth and home**.

Writer's Journal

- ⚜ Discuss this week's reading with your teacher, along with all your notes and observations. Narrate the main action of the book, and discuss any parts you did not understand. How was this reading **delightful**? What **wisdom** does this reading furnish?

Lesson 11.2

Language Logic

VERB PROPERTY – MOOD

 Study these lessons in *Sentence Sense.*

I. Etymology – Verbs

- 3.9A Property – Mood
- 3.9B Indicative Mood
- 3.9E The Imperative Mood
- 3.9F The Infinitive Mood

GRAMMAR TERMS & DEFINITIONS: VERB TERMS

 Grammar Terms to Master: In the Quizlet classroom, review or print flashcards from Verb Terms – *Poetics & Progym I.*

- ♦ Property – Mood
- ♦ Indicative Mood
- ♦ Imperative Mood
- ♦ Infinitive Mood

DIAGRAMMING & PARSING

 In your Writer's Journal, copy these sentences. Mark the prepositional phrases, subjects, and verbs. Bracket the clauses. Classify the sentence as simple, compound, complex, or compound-complex. Then diagram each one. Refer to *Sentence Sense* as needed.

Writer's Journal

Nothing useless is, or low;

Each thing in its place is best;

And what seems but idle show

Strengthens and supports the rest.

For the structure that we raise,

Time is with materials filled;

Our to-days and yesterdays

Are the blocks with which we build.

 Orally parse these words with your teacher. Use the charts in *Sentence Sense,* Chapter IV to guide you.

useless, or, its, seems, show, supports, we, with materials, is filled, which

Lesson 11.3

Eloquent Expression

FIGURES OF SPEECH – PARALLELISM AND ANTITHESIS

Parallelism is the use of related elements that are similar in grammatical form or grammatical structure. These elements may be words, phrases, or clauses in pairs or in a series. This figure creates symmetry, balance, and rhythm in a literary work. A few literary examples:

> I will go down to my grave unwept, unhonored, and unsung. — L. M. Montgomery, *Anne of the Island*

> We mutually pledge to each other our Lives, our Fortunes, and our sacred Honor. — The Declaration of Independence

> Men become builders by building and lyreplayers by playing the lyre; so too we become just by doing just acts, temperate by doing temperate acts, brave by doing brave acts.— Aristotle, *Nicomachean Ethics*

Antithesis is a juxtaposition of two opposite or contrary ideas in adjacent phrases, clauses, or sentences, often structured with parallelism.

> Art is long, and Time is fleeting.

> It was the best of times, it was the worst of times. — Charles Dickens, *A Tale of Two Cities*

> Outside the will of God, there's nothing I want. Inside the will of God, there's nothing I fear. — A. W. Tozer

Discuss the examples of parallelism and antithesis with your teacher. Can you identify any additional figures? Scan selections from earlier lessons in this book to see if they contain this figure.

Enter the following items in the Figures division of your Prose & Poetry Handbook.

Prose & Poetry Handbook

◆ Parallelism, P&P 77: Subtitle BALANCE. Add Parallelism, its definition and one literary example.

◆ Antithesis, P&P 77: Leave about 10 lines blank for future additions to the parallelism entry. Add <u>Antithesis</u>, its definition and one literary example.

LITERARY IMITATION

Work with the sentence below that you diagrammed in Language Logic. Copy the **diagram skeleton**, construct a new sentence, and write the new sentence below the diagram. The topic of your new sentence is perseverance and diligence in completing a task. Do not worry about keeping the meter or rhyme; you will work with that in a later lesson.

For the structure that we raise,

Time is with materials filled;

Our to-days and yesterdays

Are the blocks with which we build.

Lesson 11.4

Classical Composition

PROGYMNASMA NARRATIVE: PLOT OBSERVATION – THEON'S SIX AND SUMMARY

Observe and summarize Homer's *Odyssey*, Book Nine. Refer to the instructions and example in the Appendix under "Narrative Plot Observation" and "Example Narrative Plot Observation."

Complete the steps for Plot Observation – Theon's Six on the original narrative and in your Writer's Journal.

Write a one paragraph summary of this book, following the steps for Plot Observation – Summary. Work either in your Writer's Journal or on the computer. Add this summary to your running file of *Odyssey* summaries, and save the file.

ANECDOTE/PROVERB ELABORATION: PARAPHRASE

Paraphrase restates the anecdote or proverb in other words. The Paraphrase[4] is crucial because it sets the stage for the rest of the elaboration. Each of the other paragraphs in the elaboration will flow from this stated understanding of the anecdote or proverb.

Notice that these two ancient Paraphrases end with a statement of the wisdom (or wit) of the person and his statement or action. (In some ancient essays, this kind of a statement is located at the end of the Encomion paragraph instead.) This is analogous to the **thesis statement** in a modern composition; it reveals the overarching theme for the rest of the elaboration.

> This is why, when he had entered the marketplace and chanced upon a boy who was showing a lack of self-control although his paedagogus was in attendance, he disregarded the boy, went after the paedagogus, and chastised the guardian instead of the boy. Nor did he conceal the reason for his blow: "This much at least," he said, "anyone who is not a good paedagogus will understand." And so this is what he has done, but it is possible from what follows to understand that he has acted properly.[5]

> The lover of education,' he says, 'labours at first, but those labours end in profit.' That was his wise saying; and we shall show our admiration in what follows.[6]

To write a Paraphrase paragraph, use copia of words and copia of construction. (See the Copia In Your Writing chart in the Appendix.) Start with synonyms. Then, consider changing a direct quotation of the wise or witty saying to an indirect one, or vice versa. Your analysis and inflection work with the anecdote (proverb) will lay the groundwork for this paragraph.

 Discuss the meaning of the Plutarch proverb, "Character is habit long continued," with your teacher and classmates, your parents, siblings, or any other interested and helpful parties. Make notes on words, phrases, and ideas that might help you write your Paraphrase of this proverb.

Writer's Journal

IMITATING THE ANCIENT ELABORATION: PARAPHRASE

The original Paraphrase below is also from the Isocrates elaboration, and the close Paraphrase imitation is for an elaboration of the proverb *Look Before You Leap* (from a fable by Aesop). Again, notice how the underlined phrases in the original are replaced in the imitation with

---

4 We capitalize *Paraphrase* when referring the the elaboration paragraph; we use lowercase *paraphrase* when speaking of the composition skill.
5 Hock & O'Neil, *The Chreia and Ancient Rhetoric*, 213.
6 "Aphthonius' Progymnasmata," translated by Malcolm Heath.

phrases appropriate to the new subject, but the rest of the words are retained as much as possible.

'The lover of education,' he says, 'labours at first, but those labours end in profit.' That was his wise saying; and we shall show our admiration in what follows.[7]

The prudent man,' he says, 'will carefully evaluate his course of action before he proceeds.' That was his wise saying and we shall show our admiration in what follows.

 Open the file with your Encomion paragraph from Lesson 10.4, and add a Paraphrase paragraph for the Plutarch proverb in close imitation of an ancient Paraphrase paragraph. Follow the example above. For the original to imitate, you may choose either the Paraphrase paragraph from Pseudo-Nicolaus (Lesson 8) or from Aphthonius (Lesson 9). Save and print the document.

ANECDOTE/PROVERB ELABORATION: CAUSE

Cause is a discussion of the rationale behind the words and/or action in the anecdote (proverb). This may take the form of logical reasons, as in the first Cause paragraph below where Aphthonius examines reasons why the educational experience might be thought of as "bitter." Another approach, as in the second Cause paragraph below is to consider the knowledge or life experience that the person must have in order to do or say such wise or witty things. The motivation behind the saying or action might also be examined. In the case of an anecdote, the circumstances, if they are known, might be explained.

The lovers of education are enrolled with the leaders of education, whom it is fearful to approach though to desert them is foolish; fear always waits on boys, both when they are present and in anticipation. From teachers the attendants (pedagogues) take over, fearful to behold, more fearful when inflicting punishment. Fear precedes the experience and punishment follows on fear. What the boys do wrong they punish; what the boys do well they take as a matter of course. Fathers are harsher than attendants, examining their ways, telling them to make progress, viewing the market-place with suspicion; and if punishment is needed they take no account of human nature. But by these experiences the boy, when he reaches adulthood, is crowned with virtue.[8]

Diogenes understood that youth is an irrational sort of being, whereas old men have acquired, if nothing else, the experience of old age. He also knew that parents pay a high price for old men and set them as guardians over their young men, so that they correct the thoughtless nature of youth by the thoughtfulness of their elders.

7 *Ibid.*
8 "Aphthonius' Progymnasmata," translated by Malcolm Heath.

Knowing these things, he ignored the young man and went after the paedagogus, on whom the parents were relying to discipline their boy, and deliberately chose the man instead of the boy.[9]

The Cause paragraph requires some thought. In a given elaboration, the content of the Cause paragraph will affect the content for the rest of the essay, so it is very important that it be well considered. This should be a discussion exercise well before it is a written one. Discuss the anecdote or proverb with your teacher, your family, your friends. Think about following and make lots of notes before you begin to write:

♦ Logical reasons why the words and/or action is wise or witty. These may take into account both the way things are, and the way things ought to be.

♦ Knowledge or life experience needed to speak or act in this way.

♦ Motivation of person who spoke or acted in such a way.

♦ Circumstances behind the words or action (these may be included in the Cause in the case of an anecdote).

 Discuss ideas for the Cause paragraph of your Plutarch proverb elaboration with your teacher and classmates, your parents, siblings, or any other interested and helpful parties. Make a list of ideas in your Writer's Journal.

Writer's
Journal

IMITATING THE ANCIENT ELABORATION: CAUSE

The original Cause was taken from an Anecdote elaboration written by Nikephorous Xanthopoulos, a Greek scholar writing in the fourteenth century. The proverb he elaborates is *A man who is a counselor should not sleep all night*, which is is a quote from the beginning of Homer's *Iliad*. The point of the proverb is that those who lead the people should be alert and prepared at all times, and not give in to excessive sleep. It might make more sense to today's audience if you substitute general or commander or even king for counselor. You might question the wisdom of this proverb, as you should of many ancient pagan proverbs, but you must consider it in the context of the times—truly a king often could trust no one else to watch out for his interests. The underlined phrases are replaced in the imitation.

It is the proper concern of the man who has the burden of the folk resting on his shoulders to give counsel and to carry out his counsel according to this concern. But above all he must keep watch against the treachery of his opponents, not only by day, but especially by night, so that when he has offered counsel his personal affairs will prosper, and he may inflict defeat on his enemies by making his own people victor over

9 Hock & O'Neil, *The Chreia and Ancient Rhetoric*, 213-14.

these enemies. — Nikephorous Kallistos Xanthopoulos[10]

It is the proper concern of the man who wants to avoid unexpected pitfalls to consider possible adverse consequences and to make provision to avoid them according to this concern. But above all he must remain alert and be prepared, not only when making important decisions, but especially in those that seem small or mundane, so that he will not be overtaken by unanticipated outcomes.

 Open the file with your other paragraphs for this proverb, and add Cause paragraph for the Plutarch proverb in close imitation of an ancient Cause paragraph. Follow the example above. For the original to imitate, you may choose from the Cause paragraph from Pseudo-Nicolaus (Lesson 8), or from Aphthonius (Lesson 9), or from Xanthopolous in this lesson. Save and print the document.

Lesson 11.5

Reflection & Review

Commonplace Book

COMMONPLACE BOOK

Enter in your Commonplace Book:

◆ a favorite passage or two from your reading in Homer's *Odyssey*

◆ an example or two of epithet and/or epic simile

◆ a few lines of iambic poetry from your anthology

◆ examples from your reading of parallelism and antithesis

◆ examples from your reading of other figures you have learned (see Figures and Literary Devices list in *Poetics & Progym I* Appendix)

BOOK OF CENTURIES

Record in your Book of Centuries:

◆ Henry Wadsworth Longfellow

10 Hock & O'Neil, *The Chreia and Ancient Rhetoric*, 357-359.

MEMORY WORK

Review to mastery:

- Verb Terms – *Poetics & Progym I* *

Continue to review each set once a week (more if needed):

- Parts of Speech – *Bards & Poets* Review
- Sentence Terms – *Bards & Poets* Review
- Noun Terms – *Poetics & Progym I*
- Figures – Set #1 – *Poetics & Progym I*

Lesson 12

CR

JERUSALEM

And did those feet in ancient time
Walk upon England's mountains green:
And was the holy Lamb of God,
On England's pleasant pastures seen!

And did the Countenance Divine,
Shine forth upon our clouded hills?
And was Jerusalem builded here,
Among these dark Satanic Mills?

Bring me my Bow of burning gold:
Bring me my arrows of desire:
Bring me my Spear: O clouds unfold!
Bring me my Chariot of fire!

I will not cease from Mental Fight,
Nor shall my sword sleep in my hand:
Till we have built Jerusalem,
In England's green & pleasant Land.

— WILLIAM BLAKE

CR

Lesson 12.1

Prose & Poetry

LITERARY ELEMENTS IN THE POEM: JERUSALEM

1 Read
- ◆ Follow along and listen carefully as the poem is read aloud, OR read it aloud yourself. Read it at least two or three times. **Delight** in the meter, the rhyme, and the images.

2 Inquire
- ◆ Does the **title** give any hint as to the content or message of the poem? If this work was published by the poet in a larger book or anthology, does that title give any hint?
- ◆ Are there any unfamiliar persons, places, or things mentioned in the poem? Discuss these with your teacher.
- ◆ Look up the meaning of any words in the work that are not familiar to you; conduct a complete Vocabulary Study for **key words**.
- ◆ Was there any part of the poem you did not understand? If so, discuss this with your teacher and classmates.

3 Observe the Invention, Arrangement, and Style
- ◆ **Lyrical Elements**
  - ▪ What does the poet describe?
  - ▪ Does the poet make you see, hear, smell, taste, or touch anything?
  - ▪ Does the poet compare something in the poem to some other thing?
- ◆ **Narrative Elements** Does this poem tell a story? If so, observe the
  - ▪ **Setting** When and where does this story take place?
  - ▪ **Characters** Who is (are) the main character(s) in this story?
  - ▪ **Conflict** What is the main problem or crisis for the character(s)?
  - ▪ **Resolution** Is the problem solved? If so, how? If not, why not?
  - ▪ **Sequence** Is this story told *ab ovo*, or *in medias res*, or some other way?
  - ▪ **Point of View** Identify the **person** (and **level of omniscience** if applicable).
- ◆ **Figures** Look for figures of speech and figures of description. (See Appendix for the list of figures taught in *Poetics & Progym*.) Why did the poet choose these particular figures?

4 Investigate the Context

◆ Research a bit about the poet. Make notes in your Writer's Journal about William Blake's

Writer's Journal

- **Origin** Who were the poet's parents/ancestors? Where was his homeland?
- **Historical Time Period** When did the poet live? What events happened around the time that the poet lived?
- **Influences** What education, training, books, ideas, and other people or events shaped the poet's thinking?
- **Constraint** What are the requirements based on the audience and the occasion?

◆ **Identify the poem's Literary Genre**

- **Genre by literary period** In which century (time period) and country was this work written?
- **Genre by poetic/narrative category** Is this poem chiefly **lyrical** (describes an event, or a person, or a feeling, or a time and place, etc., but it does not tell a particular story) or **narrative** (tells a story)? If narrative, is it primarily **non-fiction** (a story that really happened) or **fiction** (a story told as if it really happened)?

5 Connect the Thoughts

◆ Does this poem remind you of other poems, or of stories with similar plots, messages, or characters?

◆ Does this poem remind you of any proverbs or other well-known quotations? If so, enter these in your Commonplace Book.

Commonplace Book

6 Profit and Delight

◆ **Delight** What are the sources of delight in this poem?

◆ **Wisdom** What wisdom does this poem furnish?

◆ **Read** the poem to your teacher with expression and proper pauses. (See Lesson 10.1.)

◆ **Read** other works by this poet.

◆ **Memorize** this poem and recite it before an audience.

POETIC FORM AND GENRE

As with all literature, there are many different way to classify a poem's genre. You have already been introduced to two broad genres based on a poem's content: **narrative poetry** that tells a story, and **lyrical poetry** that describes an event, person, feeling, time, place, or any number of other things, but it does not tell a particular story. Virtually all poetry will fall into one category or another, although they are not completely exclusive. A lyrical poem may have narrative elements, and a narrative poem may have lyrical elements.

Other classifications of poetic genre are tied to stanza form and rhyme scheme. A few are listed below in order of the number of lines in each stanza. We will add to this list in the next lesson.

Closed Couplet: pair of rhymed lines that form a complete thought or syntactical unit (usually a sentence).

Heroic Couplet: pair of rhymed lines written in iambic pentameter.

Triplet: three lines that rhyme AAA.

Haiku: three line poem with 5 syllables, 7 syllables, 5 syllables (Japanese).

Terza Rima: tercet with interlocking rhyme; *e.g.* ABA BCB CDC DED (Italian).

Quatrain Rhyme Schemes: Certain rhyme patterns within a particular stanza form also are named. Quatrains are categorized by rhyme pattern:

- ABAB   cross-rhymed
- ABBA   envelope rhyme
- AAAA   mono-rhymed
- AAXA   rubai (Persian form) – *X* can vary
- AABB   elegiac

Ballad: a narrative poem, usually a quatrain.

Elegy: poem written in response to a death; in English poetry, often iambic pentameter cross-rhymed quatrians.

Hymn: song of praise, often in quatrain form.

- **Short Meter** – iambic trimeter in 1st, 2nd, and 4th lines, iambic tetrameter in the 3rd; noted by number of syllables: 6.6.8.6
- **Long Meter** – four iambic tetrameters in each line; noted by number of syllables: 8.8.8.8
- **Common Meter** – alternating lines of iambic tetrameter and iambic trimeter; noted by number of syllables: 8.6.8.6.

Prose & Poetry Handbook

Make the entries indicated below in the Poetry division (P&P).

◆ Stanza Forms P&P 66-67: Title POETIC FORM AND GENRE, add definitions of narrative and lyrical poetry and the list of genres/forms, leaving a blank line between each one. This will probably spill over onto P&P 67. Do not worry if you do not understand all of these definitions. Some of these we will study in *Poetics & Progym*, the rest are meant to be a handy reference for your future studies.

SCANSION AND ANALYSIS: JERUSALEM

Scan and analyze the poetic form of the stanzas below.

A. Scan the lines. Refer back to Lesson 11 if you need a refresher on the steps.

B. Mark the end rhyme. Name the rhyme scheme:

C. Write the stanza name, along with any form/genre designation that may apply:

And did those feet in ancient time

Walk upon England's mountains green:

And was the holy Lamb of God,

On England's pleasant pastures seen!

And did the Countenance Divine,

Shine forth upon our clouded hills?

And was Jerusalem builded here,

Among these dark Satanic Mills?

Bring me my Bow of burning gold:

Bring me my arrows of desire:

Bring me my Spear: O clouds unfold!

Bring me my Chariot of fire!

I will not cease from Mental Fight,

Nor shall my sword sleep in my hand:

Till we have built Jerusalem,

In England's green & pleasant Land.

THE ODYSSEY

○ Read

◆ *The Odyssey of Homer*, Book Ten

○ As you read, continue to mark the text and make notes:

◆ Literary concepts and terms you observe in the narrative. Do any of your earlier thoughts need revision?
◆ Instances of **epic simile**.
◆ **Epithets** to add to your running list.
◆ Passages reflecting on the value of **hearth and home**.

Writer's Journal

○ Discuss this week's reading with your teacher, along with all your notes and observations. Narrate the main action of the book, and discuss any parts you did not understand. How was this reading **delightful**? What **wisdom** does this reading furnish?

Lesson 12.2

Language Logic

VERB PROPERTY – MOOD

 Study these lessons in *Sentence Sense*.

I. Etymology – Verbs
◆ 3.9C Subjunctive Mood
◆ 3.9D Potential Mood

V. Exercises
◆ Harvey's 100 *Complete this exercise orally with your teacher.*

GRAMMAR TERMS & DEFINITIONS: VERB TERMS

 Grammar Terms to Master: In the Quizlet classroom, review or print flashcards from Verb Terms – *Poetics & Progym I.*

- ◆ Subjunctive Mood
- ◆ Potential Mood

DIAGRAMMING & PARSING

 In your Writer's Journal, copy these sentences. Mark the prepositional phrases, subjects, and verbs. Bracket the clauses. Classify the sentences as simple, compound, complex, or compound-complex. Then diagram each one. Refer to *Sentence Sense* as needed. Hint: treat the colons in the first and second lines of the third verse as semi-colons joining principal clauses.

And did those feet in ancient time

Walk upon England's mountains green:

And was the holy Lamb of God,

On England's pleasant pastures seen!

And did the Countenance Divine,

Shine forth upon our clouded hills?

And was Jerusalem builded here,

Among these dark Satanic Mills?

Bring me my Bow of burning gold:

Bring me my arrows of desire:

Bring me my Spear: O clouds unfold!

Bring me my Chariot of fire!

I will not cease from Mental Fight,

Nor shall my sword sleep in my hand:

Till we have built Jerusalem,

In England's green & pleasant Land.

Orally parse these words with your teacher. Use the charts in *Sentence Sense*, Chapter IV to guide you. Add Verb Property – Mood to your noun parsing.

And, ancient, England's, was seen, forth, clouded, Bring, will cease, have built

Lesson 12.3

Eloquent Expression

COPIA OF CONSTRUCTION: SENTENCE COMBINATION – COMPOUND ELEMENTS

Writers often need to refer to a person, place, thing, or idea repeatedly. Consider these simple sentences:

> The friend sent kind greetings. He related interesting news. He promised to visit. Erasmus was filled with joy.

You could simply add other nouns and pronouns to avoid too much repetition. But you are still left with a series of short, simple sentences with the same structure. A better option in this case is to create more sophistication by varying the sentence structure and length. To do this, combine sentences with **conjunctions** and **compounds**. Any elements of a sentence can be compounded in this way: subjects, predicates, objects, or modifiers.

> Kind greetings, interesting news, and the promise of a visit brought Erasmus great joy. (compound subject)

> The friend sent kind greetings, related interesting news, and promised to visit. (compound predicate)

> Erasmus was filled with great joy by the kind greetings, the interesting news, and the promise of a visit. (compound objects of prepositions)

 Review comma rules regarding the proper use of commas in *Sentence Sense* as directed:

II. Syntax – Capitalization and Punctuation

- ◆ 11.3C Rule I Items in a Series
- ◆ 11.3C Rule II Compound Sentences
- ◆ 11.3C Rule X Adjective, Participial, Appositive, and Absolute Phrases
- ◆ 11.3C Rule XVI Clauses of a Complex Sentence

Avoid these two common errors when combining sentences:

◆ Run-on Sentence: *Erasmus received a letter from a friend he was delighted.* Correct this with a comma and conjunction: *Erasmus received a letter from a friend, and he was delighted.*

◆ Comma Splice: *The delighted scholar wrote a reply, he sent it to his friend.* Two principal clauses, each with its own subject and verb, cannot be combined into a compound sentence by just sticking a comma between them. You must either add a conjunction or replace the comma with a semi-colon. *The delighted scholar wrote a reply, and he sent it to his friend. The delighted scholar wrote a reply; he sent it to his friend.*

Disclaimer: There are fashions is writing, just as in clothing. Comma splices have not always been considered poor style. Great authors of the past used them quite often—Charles Dickens comes to mind. But since the comma splice is academically proscribed, we have emphasized this quite a bit so that you will remember.

Sometimes, in order to create a particular figure of speech, a good writer will use a comma splice on purpose. We will learn to use such a figure later. Once you know and consistently follow the rules, you may rarely have occasion to break them, but always by intention, never by mistake.

COPIA OF CONSTRUCTION: SENTENCE COMBINATION WITH PARTICIPLES
Another way to combine a series of simple sentences is by converting a main verb to a participle. Remember to avoid dangling participles, though.

Erasmus received a letter from a friend. Erasmus read the letter many times. Erasmus wrote a reply. Erasmus addressed the reply to his friend.

Erasmus, receiving a letter from a friend, read it many times. Writing a reply, the delighted scholar addressed it to his friend.

Another possibility is to use a combination of participles and conjunctions:

Having received a letter from a friend, Erasmus read it many times, wrote a reply, and addressed it to his friend.

Paraphrase the series of sentences below into two simple sentences with compound elements using commas and conjunctions. Then write a second set of simple sentences with compound elements and participles. Your topic for these sentences comes from Odysseus's account of their time in the house of Circe.

Ailos gave Odsysseus the bag of winds. He left the west wind free to blow them gently home. Odysseus's crew did not trust him. They opened the bag of winds. The bag of winds blew them off course.

LITERARY IMITATION

Work with one of the the stanzas from "Jerusalem" that you diagrammed in Language Logic. Copy the **diagram skeleton**, construct a new sentence, and write the new sentence below the diagram. Base your new sentence on Book Ten of *The Odyssey*. Do not worry about keeping the meter or rhyme.

Lesson 12.4

Classical Composition

PROGYMNASMA NARRATIVE: PLOT OBSERVATION – THEON'S SIX AND SUMMARY

Observe and summarize Homer's *Odyssey*, Book Ten Refer to the instructions and example in the Appendix under "Narrative Plot Observation" and "Example Narrative Plot Observation."

Complete the steps for Plot Observation – Theon's Six on the original narrative and in your Writer's Journal.

Write a one paragraph summary of this book, following the steps for Plot Observation – Summary. Work either in your Writer's Journal or on the computer. Add this summary to your running file of *Odyssey* summaries, and save the file.

ANECDOTE/PROVERB ELABORATION: CONTRAST

Contrast is a consideration of contrasting words or actions. This is sometimes called arguing from the opposite. Here you consider implications or results that would arise from antithetical words or actions. This may take the form of elaborating upon the person who would act in a manner opposite to the essential wisdom or wit of the anecdote or proverb, as we see in the first paragraph. Or the Contrast may consider the result of speaking or acting in a manner opposite to the way in which the wise or witty person spoke or acted, as we see in the second paragraph.

Usually the Contrast paragraph argues from the opposite of what was just stated in the Cause paragraph, making the whole elaboration cohesive.

> But if someone, because he fears these things, flees from his teachers, absconds from his parents, avoids his attendants, he is utterly deprived of eloquence; along with his fear he has set aside eloquence. All these things swayed Isocrates's judgement when he called the root of education bitter.

> Indeed, if he had inflicted the blow, not on the paedagogus, but on the boy, who would not fault Diogenes's discipline? For youth understands nothing but is always impressed by what has happened in matters where he lacks judgement.

To write the constrast paragraph, consider a contrasting scenario from that which you explored in your Cause paragraph.

- ◆ What would have been the logical result or implication of acting or speaking in a manner contrary to the essential wisdom or wit of the anecdote (proverb)?
- ◆ What would be lacking in the knowledge or life experience of a person who acts or speaks in a manner contrary to the essential wisdom or wit of the anecdote (proverb)?
- ◆ What would motivate someone to act or speak in a manner contrary to the essential wisdom or wit of the anecdote (proverb)?

Discuss ideas for the Contrast paragraph of your Plutarch Proverb elaboration with your teacher and classmates, your parents, siblings, or any other interested and helpful parties. Make a list of ideas in your Writer's Journal.

Writer's Journal

IMITATING THE ANCIENT ELABORATION: CONTRAST
The original Contrast paragraph is taken from the Isocrates elaboration in Lesson 9. The underlined phrases are replaced in the imitation.

> If, on the other hand, out of fear of these things someone were to flee from teachers, run away from parents, and shun pedagogues, he is completely deprived of training in speech and has lost ability in speech with his loss of fear. All these considerations influenced Isocrates's thought in calling the root of education bitter.[1]

> If, on the other hand, due to lack of forethought someone were to jump into a situation without due consideration, he is completely deprived of a plan to overcome the obstacles that may arise and has lost the ability to act accordingly. All these considerations influenced Aesop's thought in calling for the necessity of thinking ahead.

1 Kennedy, *Progymnasmata*, 98.

Open the file with your elaboration paragraphs for the Plutarch proverb, and add a Contrast paragraph in close imitation of an ancient Contrast paragraph. Follow the example above. For the original to imitate, you may choose from the Contrast paragraph from Pseudo-Nicolaus (Lesson 8), or from Aphthonius (Lesson 9 or this lesson). Save and print the document.

ANECDOTE/PROVERB ELABORATION: COMPARISON

Comparison, or **analogy**, is a consideration of an similar or analogous situation. This provides the reader with another way to think about the wise or witty saying and/or action. It may be a more concrete idea than that presented in the anecdote or proverb. One way to create a Comparison is by inventing a metaphor or a simile. The first ancient paragraph below uses the metaphor of a farmer sowing and reaping. In this case, the original anecdote already contains an agricultural metaphor, but the additional comparison makes it even more detailed and concrete.

Another type of Comparison may be a similar situation from another sphere that would be familiar to the reader, as we see in the second paragraph below where the author compares the situation in the anecdote to similar situations in navigation, musical performance, and military life.

> For just as those who work the land laboriously sow the seed in the earth and gather the crops with greater joy, in the same way those who strive for education by their toil acquire the subsequent renown.[2]

> Just as the mistakes of sailors are attributed to pilots, and a chorus, when it hits a false note, allows the trainer to be blamed, and an army, when it is disorderly, causes the general to be blamed, so a boy, when he makes a mistake, causes his paedagogus to be accused.[3]

The best of all analogies are found in the parables of Jesus, where He explained deep theological truths using ordinary, everyday things that his hearers would fully understand.

> The kingdom of heaven is like leaven, which a woman took and hid in three measures of meal till it was all leavened. — Matthew 13:33

> Again, the kingdom of heaven is like treasure hidden in a field, which a man found and hid; and for joy over it he goes and sells all that he has and buys that field. — Matthew 13:44

2 "Aphthonius' Progymnasmata," translated by Malcolm Heath.
3 Hock & O'Neil, *The Chreia and Ancient Rhetoric*, 215.

Again, the kingdom of heaven is like a merchant seeking beautiful pearls, who, when he had found one pearl of great price, went and sold all that he had and bought it. — Matthew 13:45

To write a Comparison, you will need to spend some time in thought and discussion—in the schoolroom, at the dinner table, in the car. Remember that you should choose a Comparison that will be familiar to your audience. Jot down several metaphorical ideas. Think of other spheres where the principle of the anecdote or proverb may be seen. Some possiblilities:

- agriculture
- education
- sports
- music or art
- business
- military

- fishing or hunting
- household tasks
- travels
- the human body
- the animal kingdom
- a hobby

Writer's Journal

⟨⟩ Discuss ideas for the Comparison paragraph of your Plutarch Proverb elaboration with your teacher and classmates, your parents, siblings, or any other interested and helpful parties. Make a list of ideas in your Writer's Journal.

IMITATING THE ANCIENT ELABORATION: COMPARISON

Again, the original Comparison paragraph is taken from the Isocrates anecdote by Aphthonius, and was translated from the Greek by a different author, so the wording is slightly different. The underlined phrases are replaced in the imitation.

Just as those who work the earth cast the seeds in the ground with toil but reap the fruits with greater pleasure, in the same way those exchanging toil for education have by toil acquired future renown.[4]

Just as those who wish to build a house must make a careful blueprint before beginning in order to budget the necessary funds and forsee possible hindrances, in the same way those who consider a situation carefully before jumping in with both feet will not find themselves facing unintended consequences without resources or a means of escape.

⟨⟩ Open the file with your elaboration paragraphs for the Plutarch proverb, and add a Comparison paragraph in close imitation of an ancient Comparison paragraph. Follow the example above. For the

4 Kennedy, *Progymnasmata*, 99.

original to imitate, you may choose from the Comparison paragraph from Pseudo-Nicolaus (Lesson 8), or from Aphthonius (Lesson 9 or this lesson). Save and print the document.

Lesson 12.5

Reflection & Review

COMMONPLACE BOOK

Commonplace Book

Enter in your Commonplace Book:

◆ a favorite passage or two from your reading in Homer's *Odyssey*

◆ an example or two of epithet and/or epic simile

◆ a few lines of trochaic poetry from your anthology

◆ examples from your reading of other figures you have learned (see Figures and Literary Devices list in *Poetics & Progym I* Appendix)

BOOK OF CENTURIES

Record in your Book of Centuries:

◆ William Blake

MEMORY WORK

GRAMMAR FLASHCARDS

Review to mastery:

◆ Verb Terms – *Poetics & Progym I*

◆ Figures – Set #2 – *Poetics & Progym I*

Use the test features at Quizlet for an online or printed quiz over Figures Set #2. If you wish, combine with previous Figure sets.

Continue to review each set once a week (more if needed):

◆ Parts of Speech – *Bards & Poets* Review

◆ Sentence Terms – *Bards & Poets* Review

◆ Noun Terms – *Poetics & Progym I*

◆ Figures – Set #1 – *Poetics & Progym I*

CR

LIMERICKS

There was once an old man with a beard,
Who said, "It is just as I feared!—
  Two Owls and a Hen,
  Four Larks and a Wren
Have all built their nests in my beard."

— EDWARD LEAR

There was a small boy of Quebec,
Who was buried in snow to his neck;
  When they said. "Are you friz?"
  He replied, "Yes, I is—
But we don't call this cold in Quebec."

— RUDYARD KIPLING

CR

Lesson 13.1

Prose & Poetry

LITERARY ELEMENTS IN LIMERICKS

1 **Read**
   ◆ Follow along and listen carefully as the poems are read aloud, OR read
     them aloud yourself. Read them at least two or three times. **Delight** in
     the meter, the rhyme, and the images.

2 **Inquire**
   ◆ If these poems were published by the poets in a larger book or
     anthology, does that title give any hint?

   ◆ Are there any unfamiliar persons, places, or things mentioned in the
     poems? Discuss these with your teacher.

   ◆ Look up the meaning of any words in the work that are not familiar to you; conduct a
     complete Vocabulary Study for **key words.**

   ◆ Was there any part of either poems you did not understand? If so, discuss this with your
     teacher and classmates.

3 **Observe the Invention, Arrangement, and Style**
   ◆ **Lyrical Elements**
       ■ What do the poets describe?
       ■ Do the poets make you see, hear, smell, taste, or touch anything?
       ■ Do the poets compare something in the poem to some other thing?

   ◆ **Narrative Elements** Does either poem tell a story? If so, observe the
       ■ **Setting** When and where does this story take place?
       ■ **Characters** Who is (are) the main character(s) in this story?
       ■ **Conflict** What is the main problem or crisis for the character(s)?
       ■ **Resolution** Is the problem solved? If so, how? If not, why not?
       ■ **Sequence** Is this story told *ab ovo*, or *in medias res*, or some other way?
       ■ **Point of View** Identify the **person** (and **level of omniscience** if applicable).

   ◆ **Figures** Look for figures of speech and figures of description. (See Appendix for the list of
     figures taught in *Poetics & Progym*.) Why did the poet choose these particular figures?

Writer's Journal

4 Investigate the Context

♦ Research a bit about Edward Lear. Make notes about his

  ■ **Origin** Who were the poet's parents/ancestors? Where was his homeland?

  ■ **Historical Time Period** When did the poet live? What events happened around the time that the poet lived?

  ■ **Influences** What education, training, books, ideas, and other people or events shaped the poet's thinking?

♦ **Identify the poem's Literary Genre**

  ■ **Genre by literary period** In which century (time period) and country was this work written?

  ■ **Genre by poetic/narrative category** Is this poem chiefly **lyrical** (describes an event, or a person, or a feeling, or a time and place, etc., but it does not tell a particular story) or **narrative** (tells a story)? If narrative, is it primarily **non-fiction** (a story that really happened) or **fiction** (a story told as if it really happened)?

5 Connect the Thoughts

♦ Do these poems remind you of other poems, or of stories with similar plots, messages, or characters?

♦ Do these poems remind you of any proverbs or other well-known quotations? If so, enter these in your Commonplace Book.

Commonplace Book

6 Profit and Delight

♦ **Delight What are the sources** of delight in these poems?

♦ **Wisdom What wisdom** do these poems furnish?

♦ **Read** the poems to your teacher with expression and proper pauses. (See Lesson 10.1.)

♦ **Read** other works by these poets.

♦ **Memorize** these poems and recite them before an audience.

POETIC FORM AND GENRE

Study these classifications of poetic genre tied to stanza form and rhyme scheme:

Limerick: Quintain written in anapestic meter; lines 1, 2, and 5 are trimeter, lines 3 and 4 are dimeter; rhyme scheme is usually AABBA. Most limericks are meant to be amusing.

Rhyme Royale (Rime Royal or Troilus stanza): Seven lines of ten syllables; usually written in iambic pentameter; rhyme scheme is ABABBCC.

Spenserian Stanza: Nine line stanza: eight lines of iambic pentameter, last line is an alexandrine (iambic hexameter); rhyming ABABBCBCC.

Sonnet: Fourteen line poem, usually in iambic pentameter. Rhyme scheme depends on the type of sonnet.

- **Petrarchan sonnet**: octave rhyming ABBAABBA plus sestet rhyming CDCDCD or CDECDE
- **Shakespearean sonnet**: three quatrains plus a couplet, rhyming ABAB CDCD EFEF GG
- **Spenserian sonnet**: similar to Shakespearean, with interlocking rhyme ABAB BCBC CDCD EE

Ode: A formal lyric poem that addresses, exalts, and/or celebrates a person, place, thing, or idea; stanza forms vary.

Epic Poem: A long narrative poem written with epic conventions and in epic style.

Blank Verse: metrical verse with no rhyme.

Free Verse: Lines closely following the natural rhythm of speech. Lines are not metrical and do not rhyme. Though a regular pattern of sound or rhythm may be discerned, the poet does not compose free verse in a particular meter.

Make the entries indicated below in the Poetry division.

Prose & Poetry Handbook

- Stanza Forms P&P 67-68: Starting after the last entry on page 67 (or 68), add the list of genres/forms, leaving a blank line between each one. This will spill over onto P&P 68. Again, do not worry if you do not understand all of these definitions. Some of these we will study in *Poetics & Progym*, the rest are meant to be a handy reference for your future studies.

SCANSION: LIMERICKS

As you just learned, a **limerick** has a very specific metrical and stanza form. The humor in limericks is often achieved through **puns** and other forms of **wordplay**. Limericks are catchy and easy to remember because of the singsong effect of anapestic meter, along with the humorous content. Some nursery rhymes are written in limerick form. Can you think of any?

Scan and analyze the poetic form of the stanzas below.

A. Scan the lines. Refer back to Lesson 11 if you need a refresher on the steps. Note that the first foot in a line sometimes drops an unstressed syllable in this poem.

B. Mark the end rhyme. Name the rhyme scheme:

C. Write the stanza name, along with any form/genre designation that may apply:

There was once an old man with a beard,

Who said, "It is just as I feared!—

  Two Owls and a Hen,

  Four Larks and a Wren

Have all built their nests in my beard."

There was a small boy of Quebec,

Who was buried in snow to his neck;

  When they said. "Are you friz?"

  He replied, "Yes, I is—

But we don't call this cold in Quebec."

THE ODYSSEY

🏆 Read

◆ *The Odyssey of Homer*, Book Eleven

🏆 As you read, continue to mark the text and make notes:

◆ Literary concepts and terms you observe in the narrative. Do any of your earlier thoughts need revision?
◆ Instances of **epic simile**.
◆ **Epithets** to add to your running list.
◆ Passages reflecting on the value of **hearth and home**.

🏆 Discuss this week's reading with your teacher, along with all your notes and observations. Narrate the main action of the book, and discuss any parts you did not understand. How was this reading **delightful**? What **wisdom** does this reading furnish?

Writer's Journal

Lesson 13.2

Language Logic

VERB PROPERTY – TENSE

 Study/review these lessons in *Sentence Sense*.

I. Etymology – Verbs

◆ 3.7A Property – Tense
◆ 3.7B Divisions of Tenses
◆ 3.7C The Present Tense
◆ 3.7D The Present Perfect Tense

◆ 3.7E The Past Tense
◆ 3.7F The Past Perfect Tense
◆ 3.7G The Future Tense
◆ 3.7H The Future Perfect Tense

DIAGRAMMING & PARSING

Writer's Journal

In your Writer's Journal, copy these sentences. Mark the prepositional phrases, subjects, and verbs. Bracket the clauses. Classify each sentence as simple, compound, complex, or compound-complex. Then diagram each one. Refer to *Sentence Sense* as needed.

1. Can storied urn, or animated bust,

   Back to its mansion call the fleeting breath? — Thomas Gray

2. O God, we are but leaves on thy stream, clouds in thy sky. — Dinah Craik

3. I am the bread of life: he that cometh to me shall never hunger; and he that believeth on me shall never thirst. — John 6:35, King James Version

Orally parse these words with your teacher. Use the charts in *Sentence Sense*, Chapter IV to guide you.

(1) animated, mansion, Can call; (2) O, God, but; (3) I, am, cometh, shall hunger, believeth

Lesson 13.3

Eloquent Expression

COPIA OF CONSTRUCTION: SCHEME – PARALLELISM

Parallelism is a basic principle of grammatical construction, and also a figure of speech as we learned in Lesson 11.3. When you have compound elements in which two or more items (words, phrases, or clauses) share a similar grammatical structure, you should generally construct those items in parallel structure.

Erasmus received, opened, and read your letter.

Your letter to Erasmus was received in the morning, opened in the afternoon, and reread throughout the evening.

Erasmus received the letter with joy, he opened it with haste, and he read it with great pleasure.

In the first sentence, the compound verbs are parallel, because they are all transitive, active, past tense, and share a common object. In the second sentence, parallel compound passive verbs are followed by parallel adverbial prepositional phrases. In the third sentence, each clause contains the parallel structure subject-verb-adverbial prepositional phrase. To "see" this parallel structure, diagram these three sentences with your teacher. Take a look also at the sentences you diagrammed in Lesson 13.2 also – they all have some kind of parallel structure.

Correct each sentence below by rewriting it in parallel format. Add modifiers and prepositional phrases if needed. Then, look through earlier compositions of your own. Find one or two sentences that could be improved or corrected with with parallelism. Copy the original and the corrected version into your Writer's Journal.

Writer's Journal

1. After the Cyclops killed his men, Odyesseus made a plan, was considering how to escape, and became prepared.

2. Because the Cyclops said that No Man hurt him, the other Cyclops did not come help; they also laughed at him.

3. The rocks landed near the ship and almost swamped it, then Odysseus and his men were frightened.

LITERARY IMITATION

Work with one of the sentences that you diagrammed in Language Logic. Copy the **diagram skeleton**, construct a new sentence, and write the new sentence below the diagram. Base your new sentence on Book Eleven of the *Odyssey*.

Lesson 13.4

Classical Composition

PROGYMNASMA NARRATIVE: PLOT OBSERVATION – THEON'S SIX AND SUMMARY
Observe and summarize Homer's *Odyssey*, Book Twelve. Refer to the instructions and example in the Appendix under "Narrative Plot Observation" and "Example Narrative Plot Observation."

Writer's Journal

◯ Complete the steps for Plot Observation – Theon's Six on the original narrative and in your Writer's Journal.

◯ Write a one paragraph summary of this book, following the steps for Plot Observation – Summary. Work either in your Writer's Journal or on the computer. Add this summary to your running file of *Odyssey* summaries, and save the file.

ANECDOTE/PROVERB ELABORATION: EXAMPLE

Example is a discussion of a relevant illustration from history or literature. Note in the Example paragraphs below, as in the Encomion, the ancient authors did not give a full retelling of the story, but instead give only enough information to call the incident to mind. Again, this is because the author expects his audience to understand his reference. Both also examine the connection between the illustration and the anecdote or proverb. This may be done either directly as in the the second paragraph, or more indirectly as in the first. Notice also that there are two separate, but related examples from Greek history included in the second paragraph.

The Example is more specific than the Comparison because it refers to a particular story from history or literature. The Example is generally composed with at least some proper nouns, while the Comparison usually only requires common nouns.

> Consider Demosthenes's career, which was more devoted to toil than that of any orator and more glorious than that of any. So great was his commitment that he even deprived his head of its adornment, thinking the best adornment is that from virtue. And he devoted to toil what others devote to enjoyment.[1]

> Consider, if you will, the city of the Athenians which, when its soldiers died in the Hellespont, passed judgment on the generals, rather than on the Hellespont, because they had not retrieved the soldiers who had died. And so what occurred because of other factors was alleged to be the faults of the generals. The Athenians also credited Themistocles with the victory at Salamis, even though the people and the city fought, too. Thus, in either case, the Athenians held responsible those in charge, both when they succeeded and when they blundered.[2]

Examples are fundamental to communication. In virtually every situation where a speaker

---

1 "Aphthonius' Progymnasmata," translated by Malcolm Heath.
2 Hock & O'Neil, *The Chreia and Ancient Rhetoric*, 215.

or writer is aiming to explain or persuade, he or she will include some kind of an example (illustration, narrative, or story). Every writer needs to have a large "storehouse of stories." Cottage Press students spend several years learning to retell some of the best stories of all time. In *Voyage of the Dawn Treader*, Eustace, having "read only the wrong books," was unable to make sense of the situation in the dragon's cave. Those books "were weak on dragons," and left him thoroughly unequipped to understand the terrible danger in which he had placed himself. Stories (examples) are a powerful tool in the writer's invention toolbox!

To write an Example, once more you must begin with reflection and discussion. Consider your audience and choose a story that should be at least somewhat familiar to them. Jot down several possibilities. Historical sources for relevant Examples might include:

- ◆ biographical stories
- ◆ accounts of battles
- ◆ accounts of other events

- ◆ life of Jesus
- ◆ acts of the apostles
- ◆ Old Testament narratives

Literary sources might include:

- ◆ fables
- ◆ legends
- ◆ myths

- ◆ fairy tales
- ◆ historical fiction
- ◆ novels

Discuss ideas for the Example paragraph of your Plutarch Proverb elaboration with your teacher and classmates, your parents, siblings, or any other interested and helpful parties. Make a list of ideas in your Writer's Journal.

Writer's Journal

IMITATING THE ANCIENT ELABORATION: EXAMPLE

The original Example paragraph is taken from the Isocrates anecdote by Aphthonius, translated from the Greek by a different author. The underlined phrases are replaced in the imitation. Notice that the imitation here has very little of the original wording, but retains the style of the original.

> Look, I ask you, at the life of Demosthenes, which was the most filled with labor of any orator but became the most glorious of all. He showed such an abundance of zeal that he took the ornament from his head, because he thought the ornament that comes from virtue was the best; and he expended in toils what others lavished on pleasures.[3]

3   Kennedy, *Progymnasmata*, 99.

Look, I ask you, at the famous fable. A goat came upon a well into which a fox had fallen, and the goat inquired of the fox whether the water was good. The crafty fox, seeing a way of escape, encouraged the thirsty goat to come and see for himself. The foolish goat, thinking only of his thirst, impulsively jumped into the well. Whereupon the fox promptly jumped on the goat's back and used him as a ladder to escape, leaving the goat stranded in the well.

 Open the file with your elaboration paragraphs for the Plutarch proverb, and add an Example paragraph in close imitation of an ancient Example paragraph. Follow the example above. For the original to imitate, you may choose from the Example paragraph from Pseudo-Nicolaus (Lesson 8), or from Aphthonius (Lesson 9 or this lesson). Save and print the document.

ANECDOTE/PROVERB ELABORATION: AUTHORITY

Authority (testimony of the ancients) cites a wise person of the past whose testimony supports the wisdom or wit behind the anecdote or proverb. Often the authority paragraph will include some explanation of how the quote supports the wisdom. We see from the lack of explanation in the paragraphs below that these ancient authors expected that their audience would recognize the referenced person of the past, and perhaps even knew the source of the quotation.

> For this reason one must admire Hesiod, who said that the road to virtue is hard but the summit easy, expressing the same wise judgement as Isocrates. For what Hesiod represented as a road Isocrates called the root; both disclosed the same opinion, though in different words.[4]

> For this reason, it is necessary to admire Sophocles, who said that every city is under the influence of its leaders, and people who are unruly become wicked through the character of their teachers.[5]

To write an authority paragraph, you will need to find a relevant quotation from a recognized person of the past (an authority). Where do you find such quotations? To begin with, check your Commonplace Book. If you have not recorded any quotes that are relevant to the anecdote or proverb, the next step might be to check a book of quotes like Bartlett's Quotations or an equivalent online resource. In order to do this, you may need to think carefully about your search term. For example, if you were looking for a quotation to support the Isocrates anecdote, you would not get very far if you search for *root* and *fruit*. Instead, you would need to think of a term that relates to the essential wisdom of the anecdote or proverb, such as *diligence* or *toil* or *industry* or *effort*.

4 "Aphthonius' Progymnasmata," translated by Malcolm Heath.
5 Hock & O'Neil, *The Chreia and Ancient Rhetoric*, 215.

You must choose an authority that your audience will consider credible. Credible authorities have some kind of expertise or recognized reason to speak on the topic under consideration. In order for the authority's testimony to be persuasive, you must choose someone that your audience respects and even reveres. The testimony of George Washington would probably be more persuasive to most Americans than would the testimony of Benedict Arnold, even if they were equally knowledgeable about a particular subject.

Choose your authority from one of these areas:

- Scripture
- authors
- poets

- historical figures, particularly leaders
- proverbs or maxims
- other revered religious sources*

*The Apostle Paul used this kind of a source when he preached on Mars Hill. Even though Christians do not give these sources an equal footing with Scripture, there is sometimes truth to be gained from pagan sources. In general, this kind of testimony will be most effective with non-Christians, but it may give you additional credibility as a person who seeks to understand the influences and authorities that others may consider significant.

Research answers to the same kinds of questions you used for the Encomion:

- **Who** is the person you are quoting?
- **What** is he or she known for? **What** was this person's profession? **What** is this person's legacy?
- **Where** did he or she live? **Where** did this person work?
- **When** did he or she live?
- **Why** is he or she authoritative in this matter?
- **How** does the quote relate to the essence or principle of the wise or witty saying and/or action?

Discuss ideas for the authority paragraph of your Plutarchs Proverb elaboration with your teacher and classmates, your parents, siblings, or any other interested and helpful parties. Make a list of ideas in your Writer's Journal.

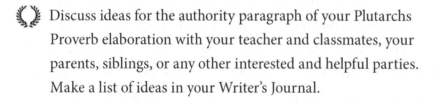

Writer's Journal

IMITATING THE ANCIENT ELABORATION: AUTHORITY

The original paragraph for authority was taken from the Diogenes Anecdote elaboration by Pseudo-Nicolaus. The underlined phrases are replaced in the imitation.

For this reason it is necessary to admire Sophocles, who said that every city is under the influence of its leaders, and people who are unruly become wicked through the character of their teachers.[6]

For this reason it is necessary to admire Victor Hugo, the nineteenth century French literary master, who said that caution is the eldest child of wisdom.

In this Paraphrase, the author information *the nineteenth century French literary master* is added since the modern audience may not be as familiar with Hugo's work as the ancient audience was with that of Sophocles.

 Open the file with your elaboration paragraphs for the Plutarch proverb, and add an authority paragraph in close imitation of an ancient authority paragraph. Follow the example above. For the original to imitate, you may choose from the authority paragraph from Pseudo-Nicolaus (Lesson 8), or from Aphthonius (Lesson 9). Save and print the document.

ANECDOTE/PROVERB ELABORATION: EXHORTATION

Exhortation is a brief epilogue exhorting the reader to admire the wit and/or emulate the wisdom. It is often just one sentence. The underlined phrases are replaced in the imitation.

Those who consider these points must admire Isocrates for his outstandingly wise saying on education.[7]

After looking at all these points, we have to admire Diogenes as the best disciplinarian.[8]

This should be the easiest paragraph of all to write. It is really just a reiteration or restatement of the thesis statement, which was usually found at the end of the Encomion or paraprhase. The key here is brevity. This will be a relief for most of you, and an enormous challenge for a few!

 Discuss ideas for the Exhortation paragraph of your Plutarch Proverb elaboration with your teacher and classmates, your parents, siblings, or any other interested and helpful parties. Make a list of ideas in your Writer's Journal.

Writer's Journal

IMITATING THE ANCIENT ELABORATION: EXHORTATION

The original Exhortation paragraph was taken from the Isocrates

6 Hock & O'Neil, *The Chreia and Ancient Rhetoric*, 215.
7 "Aphthonius' Progymnasmata," translated by Malcolm Heath.
8 Hock & O'Neil, *The Chreia and Ancient Rhetoric*, 216.

Anecdote elaboration by Aphthonius. The underlined phrases are replaced in the imitation.

> Those who consider these points must admire Isocrates for his outstandingly wise saying on education.

> Those who consider these points must admire Aesop for his outstandingly wise saying on the importance of carefully evaluating any course of action.

Open the file with your elaboration paragraphs for the Plutarch proverb, and add an Exhortation for the Plutarch proverb in close imitation of an ancient Exhortation. Follow the example above. For the original to imitate, you may choose from the Exhortation from Pseudo-Nicolaus (Lesson 8), or from Aphthonius (Lesson 9). Save and print the document.

Lesson 13.5

Reflection & Review

Commonplace Book

COMMONPLACE BOOK

Enter in your Commonplace Book:

- ◆ a favorite passage or two from your reading in Homer's *Odyssey*
- ◆ an example or two of epithet and/or epic simile
- ◆ a few lines of anapestic poetry from your anthology
- ◆ examples from your reading of other figures you have learned (see Figures and Literary Devices list in *Poetics & Progym I* Appendix)

BOOK OF CENTURIES

Record in your Book of Centuries:

- ◆ Edward Lear, Rudyard Kipling

◯ Review to mastery:

- Verb Terms – *Poetics & Progym I*

◯ Continue to review each set once a week (more if needed):

- Parts of Speech – *Bards & Poets* Review
- Sentence Terms – *Bards & Poets* Review
- Noun Terms – *Poetics & Progym I*
- Figures – Set #1 – *Poetics & Progym I*
- Figures – Set #2 – *Poetics & Progym I*

THE LOST LEADER

Just for a handful of silver he left us,

    Just for a riband to stick in his coat—

Found the one gift of which fortune bereft us,

    Lost all the others she lets us devote;

They, with the gold to give, doled him out silver,

    So much was theirs who so little allowed:

How all our copper had gone for his service!

    Rags—were they purple, his heart had been proud!

We that had loved him so, followed him, honoured him,

    Lived in his mild and magnificent eye,

Learned his great language, caught his clear accents,

    Made him our pattern to live and to die!

Shakespeare was of us, Milton was for us,

    Burns, Shelley, were with us,—they watch from their graves!

He alone breaks from the van and the freemen,

    —He alone sinks to the rear and the slaves!

We shall march prospering,—not thro' his presence;

    Songs may inspirit us,—not from his lyre;

Deeds will be done,—while he boasts his quiescence,

    Still bidding crouch whom the rest bade aspire:

Blot out his name, then, record one lost soul more,

    One task more declined, one more footpath untrod,

One more devils'-triumph and sorrow for angels,

    One wrong more to man, one more insult to God!

Life's night begins: let him never come back to us!

There would be doubt, hesitation and pain,

Forced praise on our part—the glimmer of twilight,

Never glad confident morning again!

Best fight on well, for we taught him—strike gallantly,

Menace our heart ere we master his own;

Then let him receive the new knowledge and wait us,

Pardoned in heaven, the first by the throne!

— ROBERT BROWNING

C8

Lesson 14.1

Prose & Poetry

LITERARY ELEMENTS IN THE POEM: THE LOST LEADER

1 Read
- ◆ Follow along and listen carefully as the poem is read aloud, OR read it aloud yourself. Read it at least two or three times. **Delight** in the meter, the rhyme, and the images.

2 Inquire
- ◆ Does the **title** give any hint as to the content or message of the poem? If this work was published by the poet in a larger book or anthology, does that title give any hint?
- ◆ Are there any unfamiliar persons, places, or things mentioned in the poem? Discuss these with your teacher. Who is the *Lost Leader*?
- ◆ Look up the meaning of any words in the work that are not familiar to you; conduct a complete Vocabulary Study for **key words.**
- ◆ Was there any part of the poem you did not understand? If so, discuss this with your teacher and classmates.

3 Observe the Invention, Arrangement, and Style

◆ **Lyrical Elements**

- What does the poet describe?

- Does the poet make you see, hear, smell, taste, or touch anything?

- Does the poet compare something in the poem to some other thing?

◆ **Narrative Elements** Does this poem tell a story? If so, observe the

- **Setting** When and where does this story take place?

- **Characters** Who is (are) the main character(s) in this story?

- **Conflict** What is the main problem or crisis for the character(s)?

- **Resolution** Is the problem solved? If so, how? If not, why not?

- **Sequence** Is this story told *ab ovo*, or *in medias res*, or some other way?

- **Point of View** Identify the **person** (and **level of omniscience** if applicable).

◆ **Figures** Look for figures of speech and figures of description. (See Appendix for the list of figures taught in *Poetics & Progym*.) Why did the poet choose these particular figures?

4 Investigate the Context

Writer's Journal

◆ Research a bit about the poet. Make notes in your Writer's Journal about Robert Browning's

- **Origin** Who were the poet's parents/ancestors? Where was his homeland?

- **Historical Time Period** When did the poet live? What events happened around the time that the poet lived?

- **Influences** What education, training, books, ideas, and other people or events shaped the poet's thinking?

◆ **Identify the poem's Literary Genre**

- **Genre by literary period** In which century (time period) and country was this work written?

- **Genre by poetic/narrative category** Is this poem chiefly **lyrical** (describes an event, or a person, or a feeling, or a time and place, etc., but it does not tell a particular story) or **narrative** (tells a story)? If narrative, is it primarily **non-fiction** (a story that really happened) or **fiction** (a story told as if it really happened)?

5 Connect the Thoughts

Commonplace Book

◆ Does this poem remind you of other poems, or of stories with similar plots, messages, or characters?

◆ Does this poem remind you of any proverbs or other well-known quotations? If so, enter these in your Commonplace Book.

6 **Profit and Delight**

◆ **Delight** What are the sources of delight in this poem?

◆ **Wisdom** What wisdom does this poem furnish?

◆ **Read** the poem to your teacher with expression and proper pauses.

◆ **Read** other works by this poet.

◆ **Memorize** this poem and recite it before an audience.

SCANSION AND ANALYSIS: THE LOST LEADER

Scan and analyze the poetic form of the stanzas below.

A. Scan the lines. Note that in dactylic meter, it is very common for the final foot of each line to drop one or both unstressed syllables. The sixth line from the bottom has a trochee in the middle, and the third line from the bottom has an unstressed syllable at the beginning of the first foot.

B. Mark the end rhyme. Name the rhyme scheme:

C. Write the stanza name, along with any form/genre designation that may apply:

Just for a handful of silver he left us,

Just for a riband to stick in his coat—

Found the one gift of which fortune bereft us,

Lost all the others she lets us devote;

They, with the gold to give, doled him out silver,

So much was theirs who so little allowed:

How all our copper had gone for his service!

Rags—were they purple, his heart had been proud!

We that had loved him so, followed him, honoured him,

Lived in his mild and magnificent eye,

Learned his great language, caught his clear accents,

Made him our pattern to live and to die!

Shakespeare was of us, Milton was for us,

Burns, Shelley, were with us,—they watch from their graves!

He alone breaks from the van and the freemen,

—He alone sinks to the rear and the slaves!

THE ODYSSEY

THE
ODYSSEY
OF
HOMER

◆ Read

   ◆ *The Odyssey of Homer,* Book Twelve

◆ As you read, continue to mark the text and make notes:

   ◆ Literary concepts and terms you observe in the narrative. Do any of your earlier thoughts need revision?
   ◆ Instances of **epic simile**.
   ◆ **Epithets** to add to your running list.
   ◆ Passages reflecting on the value of **hearth and home**.

Writer's
Journal

◆ Discuss this week's reading with your teacher, along with all your notes and observations. Narrate the main action of the book, and discuss any parts you did not understand. How was this reading **delightful**? What **wisdom** does this reading furnish?

Lesson 14.2

Language Logic

Writer's
Journal

DIAGRAMMING & PARSING

◆ In your Writer's Journal, copy this sentence. Mark the prepositional phrases, subjects, and verbs. Bracket the clauses.

Classify the sentence as simple, compound, complex, or compound-complex. Then diagram it. Refer to *Sentence Sense* as needed. Hint: There is actually more than one way to diagram this sentence. It will all depend on how you assign subjects to the compound predicates. In this case, you will need to make some informed interpretive decisions. Sentence diagramming is an art, not a science!

> We that had loved him so, followed him, honoured him,
>> Lived in his mild and magnificent eye,
> Learned his great language, caught his clear accents,
>> Made him our pattern to live and to die!

Orally parse these words with your teacher, using the charts in *Sentence Sense* to guide you.

We, that, had loved, so, followed, lived, mild, and, language, him, pattern

Lesson 14.3

Eloquent Expression

COPIA OF CONSTRUCTION: SCHEME – ANTITHESIS

In the figure of **antithesis,** two contrasting things are set side by side. Parallel format is often used to create antithesis.

Your letter brought both joy and sorrow to Erasmus.

Your letter brought joy to Erasmus, though it brought sorrow to him also.

Your letter brought to Erasmus the joy of your concern for him, yet the grief of your absence from him.

Complete these exercises in your Writer's Journal.

Write a sentence using antithesis and parallel structure to tell how Odysseus could listen to the Sirens according to Circe (or a sentence based on some other event from Book XII).

Write a sentence using antithesis and parallel structure telling how Odysseus responded to the poet Demodocus the bard in Book Eight.

Writer's Journal

LITERARY IMITATION

Work with the stanza that you diagrammed in Language Logic. Copy the **diagram skeleton**, construct a new sentence, and write the new sentence below the diagram. Base your new sentence on a character from *The Odyssey*. Do not worry about keeping the meter or rhyme.

Lesson 14.4

Classical Composition

PROGYMNASMA NARRATIVE: PLOT OBSERVATION – THEON'S SIX AND SUMMARY

Observe and summarize Homer's *Odyssey*, Book Twelve. Refer to the instructions and example in the Appendix under "Narrative Plot Observation" and "Example Narrative Plot Observation."

Complete the steps for Plot Observation – Theon's Six on the original narrative and in your Writer's Journal.

Writer's Journal

Write a one paragraph summary of this book, following the steps for Plot Observation – Summary. Work either in your Writer's Journal or on the computer. Add this summary to your running file of *Odyssey* summaries, and save the file.

ANECDOTE/PROVERB ELABORATION: COMPLETE ESSAY

Open the file with your elaboration paragraphs for this proverb. Check to see that you have eight paragraphs in order: Encomion, Paraphrase, Cause, Contrast, Comparison, Example, Authority, and Exhortation. The final step is to develop a title for your elaboration. This time, simply use the wise saying from the anecdote/proverb as your title. Format the heading at the top of your elaboration as follows. Headings are usually either left-aligned or centered. Follow the requirements of your teacher in this. Note: The second line of this heading is added for academic integrity. Although the ancients would have not been concerned in the least about imitating another rhetorician, modern academia thinks much differently in this regard. Because you will need to learn to function in this setting, we think it prudent to practice scrupulous integrity in this area.

Title
Imitation of Ancient Anecdote/Proverb elaboration
by [your name]
Date

Revise your elaboration using the checklist below. Work through the checklist once on your own, and then a second time with your writing mentor, making notes on the print copy of your narrative. Transfer all additions and corrections from your print copy to the computer file. Save and print the document.

Editor's Pen – The Big Picture

✓ All paragraphs included in order, and on topic:
   ◆ **Encomion**: brief praise of the person represented as speaking or acting
   ◆ **Paraphrase**: restatement of the anecdote (proverb) in your own words
   ◆ **Cause**: discussion of the rationale behind the words and/or action in the anecdote (proverb)
   ◆ **Contrast**: consideration of contrasting words or action
   ◆ **Comparison**: consideration of an analogous situation
   ◆ **Example**: discussion of relevant illustration(s) from history or literature (not a complete retelling!)
   ◆ **Authority**: credible testimony that supports the wisdom or wit behind the anecdote or proverb
   ◆ **Exhortation**: brief epilogue exhorting the reader to admire the wit and/or emulate the wisdom

✓ Ancient elaboration imitated very closely

✓ Length: very close to the ancient elaboration

✓ Figures of speech (at least one instance of each): *parallelism, antithesis*

Editor's Pen – Zoom 5x: Paragraphs

Refer to Copia In Your Writing (Prose & Poetry Handbook or Appendix) as needed

✓ Formatting: *proper indentation*

✓ Length: *neither too wordy nor too short*

✓ Sentence class by use: *effective use*

✓ Sentence openers: *varied*

✓ Dialogue: *none*

✓ Sentence length and class by form: *varied*

✓ Verb Tense: *consistent*

✓ Pronouns clear: *easily identified antecedents*

✓ Person for Nouns & Pronouns: *similar to ancient elaboration*

Editor's Pen – Zoom 10x: Sentences

Refer to Copia In Your Writing (Prose & Poetry Handbook or Appendix) as needed

✓ Complete thought expressed
✓ Subject and predicate agree in number
✓ Correct capitalization and punctuation
   ◆ No comma splices!
✓ Items in a series constructed in parallel form

Editor's Pen – Fine Focus: Words

✓ Word choices varied; word meanings clear; consider denotation AND connotation
   ◆ Verbs: *strong, specific, fitting, mostly active (vs. passive); appropriate adverbs if needed*
   ◆ Nouns: *clear, descriptive; appropriate adjectives if needed*
   ◆ Dialogue: *dialogue tags varied if appropriate*
✓ Correct spelling
✓ Final read-through

POETRY ANALYSIS ESSAY: THE BUILDERS

Now we are going to take all those poetry terms and apply them to Longfellow's poem. A college literature professor might well ask for a similar essay in class or on a test. Other disciplines might require a similar integration of theory, terms, and content. Read this example essay, written by a college student. The requirements of the assignment include using the particular terms in italic type and at least one instance of parallelism and one of antithesis.

"Stopping By Woods on a Snowy Evening" is a *lyrical poem* written in *1922* by the *American poet Robert Frost*. When he wrote this piece, he was probably inspired by the scenery of Franconia, the town in northern New Hampshire where he was living at the time. In this short but graceful poem, Frost *appeals to the readers' senses* to conjure up the feeling of being alone on a quiet evening in a cold, snow-laden wood, referencing the falling darkness and the jingling bells of the horse's harness. He uses soft, lilting or whispering words, such as "lovely, dark and deep" or "easy" and "downy" to give the poem a sound of peace and quietness, like gently falling snow. For all its evocative power, this poem is surprisingly straightforward; Frost does not use many figures of speech. He does effectively employ the occasional *alliteration*: "watch" and woods," "dark and deep," and "sound's the sweep." This alliteration gently muffles the lines, giving the reader a sense of the drifting snow filling the woods as described in the poem. The poem is composed of *four quatrains*, which are sets of four lines each. Each line is in *iambic tetrameter*, and the *rhyme scheme* goes AABA, BBCB, CCDC, and DDDD. The poem describes the dilemma of the narrator, a traveler passing through the woods in the gathering dusk. He has "miles to go" and "promises to keep" (parallelism). He wants to stay, but he has to go (antithesis). The poem ends with the traveler and his little horse leaving behind the quiet patch of woods to continue through the snowy evening to their journey's end.[1]

A note about verb tenses in literary analysis: When writing about a literary work, it is customary to use the historical present tense when referring to the content of the work. (See *Sentence Sense*, 3.7C, Rem. 2.) Circle each verb in the literary essay example above, and note its tense. The author uses the past participle *written* when referring to the past act of writing the poem itself, but as she begins to deal with the content of the work, the verbs are all present tense: *appeals, uses, employ*, etc. to refer to the content of the story.

Make literary analysis notes for "The Builders." You will write this essay in Lesson 15. Use the Poetry section in your Prose & Poetry Handbook as a guide. In your Writer's Journal, make notes about each of the following elements:

Writer's Journal

- ◆ Literary Context (P&P 30)
- ◆ Poetic Genre – Narrative or Lyrical (P&P 66)
- ◆ If narrative, briefly describe the narrative elements:
  - ▪ Setting
  - ▪ Characters
  - ▪ Conflict
  - ▪ Resolution
- ◆ If lyrical
  - ▪ What is the poet describing?
  - ▪ To which of the reader's senses does the poet appeal?
  - ▪ Is the thing being described compared to something else? How?
- ◆ Poetic Meter (P&P 58)
- ◆ Stanza Form (P&P 64, 66-68) and Rhyme Scheme (P&P 62, 66-68)
- ◆ Figures of Speech

1 Essay by Patrick Henry College intern Sarah Watterson, 2013. Used by permission of the author.

Lesson 14.5

Reflection & Review

Commonplace Book

COMMONPLACE BOOK

◯ Enter in your Commonplace Book:

- ◆ a favorite passage or two from your reading in Homer's *Odyssey*
- ◆ an example or two of epithet and/or epic simile
- ◆ a few lines of dactylic poetry from your anthology
- ◆ examples from your reading of other figures you have learned
  (see Figures and Literary Devices list in *Poetics & Progym I* Appendix)

BOOK OF CENTURIES

◯ Record in your Book of Centuries:

- ◆ Robert Browning

MEMORY WORK

GRAMMAR FLASHCARDS

◯ Review to mastery:

- ◆ Verb Terms – *Poetics & Progym I*

◯ Use the test features at Quizlet for an online or printed quiz over the Verb Terms set. If you wish, combine with previous Figure sets.

◯ Continue to review each set once a week (more if needed):

- ◆ Parts of Speech – *Bards & Poets* Review
- ◆ Sentence Terms – *Bards & Poets* Review
- ◆ Noun Terms – *Poetics & Progym I*
- ◆ Figures – Set #1 – *Poetics & Progym I*
- ◆ Figures – Set #2 – *Poetics & Progym I*

Lesson 15

❧

THE SIRENS
from Homer's Odyssey

Circe's Warning

"'Next, where the Sirens dwells, you plough the seas;

Their song is death, and makes destruction please.

Unblest the man, whom music wins to stay

Nigh the cursed shore and listen to the lay.

No more that wretch shall view the joys of life

His blooming offspring, or his beauteous wife!

In verdant meads they sport; and wide around

Lie human bones that whiten all the ground:

The ground polluted floats with human gore,

And human carnage taints the dreadful shore.

Fly swift the dangerous coast: let every ear

Be stopp'd against the song! 'tis death to hear!

Firm to the mast with chains thyself be bound,

Nor trust thy virtue to the enchanting sound.

If, mad with transport, freedom thou demand,

Be every fetter strain'd, and added band to band.

Odysseus and the Sirens

"'In flowery meads the sportive Sirens play,

Touch the soft lyre, and tune the vocal lay;

Me, me alone, with fetters firmly bound,

The gods allow to hear the dangerous sound.

Hear and obey; if freedom I demand,

Be every fetter strain'd, be added band to band.'
"While yet I speak the winged galley flies,
And lo! the Siren shores like mists arise.
Sunk were at once the winds; the air above,
And waves below, at once forgot to move;
Some demon calm'd the air and smooth'd the deep,
Hush'd the loud winds, and charm'd the waves to sleep.
Now every sail we furl, each oar we ply;
Lash'd by the stroke, the frothy waters fly.
The ductile wax with busy hands I mould,
And cleft in fragments, and the fragments roll'd;
The aerial region now grew warm with day,
The wax dissolved beneath the burning ray;
Then every ear I barr'd against the strain,
And from access of frenzy lock'd the brain.
Now round the masts my mates the fetters roll'd,
And bound me limb by limb with fold on fold.
Then bending to the stroke, the active train
Plunge all at once their oars, and cleave the main.
"While to the shore the rapid vessel flies,
Our swift approach the Siren choir descries;
Celestial music warbles from their tongue,
And thus the sweet deluders tune the song:
Oh cease thy course, and listen to our lay!
Blest is the man ordain'd our voice to hear,
The song instructs the soul, and charms the ear.
Approach! thy soul shall into raptures rise!
Approach! and learn new wisdom from the wise!
We know whate'er the kings of mighty name
Achieved at Ilion in the field of fame;
Whate'er beneath the sun's bright journey lies.
Oh stay, and learn new wisdom from the wise!'

"Thus the sweet charmers warbled o'er the main;

My soul takes wing to meet the heavenly strain;

I give the sign, and struggle to be free;

Swift row my mates, and shoot along the sea;

New chains they add, and rapid urge the way,

Till, dying off, the distant sounds decay;

Then scudding swiftly from the dangerous ground,

The deafen'd ear unlock'd, the chains unbound.

— BOOK VIII, TRANSLATED BY ALEXANDER POPE

☙

Lesson 15.1

Prose & Poetry

LITERARY ELEMENTS IN THE POEM: THE SIRENS

1 **Read** Alexander Pope's poetic rendering of the same lines that Richmond Lattimore translates in Book XII, Lines 39-54 and 73-200.

  ◆ Follow along and listen carefully as the poem is read aloud, OR read it aloud yourself. Read it at least two or three times. **Delight** in the meter, the rhyme, and the images.

2 **Inquire**

  ◆ Are there any unfamiliar persons, places, or things mentioned in the poem? Discuss these with your teacher.

  ◆ Look up the meaning of any words in the work that are not familiar to you; conduct a complete Vocabulary Study for **key words.**

  ◆ Was there any part of the poem you did not understand? If so, discuss this with your teacher and classmates.

3 **Observe the Invention, Arrangement, and Style**

  ◆ **Lyrical Elements**

    ▪ What does the poet describe?

    ▪ Does the poet make you see, hear, smell, taste, or touch anything?

- Does the poet compare something in the poem to some other thing? Notice the beautiful metaphorical description of the bard's blindness contrasted with his storytelling gift.

◆ **Narrative Elements** Does this poem tell a story? If so, observe the

- **Setting** When and where does this story take place?
- **Characters** Who is (are) the main character(s) in this story?
- **Conflict** What is the main problem or crisis for the character(s)?
- **Resolution** Is the problem solved? If so, how? If not, why not?
- **Sequence** Is this story told *ab ovo*, or *in medias res*, or some other way?
- **Point of View** Identify the **person** (and **level of omniscience** if applicable).

◆ **Figures** Look for figures of speech and figures of description. (See Appendix for the list of figures taught in *Poetics & Progym*.) Why did the poet choose these particular figures?

4 Investigate the Context

Writer's Journal

◆ Review the notes in your Writer's Journal about Alexander Pope's

- **Origin** Who were the poet's parents/ancestors? Where was his homeland?
- **Historical Time Period** When did the poet live? What events happened around the time that the poet lived?
- **Influences** What education, training, books, ideas, and other people or events shaped the poet's thinking?

◆ **Identify the poem's Literary Genre**

- **Genre by literary period** In which century (time period) and country was this work written?
- **Genre by poetic/narrative category** Is this poem chiefly **lyrical** (describes an event, or a person, or a feeling, or a time and place, etc., but it does not tell a particular story) or **narrative** (tells a story)? If narrative, is it primarily **non-fiction** (a story that really happened) or **fiction** (a story told as if it really happened)?

5 Connect the Thoughts

- Does this poem remind you of other poems, or of stories with similar plots, messages, or characters?

Commonplace Book

- Does this poem remind you of any proverbs or other well-known quotations? If so, enter these in your Commonplace Book.

6 **Profit and Delight**

- ◆ **Delight** What are the sources of delight in this poem?

- ◆ **Wisdom** What wisdom does this poem furnish?

- ◆ **Read** the poem to your teacher with expression and proper pauses.

- ◆ **Read** other works by this poet.

- ◆ **Memorize** this poem and recite it before an audience.

Writer's Journal

SCANSION

Copy a few lines from the poem, leaving room to scan them. Scan the lines, then note the meter and rhyme scheme in your Writer's Journal.

THE ODYSSEY

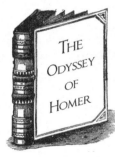

THE ODYSSEY OF HOMER

 Read

- ◆ *The Odyssey of Homer*, Book Thirteen

 As you read, continue to mark the text and make notes:

- ◆ Literary concepts and terms you observe in the narrative. Do any of your earlier thoughts need revision?

- ◆ Instances of **epic simile**.

- ◆ **Epithets** to add to your running list.

- ◆ Passages reflecting on the value of **hearth and home**.

Writer's Journal

Discuss this week's reading with your teacher, along with all your notes and observations. Narrate the main action of the book, and discuss any parts you did not understand. How was this reading **delightful**? What **wisdom** does this reading furnish?

Lesson 15.2

Language Logic

ADJECTIVES & COMPARISON

 Study/review these lessons in *Sentence Sense*.

I. Etymology – The Adjective

- ◆ 4.3B Articles
- ◆ 4.4A Comparison of Adjectives
- ◆ 4.4B Formation of Comparatives and Superlatives

GRAMMAR TERMS & DEFINITIONS: MODIFIER TERMS

 Grammar Terms to Master: In the Quizlet classroom, review or print flashcards from Modifier Terms – *Poetics & Progym I.*

- ◆ Articles
- ◆ Degrees of Comparison

DIAGRAMMING & PARSING

 In your Writer's Journal, copy these sentences. Mark the prepositional phrases, subjects, and verbs. Bracket the clauses. Classify the sentence as simple, compound, complex, or compound-complex. Then diagram each one. Refer to *Sentence Sense* as needed.

Writer's Journal

1. In verdant meads they sport; and wide around

   Lie human bones that whiten all the ground:

   The ground polluted floats with human gore,

   And human carnage taints the dreadful shore.

2. We are apt to shut our eyes against a painful truth, and listen to the song of that siren till she transforms us into beasts.

⟨❀⟩ Orally parse these words with your teacher, using the charts in *Sentence Sense* to guide you. Add Modifier Property – Comparison to your adverb parsing.

(1) sport, to shut, ground, polluted, with human gore, dreadful; (2) apt, a, transforms, us

Lesson 15.3

Eloquent Expression

FIGURE OF SPEECH – ALLUSION

Allusion is a comparison made using an indirect or figurative reference to a historical or literary source, like *cry wolf* for *tell a lie* (Aesop's Fables) or *he met his Waterloo* (reference to Napoleon's downfall). If the reference is to a biblical source, it is called a **biblical allusion**: *a good Samaritan* (Luke 10), *forbidden fruit* (Genesis 3), *turn the other cheek* (Matthew 5). An **idiom** is an allusion that has become common in everyday life: *piece of cake* for *easy*.

If adversity hath killed his thousands, prosperity hath killed his ten thousands. — Robert Burton (17th century British Scholar and author); *what other figure does this use?*

I shall be as 'umble as Uriah Heep. — L. M. Montgomery, *Anne of the Island*

How does one make a great decision? I swear that when I turned round to speak I meant to refuse. But my answer was Yes, and I had crossed the Rubicon. My voice sounded cracked and far away. — John Buchan, *Greenmantle*

Poets and preachers alike allude to the Sirens when speaking of temptation. Even Jerome, the 4th century translator of the Latin Vulgate, translated the Hebrew word for *jackals* as *sirens* (Isaiah 13:22)[1]. Read and discuss these **literary allusions** to the Sirens:

You must avoid sloth, that wicked siren. — Horace, 1st century B.C. Roman poet

We are apt to shut our eyes against a painful truth, and listen to the song of that siren till she transforms us into beasts. — Patrick Henry, St. John's Church, March 23, 1775 (Give Me Liberty or Give Me Death speech)

---

1 Murgatroyd, Paul, *Mythical Monsters in Classical Literature*, 189.

"The television, that insidious beast, . . . that Siren which called and sang and promised so much and gave, after all, so little …" — Ray Bradbury, 20th century American novelist

Discuss the examples of allusion with your teacher. Can you identify any additional figures? Scan selections from earlier lessons in this book to see if they contain this figure.

Enter the following item in the Figures division.

Prose & Poetry Handbook

◆ Allusion, P&P 83. Add <u>Allusion</u>, with its definition and one literary example. Below that, indent and add <u>biblical allusion</u> and <u>idiom</u>, with definitions and one example for each.

LITERARY IMITATION

Writer's Journal

Work with one of the the sentences that you diagrammed in Language Logic. Copy the **diagram skeleton**; construct a new sentence, and write the new sentence below the diagram. Base your new sentence on Book Thirteen of *The Odyssey*.

Lesson 15.4

Classical Composition

PROGYMNASMA NARRATIVE: PLOT OBSERVATION – THEON'S SIX AND SUMMARY

Observe and summarize Homer's *Odyssey*, Book Thirteen. Refer to the instructions and example in the Appendix under "Narrative Plot Observation" and "Example Narrative Plot Observation."

Complete the steps for Plot Observation – Theon's Six on the original narrative and in your Writer's Jourr

Writer's Journal

Write a one paragraph summary of this book, following the steps for Plot Observation – Summary. Work either in your Writer's Journal or on the computer. Add this summary to your running file of *Odyssey* summaries, and save the file.

QUOTE FOR ELABORATION: ERASMUS ON TEMPTATION

In this and upcoming lessons, you will plan, write, and edit an elaboration of your own, based on this anecdote:

> Desiderius Erasmus in his *Enchiridion Militis Christiani* said, "For we must expect one temptation after another and must never put down our arms, never desert our post, never relax our guard, while we are in this garrison of a body."

Think carefully about what Erasmus is saying here. The Latin title of Erasmus's book *Enchiridion Militis Christiani* is translated *Handbook of a Christian Knight*, which will help you understand why he employs these particular metaphors.

Writer's Journal

⚜ Copy the quote into your Writer's Journal.

⚜ Analyze and inflect just the words inside the direct quote from the anecdote, following these steps. Refer to Lesson 7 for complete instructions. and to diagramming helps in *Sentence Sense* as needed. Is this a proverb or an anecdote?

Analysis	**Inflection**
◆ Diagram	◆ Number
◆ Definitions	◆ Declension
◆ Copia of Words*	◆ Copia of Construction

*In at least one of your Copia of Words paraphrases, state the plain meaning without using metaphorical language.

⚜ Research Desiderius Erasmus using the **Five W's and an H**. Take notes in your Writer's Journal. Here are a few questions to get you started:

- **Who** was Erasmus?
- **What** is Erasmus best know for? **What** is *Enchiridion Militis Christiani*?
- **Where** did Erasmus live?
- **When** did Erasmus live?
- **Why** is Erasmus credible in this matter? **Why** is his advice worth listening to?
- **How** did Erasmus acquire his wisdom? **How** did (and does) he benefit or influence others?

ANECDOTE ELABORATION: PLAN

In your Writer's Journal, make planning notes for your elaboration based on Erasmus's quote. Work on this assignment over several days, and be sure to include lots of discussion with your teacher and your family.

Construct an outline in your Writer's Journal, with notes for each of the topics (headers) of your Elaboration. Write each topic listed below in order, leaving about a half page to jot down notes for each. Write only on the right hand pages of your Journal, so that you have room if you need to make extra notes or corrections. Once you have listed all of the topics, go back and make notes of what you plan to include in your essay for each.

Writer's
Journal

1. **Encomion** is a brief praise of the person represented as speaking or acting (Lesson 10).

    ◆ You have already researched **who, what, where, when, why**, and **how** for the person who is being praised for his/her wise or witty saying and/or action. Choose which things you will highlight from this research.
    ◆ State the essence or principle of the wisdom or wit.

2. **Paraphrase** is a restatement of the anecdote or proverb in your own words.

    ◆ Restate based on your analysis & inflection of the wise saying.

3. **Cause** is a discussion of the rationale behind the words and/or action in the anecdote or proverb. Consider:

    ◆ logical reasons
    ◆ life experience
    ◆ motivation
    ◆ circumstances.

4. **Contrast** is a consideration of contrasting words or action. In conrast to your Cause content, consider:

    ◆ logical reasons
    ◆ life experience
    ◆ motivation
    ◆ circumstances

5. **Comparison** is a consideration of an analogous situation. Possible analogies:

    ◆ a concrete comparison using simile or metaphor
    ◆ a similar situation from another sphere

6. **Example** is a discussion of relevant illustration(s) from history or literature.

   ◆ Choose an historical or literary characters that will be somewhat familiar to your audience.

   ◆ Touch on the main and relevant points; do not include too many details.

   ◆ Avoid dialogue and description.

7. **Authority** is a credible testimony supporting the wisdom or wit behind the anecdote or proverb.

   ◆ Determine the essential wisdom or principle to aid your search for testimony.

   ◆ Authority must be credible and recognizable to your audience.

   ◆ Use who, what, where, when, why, for the person cited.

   ◆ How does the Authority relate to the anecdote or proverb?

8. **Exhortation** is a brief epilogue encouraging the reader to admire the wit and/or emulate the wisdom.

   ◆ Restate the wisdom or wit in a few words.

   ◆ Exhort your reader to heed the wisdom or appreciate the wit.

Discuss your research with your teacher and classmates, your parents, siblings, or any other interested and helpful parties. Make note of any additional ideas or questions to pursue in your Writer's Journal.

POETRY ANALYSIS ESSAY: THE BUILDERS

Use your notes from Lesson 14 to write a brief poetry analysis essay (about 300 words) of "The Builders."

A. In your essay, make sure that you identify each of the literary and poetic elements listed above, using bold type to denote the literary terms you use. Include the following in your essay:

   ◆ at least one instance of parallelism and one of antithesis (underline and note the figure in parentheses as in the example essay)

   ◆ use of historical present tense when referring to content of the work

   ◆ a header, properly formatted: the title, your name, and the date

B. Revise your poetry analysis essay using the checklist below. Work through the checklist once on your own, and then a second time with your writing mentor, making notes on the print copy of your narrative. Transfer all additions and corrections from your print copy to the computer file. Save and print the document.

Editor's Pen – The Big Picture

✓ Invention and Arrangement: *all required literary and poetic elements included in bold type*

✓ Length: *around 300 words; similar to example*

✓ Title & Header: *properly formatted*

Editor's Pen – Zoom 5x: Paragraphs

Refer to Copia In Your Writing (Prose & Poetry Handbook or Appendix) as needed

✓ Flow of Ideas: *logical, not repetitive*

✓ Tone: *objective, not overly emotional or superlative (the best! the most!, etc.)*

✓ Length: *neither too wordy nor too short*

✓ Sentence class by use: *effective use*

✓ Sentence openers: *varied*

✓ Sentence length and class by form: *varied, avoid overuse of exclamatory sentences*

✓ Verb Tense: *historical present when referring to content of the work*

✓ Pronouns clear: *easily identified antecedents*

✓ Point of View: *3rd person*

Editor's Pen – Zoom 10x: Sentences

Refer to Copia In Your Writing (Prose & Poetry Handbook or Appendix) as needed

✓ Complete thought expressed

✓ Subject and predicate agree in number

✓ Correct capitalization and punctuation

  ◆ No comma splices!

✓ Items in a series constructed in parallel form

Editor's Pen – Fine Focus: Words

✓ Word choices varied; word meanings clear; consider denotation AND connotation

◆ Verbs: *strong, specific, fitting, mostly active (vs. passive); appropriate adverbs if needed*

◆ Nouns: *clear, descriptive; appropriate adjectives if needed*

◆ Dialogue: *n/a except for Authority*

◆ Level of Formality: *no contractions, no informal language, no slang or overused words (lots of, cool, awesome), acronyms adequately explained*

✓ Correct spelling

✓ Final read-through

Lesson 15.5

Reflection & Review

COMMONPLACE BOOK

 Enter in your Commonplace Book:

Commonplace
Book

◆ a favorite passage or two from your reading in Homer's *Odyssey*

◆ an example or two of epithet and/or epic simile

◆ a few lines of poetry from your anthology (identify meter)

◆ research and note quotes on character and habit from credible authorities

◆ examples from your reading of allusion, biblical allusion, or idiom

◆ examples from your reading of other figures you have learned (see Figures and Literary Devices list in *Poetics & Progym I* Appendix)

MEMORY WORK

⚜ Review to mastery:

- ◆ Modifier Terms – *Poetics & Progym I*

⚜ Use the test features at Quizlet for an online or printed quiz over the Verb Terms set. If you wish, combine with previous Figure sets.

⚜ Continue to review each set once a week (more if needed):

- ◆ Parts of Speech – *Bards & Poets* Review
- ◆ Sentence Terms – *Bards & Poets* Review
- ◆ Noun Terms – *Poetics & Progym I*
- ◆ Verb Terms – *Poetics & Progym I*
- ◆ Figures – Set #1 – *Poetics & Progym I*
- ◆ Figures – Set #2 – *Poetics & Progym I*

༖

JASON AND THE SIRENS

from THE HEROES: OR GREEK FAIRY TALES FOR MY CHILDREN, by Charles Kingsley

Then a fair wind rose, and they sailed eastward by Tartessus on the Iberian shore, till they came to the Pillars of Hercules, and the Mediterranean Sea. And thence they sailed on through the deeps of Sardinia, and past the Ausonian islands, and the capes of the Tyrrhenian shore, till they came to a flowery island, upon a still bright summer's eve. And as they neared it, slowly and wearily, they heard sweet songs upon the shore. But when Medeia heard it, she started, and cried, 'Beware, all heroes, for these are the rocks of the Sirens. You must pass close by them, for there is no other channel; but those who listen to that song are lost.'

Then Orpheus spoke, the king of all minstrels, 'Let them match their song against mine. I have charmed stones, and trees, and dragons, how much more the hearts of men!' So he caught up his lyre, and stood upon the poop, and began his magic song.

And now they could see the Sirens on Anthemousa, the flowery isle; three fair maidens sitting on the beach, beneath a red rock in the setting sun, among beds of crimson poppies and golden asphodel. Slowly they sung and sleepily, with silver voices, mild and clear, which stole over the golden waters, and into the hearts of all the heroes, in spite of Orpheus's song.

And all things stayed around and listened; the gulls sat in white lines along the rocks; on the beach great seals lay basking, and kept time with lazy heads; while silver shoals of fish came up to hearken, and whispered as they broke the shining calm. The Wind overhead hushed his whistling, as he shepherded his clouds toward the west; and the clouds stood in mid blue, and listened dreaming, like a flock of golden sheep.

And as the heroes listened, the oars fell from their hands, and their heads drooped on their breasts, and they closed their heavy eyes; and they dreamed of bright still gardens, and of slumbers under murmuring pines, till all their toil seemed foolishness, and they thought of their renown no more.

Then one lifted his head suddenly, and cried, 'What use in wandering for ever? Let us stay here and rest awhile.' And another, 'Let us row to the shore, and hear the words they sing.' And another, 'I care not for the words, but for the music. They shall sing me to sleep, that I may rest.'

And Butes, the son of Pandion, the fairest of all mortal men, leapt out and swam toward the shore, crying, 'I come, I come, fair maidens, to live and die here, listening to your song.'

When Medeia clapped her hands together, and cried, 'Sing louder, Orpheus, sing a bolder strain; wake up these hapless sluggards, or none of them will see the land of Hellas more.'

Then Orpheus lifted his harp, and crashed his cunning hand across the strings; and his music and his voice rose like a trumpet through the still evening air; into the air it rushed like thunder, till the rocks rang and the sea; and into their souls it rushed like wine, till all hearts beat fast within their breasts.

And he sung the song of Perseus, how the Gods led him over land and sea, and how he slew the loathly Gorgon, and won himself a peerless bride; and how he sits now with the Gods upon Olympus, a shining star in the sky, immortal with his immortal bride, and honoured by all men below.

So Orpheus sang, and the Sirens, answering each other across the golden sea, till Orpheus's voice drowned the Sirens', and the heroes caught their oars again.

And they cried, 'We will be men like Perseus, and we will dare and suffer to the last. Sing us his song again, brave Orpheus, that we may forget the Sirens and their spell.'

And as Orpheus sang, they dashed their oars into the sea, and kept time to his music, as they fled fast away; and the Sirens' voices died behind them, in the hissing of the foam along their wake.

But Butes swam to the shore, and knelt down before the Sirens, and cried, 'Sing on! sing on!' But he could say no more, for a charmed sleep came over him, and a pleasant humming in his ears; and he sank all along upon the pebbles, and forgot all heaven and earth, and never looked at that sad beach around him, all strewn with the bones of men.

Then slowly rose up those three fair sisters, with a cruel smile upon their lips; and slowly they crept down towards him, like leopards who creep upon their prey; and their hands were like the talons of eagles as they stept across the bones of their victims to enjoy their cruel feast.

But fairest Aphrodite saw him from the highest Idalian peak, and she pitied his youth and his beauty, and leapt up from her golden throne; and like a falling star she cleft the sky, and left a trail of glittering light, till she stooped to the Isle of the Sirens, and snatched their prey from their claws. And she lifted Butes as he lay sleeping, and wrapt him in golden mist; and she bore him to the peak of Lilybæum, and he slept there many a pleasant year.

But when the Sirens saw that they were conquered, they shrieked for envy and rage, and leapt from the beach into the sea, and were changed into rocks until this day.

$$\mathcal{CR}$$

Lesson 16.1

Prose & Poetry

RHETORICAL SITUATION

The rhetorical situation of any written or spoken work is the context in which it is created. Rhetorical situation has three parts: **exigency**, **audience**, and **constraints**.[1] Exigency is the central issue, problem, or situation that the author seeks to address, solve, or somehow change. It is the

1 Bitzer, Lloyd. "The Rhetorical Situation."

cause for the speech or composition. The audience is made up of the people to whom the author is addressing his or her work—those whom he or she wishes to inform or persuade in some way. The constraints of the oratory or composition are the requirements for invention, arrangement, and elocution based on the audience and the occasion. In terms of the audience, the author must consider things like age, educational level, religious beliefs, and cultural factors. The occasion is the format for the communication—speech, email, academic essay, letter to the editor, blog post, social media post, etc. Additional constraints include the author's own character, ways of thinking, and style. All of this together must be submitted to the ancient Greek idea of **kairos**: Is this the opportune moment? Is it fitting in this context?

Enter the first item below in the Rhetoric Section, and the second item in the Literature section.

Prose & Poetry Handbook

- ◆ Rhetoric, P&P 2: Title CANON OF INVENTION, subtitle RHETORICAL SITUATION. Define rhetorical situation and list the three components of rhetorical situation (exigency, audience, constraints), along with a description of each.
- ◆ Literature, P&P 30: Add Rhetorical Situation as the third element under LITERARY CONTEXT, and list the three compoenents of rhetorical situation (Audience, Constraints, and Exigency). Include a note here referring back to the complete notes on rhetorical situation on page 2 of the P&P Handbook.

LITERARY ELEMENTS IN THE NARRATIVE: JASON AND THE SIRENS

Here we have another famous Greek tale about the Sirens, and a man who took a different approach to avoid being tempted beyond the point of no return.

1 **Read**
- ◆ Listen carefully as your teacher reads the selection aloud. **Delight** in the story.

2 **Inquire**
- ◆ Does the **title** give any hint as to the content or message of the story? If this story was published by the author in a larger book or an anthology, does that title give any hint?
- ◆ Look up the meaning of any words in the work that are not familiar to you; conduct a complete Vocabulary Study for **key words.**
- ◆ Are there any unfamiliar persons, places, or things mentioned in the narrative? Discuss these with your teacher.

◆ Was there any part of the narrative you did not understand? If so, discuss this with your teacher and classmates.

3 Observe the Invention, Arrangement, and Style

- ◆ **Setting** When and where does this story take place?
- ◆ **Characters** Who is (are) the main character(s) in this story? Who/what is the **antagonist**? Who/what is/are the **protagonist**(s)?
- ◆ **Conflict** What is the main problem or crisis for the character(s)?
- ◆ **Resolution** Is the problem solved? If so, how? If not, why not?
- ◆ **Sequence** Is this story told *ab ovo*, or *in medias res*, or some other way?
- ◆ **Point of View** Identify the **person** and **level of omniscience**.
- ◆ **Figures** Look for figures of speech and figures of description. (See Appendix for the list of figures taught in *Poetics & Progym*.) Why did the author choose these particular figures?

4 Investigate the Context

Writer's Journal

- ◆ Research a bit about Jason, hero of Greek mythology. If you are not familiar with this delightful myth, Bulfinch's *Age of Fable* has a concise summary of his life in Chapter XVII. Make notes in your Writer's Journal about his

  - **Origin** – Who were Jason's parents/ancestors? Where was his homeland?
  - **Historical Time Period** – When did Jason live? What events happened around the time that the he lived?
  - **Influences** – What education and training shaped Jason's life and actions?

- ◆ Briefly research the same points about Charles Kingsley.
- ◆ **Rhetorical Situation**

  - **Exigency** – What is the issue, problem, or situation to be addressed?
  - **Audience** – Who is the author addressing in order to change or persuade?
  - **Constraint** What are the requirements based on the audience and the occasion?

- ◆ Identify the story's **Literary Genre**

  - **Genre by literary period** – What is the historical period/country of origin for this story (both the original myth and the retelling by Charles Kingsley)?
  - **Genre by narrative category** – Is this narrative primarily **non-fiction** (a story that really happened) or **fiction** (a story told as if it really happened)?

5   Connect the Thoughts

- Does this story remind you of other stories with similar plots, messages, or characters?
- Does this story remind you of any proverbs or other well-known quotations? If so, enter these in your Commonplace Book.

Commonplace Book

6   Profit and Delight

- **Delight** What are the sources of delight in this story?
- **Wisdom** What wisdom does this story furnish?
- **Read** a portion of the narrative aloud to your teacher with expression and with proper pauses.

THE ODYSSEY

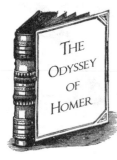

THE ODYSSEY OF HOMER

○ Read

- *The Odyssey of Homer,* Book Fourteen

○ As you read, continue to mark the text and make notes:

- Literary concepts and terms you observe in the narrative. Do any of your earlier thoughts need revision?
- Instances of **epic simile**.
- **Epithets** to add to your running list.
- Passages reflecting on the value of **hearth and home**.

Writer's Journal

○ Discuss this week's reading with your teacher, along with all your notes and observations. Narrate the main action of the book, and discuss any parts you did not understand. How was this reading **delightful**? What **wisdom** does this reading furnish?

Lesson 16.2

Language Logic

PRONOUN CLASSES

 Study/review these lessons in *Sentence Sense.*

I. Etymology – Pronouns

- ◆ 2.5A, 2.5B, and 2.5C Personal Pronouns
- ◆ 2.6 Possessive Pronouns
- ◆ 2.8A, 2.8B, and 2.8C Relative Pronouns *Pay close attention to the declension of relative pronouns; make sure you understand when to use the nominative case and when to use the objective!*
- ◆ 2.7 Interrogative Pronouns

GRAMMAR TERMS & DEFINITIONS: PRONOUN TERMS

 Grammar Terms to Master: In the Quizlet classroom, review or print flashcards from Pronoun Terms – *Poetics & Progym I.* You have already memorized the four classes of pronouns, now you should memorize the actual pronouns in each class.

- ◆ Personal Pronouns
- ◆ Possessive Pronouns
- ◆ Relative Pronouns
- ◆ Interrogative Pronouns

DIAGRAMMING & PARSING

 In your Writer's Journal, copy these sentences. Mark the prepositional phrases, subjects, and verbs. Bracket the clauses. Classify the sentence as simple, compound, complex, or compound-complex. Then diagram each one. Refer to *Sentence Sense* as needed.

1. Sing louder, Orpheus, sing a bolder strain; wake up these hapless sluggards, or none of them will see the land of Hellas more.

2. So Orpheus sang, and the Sirens, answering each other across the golden sea, till Orpheus's voice drowned the Sirens', and the heroes caught their oars again.

3. But when the Sirens saw that they were conquered, they shrieked for envy and rage, and leapt from the beach into the sea, and were changed into rocks until this day.

Orally parse these words with your teacher, using the charts in *Sentence Sense* to guide you. Add Property – Case to your pronoun parsing.

(1) Orpheus, bolder, none, will see (2) Sirens, answering, Orpheus, again; (3) when, they, for envy and rage, beach

Lesson 16.3

Eloquent Expression

FIGURE OF SPEECH – POLYSYNDETON

Poly means "many" in Greek, so think of **polysyndeton** as *many* conjunctions. It is a repetition of a conjunction between words, phrases, or clauses. Other conjunctions besides *and* can be used in this way, such as *but, nor, or*, etc. Polysyndeton emphasizes each item in the list, drawing the idea out, even to the point of frustration. It causes us to slow down and consider the ideas the writer is proposing. Sometimes it does just the opposite, creating a quick and frenetic rhythm. Sometimes it simply emphasizes each item in the list.

He hath shewed thee, O man, what is good; and what doth the LORD require of thee, but to do justly, and to love mercy, and to walk humbly with thy God? — Micah 6:8

Neither snow, nor rain, nor heat nor dark of night keeps them from completing their appointed course as swiftly as possible.[2] — Herodotus, *Histories*, VIII.98

Discuss the examples of polysyndeton with your teacher. Can you identify any additional figures? Scan selections from earlier lessons in this book to see if they contain this figure.

---

2 Herodotus' description of the ancient Persian courier system was first paraphrased and inscribed on a New York City post office building in 1924; it has become the unofficial creed of the U.S. Postal Service: "Neither snow nor rain nor heat nor gloom of night stays these couriers from the swift completion of their appointed rounds." Classical allusions abound!

Prose & Poetry
Handbook

Enter the following item in the Figures division of your Prose & Poetry Handbook.

  ◆ Polysyndeton, P&P 73: After the last entry, write Polysyndeton, and add the definition and an example.

LITERARY IMITATION

Writer's Journal

Work with one of the sentences that you diagrammed ~~Writer's~~ Logic. Copy the **diagram skeleton**, construct a new sentence, and wri ~~Journal~~ ow the diagram. Base your new sentence on Book Fourteen of *The Odyssey*.

Lesson 16.4

Classical Composition

PROGYMNASMA NARRATIVE: PLOT OBSERVATION – THEON'S SIX AND SUMMARY

Observe and summarize Homer's *Odyssey*, Book Sixteen. Refer to the instructions and example in the Appendix under "Narrative Plot Observation" and "Example Narrative Plot Observation."

Writer's Journal

Complete the steps for Plot Observation – Theon's Six on the original narrative and in your Writer's Journal.

Write a one paragraph summary of this book, following the steps for Plot Observation – Summary. Work either in your Writer's Journal or on the computer. Add this summary to your running file of *Odyssey* summaries, and save the file.

ANECDOTE ELABORATION: WRITE

Read this example elaboration:

Consider the Consequences and Act Accordingly

Look before you leap.—Aesop

Aesop hardly needs introduction, so famous is his name. Though he was a slave, his great wisdom and keen insights into human behavior have endured through the ages in his simple, unforgettable fables. The well-known morals (proverbs) that conclude a few of his fables echo in our everyday speech, encouraging people everywhere to tell the truth, avoid temptation, resist pride, and much more. Nowhere is Aesop's acumen more aptly shown than in his words about considering the consequences of our actions, "Look before you leap."

A prudent person will carefully evaluate a course of action before he proceeds. The great wisdom of these words cannot be overstated, and you shall see why in what follows.

Anyone who wants to avoid unexpected pitfalls must consider possible adverse consequences and make provision to avoid them. He must remain alert, not only when making important decisions about great matters, but even more in those matters that seem small or mundane, so that he will not be overtaken by unanticipated outcomes.

Conversely, if someone, due to lack of foresight, were to plunge into a situation without due consideration, he may find himself without recourse in the face of unexpected outcomes. He will lose the safeguard of preparedness. Aesop clearly had these things in mind when he called for the necessity of thinking ahead.

What person in his right mind would begin to build a house without first making a careful blueprint? He must budget the necessary funds and forsee possible hindrances; he cannot do this without a plan. In the same way, a man who carefully considers before committing to a course of action will avoid facing unintended consequences without resources or a means of escape..

The fable that gave rise to this proverb provides the perfect illustration. A goat came upon a well into which a fox had fallen. The goat inquired of the fox whether the water was good. Seeing a way of escape, the crafty fox encouraged the thirsty goat to come and see for himself. The foolish goat, thinking only of his thirst, impulsively jumped into the well. The fox promptly vaulted onto the goat's back and immediately out of the well, leaving the goat stranded with no egress.

Victor Hugo, the nineteenth century French novelist, author of the literary masterpiece Les Miserables, was in complete accord with Aesop's warning when he said that caution is the eldest child of wisdom.

Consider these points, admire Aesop for his outstandingly wise saying on the importance of evaluating any course of action with great care, and act accordingly.

Write your own Anecdote elaboration. For this essay, do not paraphrase an ancient elaboration so closely. Instead, use your outline and notes from your Writer's Journal to guide you as the elaboration in your own words for the anecdote:

Desiderius Erasmus in his *Enchiridion Militis Christiani* said, "For we must expect one temptation after another and must never put down our arms, never desert our post, never relax our guard, while we are in this garrison of a body."

- ◆ Length should be eight paragraphs (one for each of the topics).
- ◆ Each paragraph should be three to five sentences in length, although the Paraphrase, Authority, and Exhortation paragraphs may be shorter.
- ◆ State the anecdote as a "prequel" to your Encomion paragraph.

A. Compose your first draft. It is simplest to work on the computer, but if words flow more easily when you write by hand, use your Writer's Journal. You will want to type it up when you are done to make editing easier. Save your file, print, and save.

B. Develop a title for your elaboration. Make up your own original title. If possible, use parallelism, antithesis, and/or alliteration.

Lesson 16.5

Reflection & Review

COMMONPLACE BOOK

 Enter in your Commonplace Book:

- ◆ a favorite passage or two from your reading in Homer's *Odyssey*
- ◆ an example or two of epithet and/or epic simile
- ◆ a few lines of poetry from your anthology (identify meter)
- ◆ research and note quotes on character and habit from credible authorities
- ◆ examples from your reading of polysyndeton
- ◆ examples from your reading of other figures you have learned (see Figures and Literary Devices list in *Poetics & Progym I* Appendix)

BOOK OF CENTURIES

🏛 Record in your Book of Centuries:

◆ Charles Kingsley

MEMORY WORK

🏛 Review to mastery:

◆ Modifier Terms – *Poetics & Progym I*
◆ Pronoun Terms – *Poetics & Progym I*

🏛 Continue to review each set once a week (more if needed):

◆ Parts of Speech – *Bards & Poets* Review
◆ Sentence Terms – *Bards & Poets* Review
◆ Noun Terms – *Poetics & Progym I*
◆ Verb Terms – *Poetics & Progym I*
◆ Figures – Set #1 – *Poetics & Progym I*
◆ Figures – Set #2 – *Poetics & Progym I*

Lesson 17

❧

In Palace Beautiful
from Pilgrim's Progress **by John Bunyan**

PRUD(ENCE). Do you not find sometimes, as if those things were vanquished, which at other times are your perplexity?

CHR(ISTIAN). Yes, but that is seldom; but they are to me golden hours in which such things happen to me.

PRUD. Can you remember by what means you find your annoyances, at times, as if they were vanquished?

CHR. Yes, when I think what I saw at the cross, that will do it; and when I look upon my broidered coat, that will do it; also when I look into the roll that I carry in my bosom, that will do it; and when my thoughts wax warm about whither I am going, that will do it.

PRUD. And what is it that makes you so desirous to go to Mount Zion?

CHR. Why, there I hope to see him alive that did hang dead on the cross; and there I hope to be rid of all those things that to this day are in me an annoyance to me; there, they say, there is no death; and there I shall dwell with such company as I like best. [Isa. 25:8; Rev. 21:4] For, to tell you truth, I love him, because I was by him eased of my burden; and I am weary of my inward sickness. I would fain be where I shall die no more, and with the company that shall continually cry, "Holy, Holy, Holy!"

❧

<hr />

Lesson 17.1

Prose & Poetry

LITERARY ELEMENTS IN THE NARRATIVE: IN PALACE BEAUTIFUL

Pilgrim's Progress, by John Bunyan, was one of two most-read books in colonial America, the other being the Bible. If you are not familiar with this classic allegory of the Christian life, read "Bunyan – Pilgrim's Progress" in *English Literature for Boys and Girls*, by Henrietta Marshall. You can access it online at mainlesson.com. Then, put *Pilgrim's Progress* on your to-read list. It is a marvelous family read-aloud!

The context for our selection: Christian has just ascended the Hill Difficulty and passed the chained lions to enter the Palace Beautiful, where he is greeted and given refreshment by Piety, Prudence, and Charity. As he is waiting for supper, he talks with them about his journey thus far. Prudence here is questioning him on the temptations ("annoyances" and "vexations") that have assailed him on his way.

1 **Read**.
   - ◆ Listen carefully as your teacher reads the selection aloud. **Delight** in the story.

2 **Inquire**
   - ◆ Does the **title** give any hint as to the content or message of the story? If this story was published by the author in a larger book or an anthology, does that title give any hint?
   - ◆ Look up the meaning of any words in the work that are not familiar to you; conduct a complete Vocabulary Study for **key words.**
   - ◆ Are there any unfamiliar persons, places, or things mentioned in the narrative? Discuss these with your teacher.
   - ◆ Was there any part of the narrative you did not understand? If so, discuss this with your teacher and classmates.

3 **Observe the Invention, Arrangement, and Style**
   - ◆ **Setting** When and where does this story take place?
   - ◆ **Characters** Who is (are) the main character(s) in this story? Who/what is the **antagonist**? Who/what is/are the **protagonist**(s)?
   - ◆ **Conflict** What is the main problem or crisis for the character(s)? *For this question and the following three, think about the story of* Pilgrim's Progress *as a whole, not just this vignette.*

♦ **Resolution** Is the problem solved? If so, how? If not, why not?

♦ **Sequence** Is this story told *ab ovo*, or *in medias res*, or some other way?

♦ **Point of View** Identify the **person** and **level of omniscience**.

♦ **Figures** Look for figures of speech and figures of description. (See Appendix for the list of figures taught in *Poetics & Progym*.) Why did the author choose these particular figures?

4 Investigate the Context

♦ Research a bit about the author. Make notes in your Writer's Journal about John Bunyan's

  ▪ **Origin** – Who were the author's parents/ancestors? Where was his homeland?

  ▪ **Historical Time Period** – When did the author live? What events happened around the time that the poet lived?

  ▪ **Influences** What education, training, books, ideas, and other people or events shaped the author's thinking?

♦ **Rhetorical Situation**

  ▪ **Exigency** – What is the issue, problem, or situation to be addressed?

  ▪ **Audience** – Who is the author addressing in order to change or persuade?

  ▪ **Constraint** What are the requirements based on the audience and the occasion?

♦ Identify the story's **Literary Genre**

  ▪ **Genre by literary period** – What is the historical period/country of origin for this story?

  ▪ **Genre by narrative category** – Is this narrative primarily **non-fiction** (a story that really happened) or **fiction** (a story told as if it really happened)?

5 Connect the Thoughts

♦ Does this story remind you of other stories with similar plots, messages, or characters?

♦ Does this story remind you of any proverbs or other well-known quotations? If so, enter these in your Commonplace Book.

6 Profit and Delight

♦ **Delight** What are the sources of delight in this story?

♦ **Wisdom** What wisdom does this story furnish?

♦ **Read** a portion of the narrative aloud to your teacher with expression and with proper pauses.

THE ODYSSEY

◉ Read

◆ *The Odyssey of Homer,* Book Fifteen

◉ As you read, continue to mark the text and make notes:

◆ Literary concepts and terms you observe in the narrative. Do any of your earlier thoughts need revision?
◆ Instances of **epic simile**.
◆ **Epithets** to add to your running list.
◆ Passages reflecting on the value of **hearth and home**.

Writer's Journal

◉ Discuss this week's reading with your teacher, along with all your notes and observations. Narrate the main action of the book, and discuss any parts you did not understand. How was this reading **delightful**? What **wisdom** does this reading furnish?

Lesson 17.2

Language Logic

ADVERBS & COMPARISON

 Study/review these lessons in *Sentence Sense*.

I. Etymology – Adverb

◆ 5.3 Adverb Property – Comparison

DIAGRAMMING & PARSING

◉ In your Writer's Journal, copy these sentences. Mark the prepositional phrases, subjects, and verbs. Bracket the clauses. Classify each sentence as simple, compound, complex, or compound-complex. Then diagram each one. Refer to *Sentence Sense* as needed.

Writer's
Journal

1. When I think what I saw at the cross, that will do it; and when
   I look upon my broidered coat, that will do it; also when I
   look into the roll that I carry in my bosom, that will do it; and
   when my thoughts wax warm about whither I am going, that
   will do it.

2. He is no fool who gives what he cannot keep to gain that which he cannot lose.

Nota Bene: #1 is a very long sentence! If it were written today, it would probably be broken up into several sentences. Work through each clause systematically, and then fit them together with the coordinating and subordinating conjunctions. It is very much like putting together a puzzle!

Orally parse these words with your teacher, using the charts in *Sentence Sense* to guide you. Add Modifier Property – Comparison to your adverb parsing.

(1) When, broidered, also, warm; (2) He, who, can(not) keep, to gain, which

---

Lesson 17.3

Eloquent Expression

FIGURE OF SPEECH – ASYNDETON

When a writer purposely omits the conjunction in a compound list of elements, it is called **asyndeton** (ā sin' de ton). The prefix *a* means *no*, so you can remember asyndeton as *no conjunctions*. With asyndeton, the commas between the elements must be left in place. Perhaps the most famous example of asyndeton is Julius Caesar's "I came, I saw, I conquered." ("*Veni, vidi, vici.*" in Latin.) Notice the parallelism as well. The effect of asyndeton is to move the reader quickly from one idea to the next. The movement feels rhythmic, staccato, blunt, practical, matter-or-fact.

> We here highly resolve that these dead shall not have died in vain -- that this nation,
> under God, shall have a new birth of freedom -- and that government of the people,
> by the people, for the people, shall not perish from the earth — Abraham Lincoln,
> *Gettysburg Address*

I held ye sage men, bold men, ready-witted men; yet ye throw down wealth, honour, pleasure, all that our noble game promised you, at the moment it might be won by one bold cast! — Sir Walter Scott, *Ivanhoe*

Here is an example of effective use of polysyndeton and asyndeton together.

For as to naval power, and the number of forces, and revenues, and a plenty of martial preparations, and in a word, as to other things that may be esteemed the strength of a state, these are all both more and greater than in former times; but all these things are rendered useless, inefficacious, abortive, through the power of corruption. — Demosthenes, *Philippic III*

Discuss the examples of asyndeton with your teacher. Can you identify any additional figures? Scan selections from earlier lessons in this book to see if they contain this figure.

Enter the following item in the Figures division of your Prose & Poetry Handbook.

Prose & Poetry Handbook

Writer's Journal

◆ Asyndeton, P&P 81: Subtitle OMISSION, add Asyndeton, its definition and an example.

LITERARY IMITATION

Work with one of the sentences that you diagrammed in Language Logic. Copy the **diagram skeleton**, construct a new sentence, and write the new sentence below the diagram. Your sentence should be one that you could use in your current elaboration.

Lesson 17.4

Classical Composition

PROGYMNASMA NARRATIVE: PLOT OBSERVATION – THEON'S SIX AND SUMMARY
Observe and summarize Homer's *Odyssey*, Book Fifteen. Refer to the instructions and example in the Appendix under "Narrative Plot Observation" and "Example Narrative Plot Observation."

Writer's Journal

❦ Complete the steps for Plot Observation – Theon's Six on the original narrative and in your Writer's Journal.

❦ Write a one paragraph summary of this book, following the steps for Plot Observation – Summary. Work either in your Writer's Journal or on the computer. Add this summary to your running file of *Odyssey* summaries, and save the file.

ANECDOTE ELABORATION: REVISE

❦ Revise your elaboration using the checklist below. Work through the checklist once on your own, and then a second time with your writing mentor, making notes on the print copy of your narrative. Transfer all additions and corrections from your print copy to the computer file. Save and print the document.

Editor's Pen – The Big Picture

✓ All paragraphs included in order, and on topic:
- ◆ **Encomion**: brief praise of the person represented as speaking or acting
- ◆ **Paraphrase**: restatement of the anecdote (proverb) in your own words
- ◆ **Cause**: discussion of the rationale behind the words and/or action in the anecdote (proverb)
- ◆ **Contrast**: consideration of contrasting words or action
- ◆ **Comparison**: consideration of an analogous situation
- ◆ **Example**: discussion of relevant illustration(s) from history or literature (not a complete retelling!)
- ◆ **Authority**: credible testimony that supports the wisdom or wit behind the anecdote or proverb
- ◆ **Exhortation**: brief epilogue exhorting the reader to admire the wit and/or emulate the wisdom

✓ Length: 8 paragraphs of 3-5 sentences each (Paraphrase, Authority, and Exhortation may be shorter)

✓ Title: *original, including parallelism, antithesis, and/or alliteration*

✓ Proverb: *stated in the Encomion paragraph*

✓ Figures of speech (at least one instance of each): *parallelism, antithesis*

Editor's Pen – Zoom 5x: Paragraphs

Refer to Copia In Your Writing (Prose & Poetry Handbook or Appendix)

✓ Formatting: *proper indentation*

✓ Length: *neither too wordy nor too short*

✓ Sentence class by use: *effective use*

✓ Sentence openers: *varied*

✓ Dialogue: *none*

✓ Verb Tense: *consistent*

✓ Pronouns clear: *easily identified antecedents*

✓ Person for Nouns & Pronouns: *similar to ancient elaboration*

Editor's Pen – Zoom 10x: Sentences

Refer to Copia In Your Writing (Prose & Poetry Handbook or Appendix) as needed

✓ Complete thought expressed

✓ Subject and predicate agree in number

✓ Correct capitalization and punctuation

   ◆ No comma splices!

✓ Items in a series constructed in parallel form

Editor's Pen – Fine Focus: Words

✓ Word choices varied; word meanings clear; consider denotation AND connotation

   ◆ Verbs: *strong, specific, fitting,* mostly active (vs. passive); *appropriate adverbs if needed*

   ◆ Nouns: *clear, descriptive; appropriate adjectives if needed*

   ◆ Dialogue: *dialogue tags varied if appropriate*

✓ Correct spelling

✓ Final read-through

POETRY COMPOSITION

Now try your hand at composing a bit of your own poetry.

Writer's Journal

Imitate the meter and rhyme scheme of these lines from "The Builders"(Lesson 11). For content, use "Jason and the Sirens" or another story from literature or history that you have read recently.

Nothing useless is, or low;

Each thing in its place is best;

And what seems but idle show

Strengthens and supports the rest.

For the structure that we raise,

Time is with materials filled;

Our to-days and yesterdays

Are the blocks with which we build.

1. Copy the lines into your Writer's Journal. You diagrammed these lines in Lesson 11. If you have trouble getting started, try copying that diagram skeleton and using it to begin to construct your own lines.

2. List possible rhyming words, and write words and phrases to fit the meter. Use a rhyming dictionary and a thesaurus as needed.

3. When you are satisfied with your imitation, type the final version on the computer. Title it, add your byline, and note below your poem that it is an imitation of "The Builders."

Lesson 17.5

Reflection & Review

Commonplace Book

COMMONPLACE BOOK

Enter in your Commonplace Book:

◆ a favorite passage or two from your reading in Homer's *Odyssey*
◆ an example or two of epithet and/or epic simile

- a few lines of poetry from your anthology (identify meter)
- research and note quotes on character and habit from credible authorities
- examples from your reading of asyndeton
- examples from your reading of other figures you have learned (see Figures and Literary Devices list in *Poetics & Progym I* Appendix)

BOOK OF CENTURIES

 Record in your Book of Centuries:

- John Bunyan, *Pilgrim's Progress*

MEMORY WORK

GRAMMAR
FLASHCARDS

 Review to mastery:

- Modifier Terms – *Poetics & Progym I*
- Pronoun Terms – *Poetics & Progym I*
- Figures – Set #3 – *Poetics & Progym I*

 Continue to review each set once a week (more if needed):

- Parts of Speech – *Bards & Poets* Review
- Sentence Terms – *Bards & Poets* Review
- Noun Terms – *Poetics & Progym I*
- Verb Terms – *Poetics & Progym I*
- Figures – Set #1 – *Poetics & Progym I*
- Figures – Set #2 – *Poetics & Progym I*

❧

THE REQUEST OF KING ALCINOUS
from HOMER'S ODYSSEY

"But, friend, discover faithful what I crave;

Artful concealment ill becomes the brave:

Say what thy birth, and what the name you bore,

Imposed by parents in the natal hour?

(For from the natal hour distinctive names,

One common right, the great and lowly claims:)

Say from what city, from what regions toss'd,

And what inhabitants those regions boast?

So shalt thou instant reach the realm assign'd,

In wondrous ships, self-moved, instinct with mind;

No helm secures their course, no pilot guides;

Like man intelligent, they plough the tides,

Conscious of every coast, and every bay,

That lies beneath the sun's all-seeing ray;

Though clouds and darkness veil the encumber'd sky,

Fearless through darkness and through clouds they fly;

Though tempests rage, though rolls the swelling main,

The seas may roll, the tempests rage in vain;

E'en the stern god that o'er the waves presides,

Safe as they pass, and safe repass the tides,

With fury burns; while careless they convey

Promiscuous every guest to every bay,

These ears have heard my royal sire disclose

A dreadful story, big with future woes;

How Neptune raged, and how, by his command,

Firm rooted in a surge a ship should stand

A monument of wrath; how mound on mound

Should bury these proud towers beneath the ground.

But this the gods may frustrate or fulfil,

As suits the purpose of the Eternal Will.

But say through what waste regions hast thou stray'd

What customs noted, and what coasts survey'd;

Possess'd by wild barbarians fierce in arms,

Or men whose bosom tender pity warms?

Say why the fate of Troy awaked thy cares,

Why heaved thy bosom, and why flowed thy tears?

Just are the ways of Heaven: from Heaven proceed

The woes of man; Heaven doom'd the Greeks to bleed,

A theme of future song! Say, then, if slain

Some dear-loved brother press'd the Phrygian plain?

Or bled some friend, who bore a brother's part,

And claim'd by merit, not by blood, the heart?"

— BOOK VIII, TRANSLATED BY ALEXANDER POPE

CR

Lesson 18.1

Prose & Poetry

LITERARY ELEMENTS IN THE POEM: THE REQUEST OF KING ALCINOUS

1 **Read**
   - ◆ Follow along and listen carefully as the poem is read aloud, OR read it aloud yourself. Read it at least two or three times. **Delight** in the meter, the rhyme, and the images.

2 **Inquire**
   - ◆ Skim back through Homer's description of the feast at the end of Book Eight to refresh your memory on this request made to Odysseus. Research any persons, places, or things mentioned in this poem that are not familiar to you
   - ◆ Are there any unfamiliar persons, places, or things mentioned in the poem? Discuss these with your teacher.
   - ◆ Look up the meaning of any words in the work that are not familiar to you; conduct a complete Vocabulary Study for **key words**.
   - ◆ Was there any part of the poem you did not understand? If so, discuss this with your teacher and classmates.

3 **Observe the Invention, Arrangement, and Style**
   - ◆ **Lyrical Elements**
     - ▪ What does the poet describe?
     - ▪ Does the poet make you see, hear, smell, taste, or touch anything?
     - ▪ Does the poet compare something in the poem to some other thing?
   - ◆ **Narrative Elements** Does this poem tell a story? If so, observe the
     - ▪ **Setting** When and where does this story take place?
     - ▪ **Characters** Who is (are) the main character(s) in this story?
     - ▪ **Conflict** What is the main problem or crisis for the character(s)?
     - ▪ **Resolution** Is the problem solved? If so, how? If not, why not?
     - ▪ **Sequence** Is this story told *ab ovo*, or *in medias res*, or some other way?
     - ▪ **Point of View** Identify the **person** (and **level of omniscience** if applicable).
   - ◆ **Figures** Look for figures of speech and figures of description. (See Appendix for the list of figures taught in *Poetics & Progym*.) Why did the poet choose these particular figures?

4 Investigate the Context

- Review what you know about Homer's

  - **Origin** Who were the poet's parents/ancestors? Where was his homeland?

  - **Historical Time Period** When did the poet live? What events happened around the time that the poet lived?

  - **Influences** What education, training, books, ideas, and other people or events shaped the poet's thinking?

- **Rhetorical Situation**

  - **Exigency** – What is the issue, problem, or situation to be addressed?

  - **Audience** – Who is the author addressing in order to change or persuade?

  - **Constraint** What are the requirements based on the audience and the occasion?

- **Identify the poem's Literary Genre**

  - **Genre by literary period** In which century (time period) and country was this work written?

  - **Genre by poetic/narrative category** Is this poem chiefly **lyrical** (describes an event, or a person, or a feeling, or a time and place, etc., but it does not tell a particular story) or **narrative** (tells a story)? If narrative, is it primarily **non-fiction** (a story that really happened) or **fiction** (a story told as if it really happened)?

Writer's Journal

5 Connect the Thoughts

- Does this poem remind you of other poems, or of stories with similar plots, messages, or characters?

- Does this poem remind you of any proverbs or other well-known quotations? If so, enter these in your Commonplace Book.

Commonplace Book

6 Profit and Delight

- **Delight** What are the sources of delight in this poem?

- **Wisdom** What wisdom does this poem furnish?

- **Read** the poem to your teacher with expression and proper pauses.

- **Read** other works by this poet.

- **Memorize** this poem and recite it before an audience.

SCANSION AND ANALYSIS: THE ODYSSEY, BOOK VIII

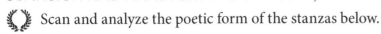 Scan and analyze the poetic form of the stanzas below.

A. Scan the lines. Notice there are times where syllables that are normally pronounced separately are **elided** or run together. For example, in several places, the word *Heaven* is elided to *Heav'n* (pronounced with one syllable). You may either mark the syllables together as one unstressed or stressed syllable, or you may mark the elision as an extra unstressed syllable.

B. Mark the end rhyme. Name the rhyme scheme:

C. Write the stanza name, along with any form/genre designation that may apply:

But say through what waste regions hast thou stray'd

What customs noted, and what coasts survey'd;

Possess'd by wild barbarians fierce in arms,

Or men whose bosom tender pity warms?

Say why the fate of Troy awaked thy cares,

Why heaved thy bosom, and why flowed thy tears?

Just are the ways of Heaven: from Heaven proceed

The woes of man; Heaven doom'd the Greeks to bleed,

A theme of future song! Say, then, if slain

Some dear-loved brother press'd the Phrygian plain?

Or bled some friend, who bore a brother's part,

And claim'd by merit, not by blood, the heart?"

THE ODYSSEY

〔 Read

◆ *The Odyssey of Homer*, Book Sixteen

〔 As you read, continue to mark the text and make notes:

◆ Literary concepts and terms you observe in the narrative. Do any of your earlier thoughts need revision?
◆ Instances of **epic simile**.
◆ **Epithets** to add to your running list.
◆ Passages reflecting on the value of **hearth and home**.

Writer's Journal

〔 Discuss this week's reading with your teacher, along with all your notes and observations. Narrate the main action of the book, and discuss any parts you did not understand. How was this reading **delightful**? What **wisdom** does this reading furnish?

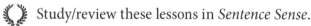

Lesson 18.2

Language Logic

SYNTAX – SENTENCE CLASSIFICATION

〔 Study/review these lessons in *Sentence Sense*.

II. Syntax – The Sentence

◆ 9.6A Phrases
◆ 9.7A and 9.7B Clauses
◆ 9.14A and 9.14B Classification by Use
◆ 9.15A and 9.15B Classification by Form

III. Sentence Diagramming – Modifiers

◆ 13.8 Adverbs Modifying Prepositional Phrases
◆ 13.9 Prepositional Phrases As Subject Complements
◆ 13.10 Prepositional Phrases As Objective Complements

DIAGRAMMING & PARSING

In your Writer's Journal, copy these sentences. Mark the prepositional phrases, subjects, and verbs. Bracket the clauses. Classify the sentence as simple, compound, complex, or compound-complex. Then diagram each one. Refer to *Sentence Sense* as needed.

1. We here highly resolve that these dead shall not have died in vain—that this nation, under God, shall have a new birth of freedom—and that government of the people, by the people, for the people, shall not perish from the earth.

2. Men become builders by building and lyreplayers by playing the lyre; so too we become just by doing just acts, temperate by doing temperate acts, brave by doing brave acts.

Orally parse these words with your teacher, using the charts in *Sentence Sense* to guide you.

(1) of the people, shall perish; (2) builders, building, temperate (first use), by doing brave acts

---

Lesson 18.3

Eloquent Expression

COPIA OF CONSTRUCTION: SENTENCE COMBINATION WITH SENTENCE CLASSES BY FORM

In addition to combining sentences with compound elements or participles, you could also combine them by working with each sentence's **classification by form**. Consider again this series of sentences:

Erasmus received a letter from a friend. Erasmus read the letter many times. Erasmus wrote a reply. Erasmus sent the reply to his friend.

As you have already seen, you could create **compound sentences** from the original **simple sentences**. In all of the sentences below, clauses are bracketed and conjunctions or relative pronouns are underlined:

[Erasmus received a letter from a friend], and [he read it many times]. [He wrote a reply], then [he sent it to his friend].

244 ◆ Lesson 18.4

POETICS & PROGYM I

Or you could create **subordinate clauses** to form a **complex sentence**:

> [When Erasmus received a letter from a friend], [he read it many times]. [The delighted scholar wrote a reply] [which he sent to his friend].

Finally, you could create a **compound-complex sentence**:

> [After Erasmus received a letter from a friend], [he read it many times], and he wrote a reply] [which he sent to his friend.]

Paraphrase this series of sentences twice. The first time, combine them into a complex sentence or two, adjusting other words in the sentence as needed. The second time, combine them into one compound-complex sentence. Then, find some sentences from one of your earlier compositions that could be improved by combining them with sentence form. Copy the original in your Writer's Journal along with your revision.

> Eumaeus sat with Odysseus. Someone approached. The dogs did did not bark. The dogs were fawning. The swineherd went out to investigate.

Writer's Journal

LITERARY IMITATION

Work with the verses that you diagrammed in Language Logic.
Copy the **diagram skeleton**, construct a new sentence, and write the new sentence below the diagram. The topic of your new sentence is the benefit of friendship; your sentence should be one you could use in your upcoming elaboration.

Lesson 18.4

Classical Composition

PROGYMNASMA NARRATIVE: PLOT OBSERVATION – THEON'S SIX AND SUMMARY
Observe and summarize Homer's *Odyssey*, Book Sixteen. Refer to the instructions and example in the Appendix under "Narrative Plot Observation" and "Example Narrative Plot Observation."

❦ Complete the steps for Plot Observation – Theon's Six on the original narrative and in your Writer's Journal.

❦ Write a one paragraph summary of this book, following the steps for Plot Observation – Summary. Work either in your Writer's Journal or on the computer. Add this summary to your running file of *Odyssey* summaries, and save the file.

QUOTE FOR ELABORATION: HOMER ON FRIENDSHIP

The quote you will use for your next elaboration is derived from these lines found at the end of Alexander Pope's translation of the *Odyssey*, Book VIII.

> ". . . some friend, who bore a brother's part,
> And claim'd by merit, not by blood, the heart."

Here are a few other translations of the same lines:

> . . . no less dear than a brother, the brother-in-arms
> who shares our inmost thoughts (translated by Robert Fagles)

> True it is, a wise friend can take a brother's place
> in our affection. (translated by Robert Fitzgerald)

> A good friend is as dear to a man as his own brother. (translated by Samuel Butler)

> One who is your companion, and has thoughts honorable towards you,
> is of no less degree than a brother (translated by Richmond Lattimore)

> For no whit worse than a brother is a comrade who has an understanding heart. (Loeb Classical Library — E Capps, T. E. Page, and W. H. D Rouse)

> . . . a knowing soul, and no unpleasing thing?
> Since such a good one is no underling
> To any brother; for, what fits true friends,

True wisdom is, that blood and birth transcends. (translated by George Chapman)

Writer's Journal

Copy this quote into your Writer's Journal. Is it a proverb or an anecdote?

Homer said a friend is one ". . . who bore a brother's part, And claim'd by merit, not by blood, the heart."

Analyze and inflect the saying, following these steps. Refer to Lesson 7 for complete instructions. and to diagramming helps in *Sentence Sense* as needed.

Analysis	**Inflection**
◆ Diagram	◆ Number (inflect *friend*)
◆ Definitions	◆ Declension (inflect *Homer*)
◆ Copia of Words	◆ Copia of Construction

Writer's Journal

Research both Homer and Alexander Pope using the **Five W's and an H**. Take notes in your Writer's Journal. Here are a few questions to get you started:

- **Who** was Homer? Pope?
- **What** is Homer best know for? Pope?
- **Where** did Homer live? Pope?
- **When** did Homer live? Pope?
- **Why** is Homer credible in this matter? **Why** is his advice worth listening to? **Why** use Pope's translation of these lines?
- **How** did Homer acquire his wisdom? **How** did he benefit or influence others then and now?

ANECDOTE ELABORATION: PLAN

In your Writer's Journal, make planning notes for your Proverb elaboration. Work on this assignment over several days, and be sure to engage in lots of discussion with your teacher and your family. Construct an outline in your Writer's Journal, with notes for each of the topics (headers) of your Elaboration Essay. Write each topic listed below in order, leaving about a half page to jot down notes for each. Write only on the right hand pages of your Journal, so that you have room if you need to make extra notes or corrections. Once you have listed all of the topics, go back and make notes of what you plan to include in your essay for each.

1. **Encomion** is a brief praise of the person represented as **speaking or acting (Lesson 10)**.

    ◆ You have already researched **who, what, where, when, why**, and **how** for the person who is being praised for his/ her wise or witty saying and/or action. Choose which things you will highlight from this research.
    ◆ State the essence or principle of the wisdom or wit.

2. **Paraphrase** is a restatement of the anecdote or proverb in your own words.

    ◆ Restate based on your analysis & inflection of the wise saying.

3. **Cause** is a discussion of the rationale behind the words and/or action in the anecdote or proverb. Consider:

    ◆ logical reasons
    ◆ life experience
    ◆ motivation
    ◆ circumstances

4. **Contrast** is a consideration of contrasting words or action. In conrast to your Cause content, consider:

    ◆ logical reasons
    ◆ life experience
    ◆ motivation
    ◆ circumstances

5. **Comparison** is a consideration of an analogous situation. Possible analogies:

    ◆ a concrete comparison using simile or metaphor
    ◆ a similar situation from another sphere

6. **Example** is a discussion of relevant illustration(s) from history or literature.

    ◆ Choose an historical or literary characters that will be somewhat familiar to your audience.
    ◆ Touch on the main and relevant points; do not include too many details.
    ◆ Avoid dialogue and description.

7. **Authority** is a credible testimony supporting the wisdom or wit behind the anecdote or proverb.

   ◆ Determine the essential wisdom or principle to aid your search for testimony.
   ◆ Authority must be credible and recognizable to your audience.
   ◆ Use who, what, where, when, why, for the person cited.
   ◆ How does the Authority relate to the anecdote or proverb?

8. **Exhortation** is a brief epilogue encouraing the reader to admire the wit and/or emulate the wisdom.

   ◆ Restate the wisdom or wit in a few words.
   ◆ Exhort your reader to heed the wisdom or appreciate the wit.

Discuss your research with your teacher and classmates, your parents, siblings, or any other interested and helpful parties. Make note of any additional ideas or questions to pursue in your Writer's Journal.

Lesson 18.5

Reflection & Review

Commonplace Book

COMMONPLACE BOOK

Enter in your Commonplace Book:

   ◆ a favorite passage or two from your reading in Homer's *Odyssey*
   ◆ an example or two of epithet and/or epic simile
   ◆ a few lines of poetry from your anthology (identify meter)
   ◆ research and note quotes on the benefits of friendship from credible authorities
   ◆ examples from your reading of other figures you have learned (see Figures and Literary Devices list in *Poetics & Progym I* Appendix)

GRAMMAR
FLASHCARDS

Review to mastery:

- Modifier Terms – *Poetics & Progym I*
- Pronoun Terms – *Poetics & Progym I*
- Figures – Set #3 – *Poetics & Progym I*

Use the combine and test features at Quizlet for an online or printed quiz over Figure Set #3. If you wish, use combine set features to include previous figure sets.

Continue to review each set once a week (more if needed):

- Parts of Speech – *Bards & Poets* Review
- Sentence Terms – *Bards & Poets* Review
- Noun Terms – *Poetics & Progym I*
- Verb Terms – *Poetics & Progym I*
- Figures – Set #1 – *Poetics & Progym I*
- Figures – Set #2 – *Poetics & Progym I*

☙

KING SOLOMON ON FRIENDSHIP

Two are better than one; because they have a good reward for their labour. For if they fall, the one will lift up his fellow: but woe to him that is alone when he falleth; for he hath not another to help him up. Again, if two lie together, then they have heat: but how can one be warm alone? And if one prevail against him, two shall withstand him; and a threefold cord is not quickly broken.

— ECCLESIASTES 4:9-12

☙

Lesson 19.1

Prose & Poetry

LITERARY ELEMENTS IN WISDOM LITERATURE: KING SOLOMON ON FRIENDSHIP
King Solomon was the son of the great Hebrew King David, and a prolific author of Scripture. He wrote the Ecclesiastes and Song of Songs, and much of the book of Proverbs.

1 **Read**
  ◆ Read the selection aloud, preferably in a group setting. **Delight** in the well-chosen words.

2 **Inquire**
  ◆ Does the **title** of the book from which this is excerpted (Ecclesiastes) give any clues as to the content or the author's message?
  ◆ Look up the meaning of any words in the work that are not familiar to you; conduct a complete Vocabulary Study for **key words.**

◆ Do a little research on Wisdom Literature in the bible. Which books are included in this genre? What is their purpose? If possible, ask you pastor about this. Ligonier Ministries also has a good online article about Wisdom Literature entitled "The Purpose of Wisdom Literature."

◆ State your first impression of the author's **message**.

3 Observe the Invention, Arrangement, and Style

◆ Outline the main points of the selection.

◆ **Point of View** Identify the **person** (P&P 50)

◆ Identify the **Figures** – both **figures of speech** and **figures of description** (See the list of figures in the Appendix.) Why did the author choose these particular figures?

4 Investigate the Context

◆ Who is the **author**? Of course, God is the author of all Scripture, but in this case, research the human author (Solomon) and make notes in your Writer's Journal. The story of Solomon's life is found in I Kings 1-11 and I Chronicles 29 – II Chronicles 8. In addition to Ecclesiastes, he authored Song of Solomon and much of the Book of Proverbs.

- **Origin** – Who were the author's parents/ancestors? Where was his homeland?
- **Historical Time Period** – When did the author live?
- **Influences** What education, training, people, events, books, or ideas shaped the author's thinking?

◆ **Rhetorical Situation** (P&P 2) for the book of Ecclesiastes

- **Exigency** – What is the issue, problem, or situation to be addressed? How does the author want the reader to respond?
- **Audience** – Who is the author addressing in order to change or persuade?
- **Constraint** What are the requirements based on the audience and the genre?

5 Respond

◆ State the message of the selection. Revisit your first impression. Has your interpretation changed?

◆ Paraphrase, summarize and/or write a précis of this selection.

6 Connect the Thoughts

◆ Does this selection remind you of other things you have **Read** in Scripture, literature, history, etc?

◆ Does this selection remind you of any proverbs or other well-known quotations? If so, enter these in your Commonplace Book.

Commonplace Book

7 Profit and Delight

◆ What are the sources of **delight** in this work?

◆ What **wisdom** does this work furnish?

◆ **Discuss** this work **in community** with family, friends, classmates.

◆ **Memorize** a portion of this work and recite it before an audience.

THE ODYSSEY

THE
ODYSSEY
OF
HOMER

◯ Read

◆ *The Odyssey of Homer,* Book Seventeen

◯ As you read, continue to mark the text and make notes:

◆ Literary concepts and terms you observe in the narrative. Do any of your earlier thoughts need revision?

◆ Instances of **epic simile**.

◆ **Epithets** to add to your running list.

◆ Passages reflecting on the value of **hearth and home**.

Writer's Journal

◯ Discuss this week's reading with your teacher, along with all your notes and observations. Narrate the main action of the book, and discuss any parts you did not understand. How was this reading **delightful**? What **wisdom** does this reading furnish?

Lesson 19.2

Language Logic

SYNTAX – SENTENCE ELEMENTS

 Study/review these lessons in *Sentence Sense.*

II. Syntax – The Sentence *This is mainly a review of what you already know.*

- ◆ 9.3 Principal Elements
- ◆ 9.8 Arrangement of Elements *What figure of speech is related to an inverted order of elements?*
- ◆ 9.9 Subordinate Elements

DIAGRAMMING & PARSING

 In your Writer's Journal, copy these sentences. Mark the prepositional phrases, subjects, and verbs. Bracket the clauses. Classify the sentence as simple, compound, complex, or compound-complex. Then diagram each one. Refer to *Sentence Sense* as needed.

Writer's Journal

1. Soon rested those who fought. — William Cullen Bryant

2. Neither snow, nor rain, nor heat nor dark of night keeps them from completing their appointed course as swiftly as possible.

3. Two are better than one; because they have a good reward for their labour.

 Orally parse these words with your teacher, using the charts in *Sentence Sense* to guide you.

(1) Soon, who; (2) Neither, nor, them, accomplishing, appointed, as (swiftly), as possible;

(3) Two, because, reward, their

Lesson 19.3

Eloquent Expression

COPIA OF CONSTRUCTION: SENTENCE COMBINATION WITH SCHEMES POLYSYNDETON & ASYNDETON

You have learned to combine sentences by using conjunctions and a comma to join three or more elements of equal rank:

> When he received your letter, Erasmus smiled delightedly, shouted gleefully, and danced joyfully.

Most of your sentences with compound elements (words, phrases, or clauses) should follow these conventions. However, as we said in that lesson, there are some "rules" that good writers occasionally break. This is one such rule.

> When he received your letter, Erasmus smiled delightedly, and shouted gleefully, and sang joyfully.

This is the same sentence constructed with the scheme of **polysyndeton**. One extra conjunction has been added between the elements. You could also leave out the commas, depending on the effect you are trying to achieve.

> When he received your letter, Erasmus smiled delightedly, shouted gleefully, sang joyfully.

This is the same sentence constructed with the scheme of **asyndeton**. The conjunction is removed, but the commas remain between the elements. Be careful here, and make sure when you use asyndeton, you use it intentionally. At all other times, be on guard against comma splices.

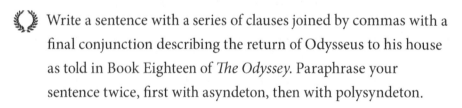 Write a sentence with a series of clauses joined by commas with a final conjunction describing the return of Odysseus to his house as told in Book Eighteen of *The Odyssey*. Paraphrase your sentence twice, first with asyndeton, then with polysyndeton.

Writer's Journal

LITERARY IMITATION

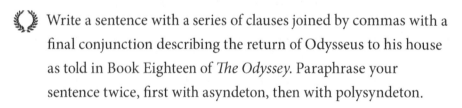 Work with another of the sentences that you diagrammed in Lesson 18.2 Language Logic. Copy the **diagram skeleton**, construct a new sentence, and write the new sentence below the diagram. The topic of your new sentence is friendship. It should be a sentence you could use in your elaboration.

Lesson 19.4

Classical Composition

PROGYMNASMA NARRATIVE: PLOT OBSERVATION – THEON'S SIX AND SUMMARY

Observe and summarize Homer's *Odyssey*, Book Seventeen. Refer to the instructions and example in the Appendix under "Narrative Plot Observation" and "Example Narrative Plot Observation."

- Complete the steps for Plot Observation – Theon's Six on the original narrative and in your Writer's Journal.

- Write a one paragraph summary of this book, following the steps for Plot Observation – Summary. Work either in your Writer's Journal or on the computer. Add this summary to your running file of *Odyssey* summaries, and save the file.

ANECDOTE ELABORATION: WRITE

- Use the outline and notes in your Writer's Journal to guide you as you write the elaboration in your own words for the anecdote:

Homer said a friend is one ". . . who bore a brother's part,
And claim'd by merit, not by blood, the heart." (*Odyssey*, Book VIII)

- ◆ Length should be eight paragraphs (one for each of the topics).
- ◆ Each paragraph should be three to five sentences in length, although the Paraphrase, Authority, and Exhortation paragraphs may be shorter.
- ◆ State the anecdote as a "prequel" to your Encomion paragraph.

A. Compose your first draft. It is simplest to work on the computer, but if words flow more easily when you write by hand, use your Writer's Journal. You will want to type it up when you are done to make editing easier. Save your file, print, and save.

B. Develop a title for your elaboration. Make up your own original title. If possible, use parallelism, antithesis, and/or alliteration.

Lesson 19.5

Reflection & Review

Commonplace
Book

COMMONPLACE BOOK

Enter in your Commonplace Book:

- ◆ a favorite passage or two from your reading in Homer's *Odyssey*
- ◆ an example or two of epithet and/or epic simile
- ◆ a few lines of poetry from your anthology (identify meter)
- ◆ research and note quotes on the benefits of friendship from credible authorities
- ◆ examples from your reading of other figures you have learned (see Figures and Literary Devices list in *Poetics & Progym I* Appendix)

BOOK OF CENTURIES

Record in your Book of Centuries:

- ◆ King Solomon, *Proverbs*

MEMORY WORK

GRAMMAR
FLASHCARDS

Review to mastery:

- ◆ Modifier Terms – *Poetics & Progym I*
- ◆ Pronoun Terms – *Poetics & Progym I*

Use the combine and test features at Quizlet for an online or printed quiz over the Modifier and Pronoun sets. If you wish, use combine set features to include previous figure sets.

Continue to review each set once a week (more if needed):

- ◆ Parts of Speech – *Bards & Poets* Review
- ◆ Sentence Terms – *Bards & Poets* Review
- ◆ Noun Terms – *Poetics & Progym I*
- ◆ Verb Terms – *Poetics & Progym I*
- ◆ Figures – Set #1 – *Poetics & Progym I*
- ◆ Figures – Set #2 – *Poetics & Progym I*
- ◆ Figures – Set #3 – *Poetics & Progym I*

ભ

ARISTOTLE ON FRIENDSHIP
from NICOMACHEAN ETHICS

[Friendship] is a virtue or implies virtue, and is besides most necessary with a view to living. For without friends no one would choose to live, though he had all other goods; even rich men and those in possession of office and of dominating power are thought to need friends most of all; for what is the use of such prosperity without the opportunity of beneficence, which is exercised chiefly and in its most laudable form towards friends? Or how can prosperity be guarded and preserved without friends? The greater it is, the more exposed is it to risk. And in poverty and in other misfortunes men think friends are the only refuge. It helps the young, too, to keep from error; it aids older people by ministering to their needs and supplementing the activities that are failing from weakness; those in the prime of life it stimulates to noble actions—'two going together'—for with friends men are more able both to think and to act. Again, parent seems by nature to feel it for offspring and offspring for parent, not only among men but among birds and among most animals; it is felt mutually by members of the same race, and especially by men, whence we praise lovers of their fellowmen. We may even in our travels how near and dear every man is to every other. Friendship seems too to hold states together, and lawgivers to care more for it than for justice; for unanimity seems to be something like friendship, and this they aim at most of all, and expel faction as their worst enemy; and when men are friends they have no need of justice, while when they are just they need friendship as well, and the truest form of justice is thought to be a friendly quality.

But it is not only necessary but also noble; for we praise those who love their friends, and it is thought to be a fine thing to have many friends;

and again we think it is the same people that are good men and are
friends.

— VIII.1 TRANSLATED BY D. P. CHASE

Cℛ

Lesson 20.1

Prose & Poetry

LITERARY ELEMENTS IN PROSE: ARISTOTLE ON FRIENDSHIP

Friendship has been a favored topic for authors in every age. Many ancient authors wrote essays
or meditations on friendship. Aristotle, in this selection, reflects on friendship as a virtue. His
words are well worth considering not only as you finish up your elaboration about Homer's words
on friendship in this lesson, but also as you are learning to navigate your own friendships.

1 Read
- Read the selection aloud, preferably in a group setting. **Delight** in the
  well-chosen words.

2 Inquire
- Does the **title** give any hint as to the content or message of the passage?
  If this work was published by the author in a larger book or anthology,
  does that title give any hint?
- Look up the meaning of any words in the work that are not familiar
  to you; conduct a complete Vocabulary Study for **key words.** *Virtue* is
  definitely a key word in Aristotle's Ethics, so make sure you include that.
- Research unfamiliar persons, places, or things mentioned in the work.
- State your first impression of the author's **message**.

3 Observe the Invention, Arrangement, and Style
- What is the topic of this passage? Outline its main points.
- **Point of View** Identify the **person** (P&P 50).
- Identify the **Figures** – both **figures of speech** and **figures of description** (See the list of
  figures in the Appendix.) Why did the author choose these particular figures?

4 **Investigate the Context**

Writer's Journal

- ◆ Research a bit about the author. Make notes in your Writer's Journal about Aristotle's

  - ■ **Origin** – Who were the author's parents/ancestors? Where was his homeland?
  - ■ **Historical Time Period** – When did the author live?
  - ■ **Influences** What education, training, people, events, books, or ideas shaped the author's thinking?

- ◆ **Rhetorical Situation** (P&P 2) Research *Nichomachean Ethics* to see what his overall aim was. Answer the questions below based on the passage under study.

  - ■ **Exigency** – What is the issue, problem, or situation to be addressed? How does the author want the reader to respond?
  - ■ **Audience** – Who is the author addressing in order to change or persuade?
  - ■ **Constraint** What are the requirements based on the audience and the genre?

5 **Respond**

- ◆ State the message of the passage. Revisit your first impression. Has your interpretation changed?
- ◆ Paraphrase, summarize and/or write a précis of this passage.

6 **Connect the Thoughts**

- ◆ Does this passage remind you of other things you have **Read** in Scripture, literature, history, etc?
- ◆ Does this passage remind you of any proverbs or other well-known quotations? If so, enter these in your Commonplace Book.

Commonplace Book

7 **Profit and Delight**

- ◆ What are the sources of **delight** in this work?
- ◆ What **wisdom** does this work furnish?
- ◆ **Discuss** this work **in community** with family, friends, classmates.
- ◆ **Memorize** a portion of this work and recite it before an audience.

THE ODYSSEY

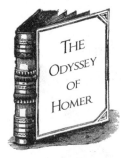

◉ Read

- *The Odyssey of Homer,* Book Eighteen

◉ As you read, continue to mark the text and make notes:

- Literary concepts and terms you observe in the narrative. Do any of your earlier thoughts need revision?
- Instances of **epic simile**.
- **Epithets** to add to your running list.
- Passages reflecting on the value of **hearth and home**.

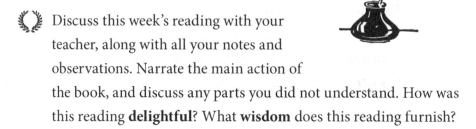

Writer's Journal

◉ Discuss this week's reading with your teacher, along with all your notes and observations. Narrate the main action of the book, and discuss any parts you did not understand. How was this reading **delightful**? What **wisdom** does this reading furnish?

Lesson 20.2

Language Logic

SYNTAX – SENTENCE ELEMENTS

 Study/review these lessons in *Sentence Sense.*

II. Syntax – The Sentence *This is mainly a review of what you already know.*

- ◆ 9.10A Objective Elements
- ◆ 9.11A Adjective Elements
- ◆ 9.12A Adverbial Elements
- ◆ 9.13A Attendant Elements

DIAGRAMMING & PARSING

◆ In your Writer's Journal, copy this sentence. Mark the prepositional phrases, subjects, and verbs. Bracket the clauses. Classify the sentence as simple, compound, complex, or compound-complex. Then diagram it. Refer to *Sentence Sense* as needed.

Writer's Journal

> Friendship is a virtue or implies virtue, and is besides most necessary with a view to living.

◆ Orally parse these words with your teacher, using the charts in *Sentence Sense* to guide you.

> Friendship, is, virtue, besides, most, necessary, with a view, living.

Lesson 20.3

Eloquent Expression

COPIA OF CONSTRUCTION: SENTENCE STRUCTURE – SENTENCE CLASSES BY FORM

Sentences can often be switched from one **classification by form** to another:

> The letter which you wrote arrived today, so was my heart delighted. (compound-complex)

> My heart was delighted because I received your letter. (complex)

> I received your letter, and my heart was delighted. (compound)

> I received your letter. My heart was delighted. (simple)

◆ Paraphrase the sentence below as a series of simple sentences. Then look for some sentences from an earlier composition that could be improved by changing the class by form. Copy the originals into your Writer's Journal, and then write the revised sentence below it.

Writer's Journal

> For without friends no one would choose to live, though he had all other goods; even rich men and those in possession of office and of dominating power are thought to need friends most of all;

for what is the use of such prosperity without the opportunity of beneficence, which is exercised chiefly and in its most laudable form towards friends?

LITERARY IMITATION

Work with the sentence below that you diagrammed in Language Logic. Copy the **diagram skeleton**, construct a new sentence, and write the new sentence below the diagram. Base your new sentence on Odysseus's homecoming in Book Eighteen.

[Friendship] is a virtue or implies virtue, and is besides most necessary with a view to living.

Lesson 20.4

Classical Composition

PROGYMNASMA NARRATIVE: PLOT OBSERVATION – THEON'S SIX AND SUMMARY

Observe and summarize Homer's *Odyssey*, Book Eighteen. Refer to the instructions and example in the Appendix under "Narrative Plot Observation" and "Example Narrative Plot Observation."

Complete the steps for Plot Observation – Theon's Six on the original narrative and in your Writer's Journal.

Writer's Journal

Write a one paragraph summary of this book, following the steps for Plot Observation – Summary. Work either in your Writer's Journal or on the computer. Add this summary to your running file of *Odyssey* summaries, and save the file.

ANECDOTE ELABORATION: REVISE

Revise your elaboration about Homer and friendship using the checklist below. Work through the checklist once on your own, and then a second time with your writing mentor, making notes on the print copy of your narrative. Transfer all additions and corrections from your print copy to the computer file. Save and print the document.

Editor's Pen – The Big Picture

✓ All paragraphs included in order, and on topic:

- ◆ **Encomion**: brief praise of the person represented as speaking or acting
- ◆ **Paraphrase**: restatement of the anecdote (proverb) in your own words
- ◆ **Cause**: discussion of the rationale behind the words and/or action in the anecdote (proverb)
- ◆ **Contrast**: consideration of contrasting words or action
- ◆ **Comparison**: consideration of an analogous situation
- ◆ **Example**: discussion of relevant illustration(s) from history or literature (not a complete retelling!)
- ◆ **Authority**: credible testimony that supports the wisdom or wit behind the anecdote or proverb
- ◆ **Exhortation**: brief epilogue exhorting the reader to admire the wit and/or emulate the wisdom

✓ Length: 8 paragraphs of 3-5 sentences each (Paraphrase, Authority, and Exhortation may be shorter)

✓ Title: *original, including parallelism, antithesis, and/or alliteration*

✓ Proverb: *stated in the Encomion*

✓ Figures of speech (at least one instance of each): *parallelism, antithesis;*

✓ Figures of speech (one or the other) *asyndeton, polysyndeton*

Editor's Pen – Zoom 5x: Paragraphs

Refer to Copia In Your Writing (Prose & Poetry Handbook or Appendix) as needed

✓ Formatting: *proper indentation*

✓ Length: *neither too wordy nor too short*

✓ Sentence class by use: *effective use*

✓ Sentence openers: *varied*

✓ Dialogue: *none*

✓ Sentence length and class by form: *varied*

✓ Verb Tense: *consistent*

✓ Pronouns clear: *easily identified antecedents*

✓ Person for Nouns & Pronouns: *similar to ancient elaboration*

Editor's Pen – Zoom 10x: Sentences

Refer to Copia In Your Writing (Prose & Poetry Handbook or Appendix) as needed

✓ Complete thought expressed

✓ Subject and predicate agree in number

✓ Correct capitalization and punctuation

◆ No comma splices!

✓ Items in a series constructed in parallel form

Editor's Pen – Fine Focus: Words

✓ Word choices varied; word meanings clear; consider denotation AND connotation

◆ Verbs: *strong, specific, fitting, mostly active (vs. passive); appropriate adverbs if needed*

◆ Nouns: *clear, descriptive; appropriate adjectives if needed*

◆ Dialogue: *dialogue tags varied if appropriate*

✓ Correct spelling

✓ Final read-through

POETRY COMPOSITION

Imitate the meter and rhyme scheme of these lines from "Jerusalem"(Lesson 12). For content, use a story from literature or history that you have read recently.

Writer's Journal

And did those feet in ancient time

Walk upon England's mountains green:

And was the holy Lamb of God,

On England's pleasant pastures seen!

And did the Countenance Divine,

Shine forth upon our clouded hills?

And was Jerusalem builded here,

Among these dark Satanic Mills?

Bring me my Bow of burning gold:

Bring me my arrows of desire:

Bring me my Spear: O clouds unfold!

Bring me my Chariot of fire!

I will not cease from Mental Fight,

Nor shall my sword sleep in my hand:

Till we have built Jerusalem,

In England's green & pleasant Land.

1. Copy the lines into your Writer's Journal. You diagrammed these lines in Lesson 12. If you have trouble getting started, try copying that diagram skeleton and using it to begin to construct your own lines.

2. List possible rhyming words, and write words and phrases to fit the meter. Use a rhyming dictionary and a thesaurus as needed.

3. When you are satisfied with your imitation, type the final version on the computer. Title it, add your byline, and note below your poem that it is an imitation of "Jerusalem."

Lesson 20.5

Reflection & Review

 Commonplace Book

COMMONPLACE BOOK

 Enter in your Commonplace Book:

- ◆ a favorite passage or two from your reading in Homer's *Odyssey*
- ◆ an example or two of epithet and/or epic simile
- ◆ a few lines of poetry from your anthology (identify meter)
- ◆ research and note quotes on the benefits of friendship from credible authorities
- ◆ examples from your reading of other figures you have learned (see Figures and Literary Devices list in *Poetics & Progym I* Appendix)

BOOK OF CENTURIES

Record in your Book of Centuries:

- ◆ Aristotle

MEMORY WORK

GRAMMAR FLASHCARDS

Continue to review each set once a week (more if needed):

- Parts of Speech – *Bards & Poets* Review
- Sentence Terms – *Bards & Poets* Review
- Noun Terms – *Poetics & Progym I*
- Verb Terms – *Poetics & Progym I*
- Modifier Terms – *Poetics & Progym I*
- Pronoun Terms – *Poetics & Progym I*
- Figures – Set #1 – *Poetics & Progym I*
- Figures – Set #2 – *Poetics & Progym I*
- Figures – Set #3 – *Poetics & Progym I*

⊗

THE SHEPHERD BOY AND THE WOLF

from THE AESOP FOR CHILDREN **by Milo Winter**

A Shepherd Boy tended his master's Sheep near a dark forest not far from the village. Soon he found life in the pasture very dull. All he could do to amuse himself was to talk to his dog or play on his shepherd's pipe.

One day as he sat watching the Sheep and the quiet forest, and thinking what he would do should he see a Wolf, he thought of a plan to amuse himself.

His Master had told him to call for help should a Wolf attack the flock, and the Villagers would drive it away. So now, though he had not seen anything that even looked like a Wolf, he ran toward the village shouting at the top of his voice, "Wolf! Wolf!"

As he expected, the Villagers who heard the cry dropped their work and ran in great excitement to the pasture. But when they got there they found the Boy doubled up with laughter at the trick he had played on them.

A few days later the Shepherd Boy again shouted, "Wolf! Wolf!" Again the Villagers ran to help him, only to be laughed at again.

Then one evening as the sun was setting behind the forest and the shadows were creeping out over the pasture, a Wolf really did spring from the underbrush and fall upon the Sheep.

In terror the Boy ran toward the village shouting "Wolf! Wolf!" But though the Villagers heard the cry, they did not run to help him as they had before. "He cannot fool us again," they said.

The Wolf killed a great many of the Boy's sheep and then slipped away into the forest.

Liars are not believed even when they speak the truth.

ℭℛ

Lesson 21.1

Prose & Poetry

REVISITING THE FABLE

Go back to Lesson 1.1 and review the section in Prose & Poetry entitled "Aesop and His Fables." Your task in Lesson 21.4 will be to compose your own fable in the spirit of Aesop, illustrating the wisdom of one of these proverbs:

Habit is like a fire, a bad master but an indispensable servant. — Charlotte Mason

Two are better than one; because they have a good reward for their labour. — Ecclesiastes 4:9

*Do not stop to argue with temptation. — Aesop

Of course, we do not want you to offend people to the point of putting your own life in peril as Aesop did, but the aim of a fable should be to cause readers to reflect, and perhaps even reform.

*This is the moral to the fable in Lesson 1, "The Dog and His Master's Dinner." If you choose this one, make up a totally different fable or parable to illustrate this proverb.

Read the familiar fable by Aesop at the beginning of this lesson as an example of how a fable may be constructed. If you have time, read additional fables by Aesop. If you do not have a volume of Aesop's fables at home, you will easily find them online. *The Aesop for Children* by Milo Winter is an excellent anthology; you may access it at gutenberg.org.

 Begin thinking about the fable you will write. In your Writer's Journal, write all three proverbs, then analyze and inflect them, following these steps. Refer to Lesson 7 for complete instructions. and to diagramming helps in *Sentence Sense* as needed. You already diagrammed the Ecclesiastes proverb in Lesson 19.2. For Mason's proverb, see *Sentence Sense* 26.1 Similes.

Analysis	Inflection
◆ Diagram	◆ Number
◆ Definitions	◆ Declension
◆ Copia of Words	◆ Copia of Construction

 Reflect on the wit or wisdom of your chosen proverb. Begin to think about possible characters. It is probably easiest to use anthropomorphic animals, but do not feel limited to these. You might invent a story that is more like a *parable*, as Jesus did to illustrate his kingdom principles. Jot down your ideas in your Writer's Journal.

THE ODYSSEY

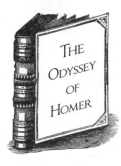

THE ODYSSEY OF HOMER

 Read

◆ *The Odyssey of Homer,* Book Nineteen

 As you read, continue to mark the text and make notes:

- Literary concepts and terms you observe in the narrative. Do any of your earlier thoughts need revision?
- Instances of **epic simile**.
- **Epithets** to add to your running list.
- Passages reflecting on the value of **hearth and home**.

Discuss this week's reading with your teacher, along with all your notes and observations. Narrate the main action of the book, and discuss any parts you did not understand. How was this reading **delightful**? What **wisdom** does this reading furnish?

Lesson 21.2

Language Logic

SYNTAX – SENTENCE ELEMENTS

 Study/review these lessons in *Sentence Sense*.

II. Syntax – The Sentence
- ◆ 9.2A Words as Elements
- ◆ 9.2B Phrases as Elements
- ◆ 9.2C Clauses as Elements
- ◆ 9.6A and 9.6B Phrases
- ◆ 9.7A and 9.7B Clauses

DIAGRAMMING & PARSING

Writer's Journal

 In your Writer's Journal, copy these sentences. Mark the prepositional phrases, subjects, and verbs. Bracket the clauses. Classify the sentence as simple, compound, complex, or compound-complex. Then diagram each one. Refer to *Sentence Sense* as needed.

1. Liars are not believed even when they speak the truth.

2. One hour beheld him since the tide he stemmed,

    Disguised, discovered, conquering, ta'en, condemned;

    A chief on land, and outlaw on the deep,

    Destroying, saving, prisoned, and asleep. — Byron

 Orally parse these words with your teacher, using the charts in *Sentence Sense* to guide you.

(1) even, when, they, speak; (2) since, stemmed, chief, on the deep, saving

Lesson 21.3

Eloquent Expression

COPIA OF CONSTRUCTION: SENTENCE STRUCTURE – SUBORDINATE AND PRINCIPAL CLAUSES

Clauses can sometimes be switched by classification. The principal clause can be made subordinate, and vice versa.

When it arrived, your letter brought joy to Erasmus.

Your letter, which brought joy to Erasmus, arrived today.

Your letter, which was filled with glad tidings, brought joy to Erasmus.

Your letter was filled with glad tidings, which brought joy to Erasmus.

As you can see in the examples above, the meaning or emphasis of the sentence may change a little (or a lot!), which may or may not be a good thing. Check the meaning of the rewritten sentence carefully to make sure it says what you want it to say.

❧ Paraphrase each sentence, switching principal and subordinate clauses.

For without friends no one would choose to live, though he had all other goods; even rich men and those in possession of office and of dominating power are thought to need friends most of all; for what is the use of such prosperity without the opportunity of beneficence, which is exercised chiefly and in its most laudable form towards friends?

Writer's Journal

LITERARY IMITATION

❧ Work with any sentence that you have diagrammed in this course for which you have not already done a literary imitation. Copy the **diagram skeleton**, construct a new sentence, and write the new sentence below the diagram. Your new sentence should be one you could use in your fable.

Lesson 21.4

Classical Composition

PROGYMNASMA NARRATIVE: PLOT OBSERVATION – THEON'S SIX AND SUMMARY

Observe and summarize Homer's *Odyssey*, Book Nineteen. Refer to the instructions and example in the Appendix under "Narrative Plot Observation" and "Example Narrative Plot Observation."

Writer's Journal

- Complete the steps for Plot Observation – Theon's Six on the original narrative and in your Writer's Journal.

- Write a one paragraph summary of this book, following the steps for Plot Observation – Summary. Work either in your Writer's Journal or on the computer. Add this summary to your running file of *Odyssey* summaries, and save the file.

ORIGINAL FABLE: PLAN

Now you will compose your own fable in the spirit of Aesop, illustrating the wisdom the proverb you chose in Lesson 21.1.

Writer's Journal

- In your Writer's Journal, write an outline for your own original fable following the template listed below. Work on this assignment over several days.

  I.   **Exposition**: present the characters and setting (Person, Place, Time)
  II. **Conflict**: complicate the situation with a catalyst; develop rising action, climax, and falling action (Action, Cause, Manner)
  III. **Denouement**: resolve the story with consequences, a reversal, and/or an epiphany (Action, Cause, Manner)

ORIGINAL FABLE: WRITE

- Write your fable. It should be brief (around 300-400 words). Some of your outline points may be covered in two or three sentences. Quote the proverb at the end of the fable as a moral. Include the following figures:

  ◆ simile

- ◆ parallelism
- ◆ at least one other figure of speech
- ◆ at least two figures of description

ORIGINAL FABLE: REVISE

Revise your elaboration using the checklist below. Work through the checklist once on your own, and then a second time with your writing mentor, making notes on the print copy of your narrative. Transfer all additions and corrections from your print copy to the computer file. Save and print the document.

Editor's Pen – The Big Picture

✓ Message: *aptly illustrates the wisdom of the proverb/moral*

✓ All major plot elements included:

   I. Exposition: present characters

   II. Conflict: develop catalyst, rising action, climax, and falling action

   III. Denouement: resolve with consequences, a reversal, and/or an epiphany

✓ Length: 300-400 words

✓ Figure of Speech: *simile, parallelism, and one other figure of speech*

✓ Figures of Description (choose two): *anemographia, chronographia, astrothesia, topographia, hydrographia*

✓ Title & Header: incorporates *parallelism, antithesis, and/or alliteration*

✓ Moral: *proverb quoted at the end of the fable*

Editor's Pen – Zoom 5x: Paragraphs

Refer to Copia In Your Writing (Prose & Poetry Handbook or Appendix) as needed

✓ Flow of ideas: *smooth and interesting*

✓ Length: *neither too wordy nor too short*

✓ Sentence class by use: *effective use*

✓ Sentence openers: *varied*

✓ Sentence class by form and length: *varied*

✓ Dialogue: *as needed*

✓ Verb Tense: *consistent past except dialogue*

✓ Point of View: *3rd person except dialogue*

✓ Tone: *storytelling informal*

Editor's Pen – Zoom 10x: Sentences

Refer to Copia In Your Writing (Prose & Poetry Handbook or Appendix) as needed

✓ Complete thought expressed

✓ Subject and predicate agree in number

✓ Correct capitalization and punctuation

   ◆ No comma splices!

✓ Items in a series constructed in parallel form

Editor's Pen – Fine Focus: Words

✓ Word choices varied; word meanings clear; consider denotation AND connotation

   ◆ Verbs: *strong, specific, fitting, mostly active (vs. passive); appropriate adverbs if needed*

   ◆ Nouns: *clear, descriptive; appropriate adjectives if needed*

   ◆ Dialogue: *dialogue tags varied as needed*

✓ Correct spelling

✓ Final read-through

If possible, present your fable by reading it aloud dramatically before an audience.

For an extra challenge, consider turning your fable into a narrative poem. Also consider drawing or painting a series of illustrations. If you are really inspired, you could even create your own little book online at a photo printing site.

Lesson 21.5

Reflection & Review

Commonplace Book

COMMONPLACE BOOK

Enter in your Commonplace Book:

   ◆ a favorite passage or two from your reading in Homer's *Odyssey*

   ◆ an example or two of epithet and/or epic simile

   ◆ a few lines of poetry from your anthology (identify meter)

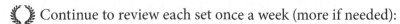

◆ examples from your reading of other figures you have learned (see Figures and Literary Devices list in *Poetics & Progym I* Appendix)

MEMORY WORK

◯ Continue to review each set once a week (more if needed):

- Parts of Speech – *Bards & Poets* Review
- Sentence Terms – *Bards & Poets* Review
- Noun Terms – *Poetics & Progym I*
- Verb Terms – *Poetics & Progym I*
- Modifier Terms – *Poetics & Progym I*
- Pronoun Terms – *Poetics & Progym I*
- Figures – Set #1 – *Poetics & Progym I*
- Figures – Set #2 – *Poetics & Progym I*
- Figures – Set #3 – *Poetics & Progym I*

Lesson 22

ॐ

THE SPACIOUS FIRMAMENT ON HIGH

The spacious firmament on high,

With all the blue ethereal sky,

And spangled heavens, a shining frame,

Their great Original proclaim.

The unwearied sun from day to day

Does his Creator's power display;

And publishes to every land

The work of an almighty hand.

Soon as the evening shades prevail,

The moon takes up the wondrous tale,

And nightly to the listening earth

Repeats the story of her birth;

While all the stars that round her burn,

And all the planets, in their turn,

Confirm the tidings, as they roll

And spread the truth from pole to pole.

What though in solemn silence all

Move round the dark terrestrial ball?

What though no real voice nor sound

Amid their radiant orbs be found?

In reason's ear they all rejoice,

And utter forth a glorious voice;

For ever singing as they shine,

'The hand that made us is divine.'

— JOSEPH ADDISON, 1712

ℭℜ

Lesson 22.1

Prose & Poetry

LITERARY ELEMENTS IN THE POEM: THE SPACIOUS FIRMAMENT ON HIGH

1 Read

◆ Follow along and listen carefully as the poem is read aloud, OR read it aloud yourself. Read it at least two or three times. **Delight** in the meter, the rhyme, and the images.

2 Inquire

◆ Does the **title** give any hint as to the content or message of the poem? If this work was published by the poet in a larger book or anthology, does that title give any hint?

◆ Are there any unfamiliar persons, places, or things mentioned in the poem? Discuss these with your teacher.

◆ Look up the meaning of any words in the work that are not familiar to you; conduct a complete Vocabulary Study for **key words**.

◆ Was there any part of the poem you did not understand? If so, discuss this with your teacher and classmates.

3 Observe the Invention, Arrangement, and Style
◆ **Lyrical Elements**
- What does the poet describe?
- Does the poet make you see, hear, smell, taste, or touch anything?
- Does the poet compare something in the poem to some other thing?

- **Narrative Elements** Does this poem tell a story? If so, observe the
  - **Setting** When and where does this story take place?
  - **Characters** Who is (are) the main character(s) in this story?
  - **Conflict** What is the main problem or crisis for the character(s)?
  - **Resolution** Is the problem solved? If so, how? If not, why not?
  - **Sequence** Is this story told *ab ovo*, or *in medias res*, or some other way?
  - **Point of View** Identify the **person** (and **level of omniscience** if applicable).
- **Figures** Look for figures of speech and figures of description. (See Appendix for the list of figures taught in *Poetics & Progym*.) Why did the poet choose these particular figures?

4 Investigate the Context

- Research a bit about the poet. Make notes in your Writer's Journal about Joseph Addison's
  - **Origin** Who were the poet's parents/ancestors? Where was his homeland?
  - **Historical Time Period** When did the poet live? What events happened around the time that the poet lived?
  - **Influences** What education, training, books, ideas, and other people or events shaped the poet's thinking?
- **Rhetorical Situation**
  - **Exigency** – What is the issue, problem, or situation to be addressed?
  - **Audience** – Who is the author addressing in order to change or persuade?
  - **Constraint** What are the requirements based on the audience and the occasion?
- **Identify the poem's Literary Genre**
  - **Genre by literary period** In which century (time period) and country was this work written?
  - **Genre by poetic/narrative category** Is this poem chiefly **lyrical** (describes an event, or a person, or a feeling, or a time and place, etc., but it does not tell a particular story) or **narrative** (tells a story)? If narrative, is it primarily **non-fiction** (a story that really happened) or **fiction** (a story told as if it really happened)?

5 Connect the Thoughts

- Does this poem remind you of other poems, or of stories with similar plots, messages, or characters?
- Does this poem remind you of any proverbs or other well-known quotations? If so, enter these in your Commonplace Book.

6 Profit and Delight

- ◆ **Delight** What are the sources of delight in this poem?

- ◆ **Wisdom** What wisdom does this poem furnish?

- ◆ **Read** the poem to your teacher with expression and proper pauses.

- ◆ **Read** other works by this poet.

- ◆ **Memorize** this poem and recite it before an audience.

THE ODYSSEY

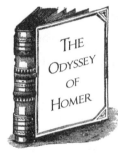

◆ Read

- ◆ *The Odyssey of Homer*, Book Twenty

◆ As you read, continue to mark the text and make notes:

- ◆ Literary concepts and terms you observe in the narrative. Do any of your earlier thoughts need revision?
- ◆ Instances of **epic simile**.
- ◆ **Epithets** to add to your running list.
- ◆ Passages reflecting on the value of **hearth and home**.

Writer's Journal

◆ Discuss this week's reading with your teacher, along with all your notes and observations. Narrate the main action of the book, and discuss any parts you did not understand. How was this reading **delightful**? What **wisdom** does this reading furnish?

HYMNS

Hymns are songs of praise. Although the word *hymn* technically can refer to any song of praise, we generally think of hymns as songs written specifically for the corporate worship of God by Christians.

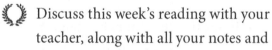

A Christian hymn is a lyric poem, reverently and devotionally conceived, which is designed to be sung and which expresses the worshiper's attitude toward God . . .

— Carl F. Price

Hymn lyrics are also poems. Many hymns were originally composed as poems and later set to music. Because hymn lyrics are also poems, we can scan them, analyze the stanza form, and note the rhyme scheme just as we do for any poem.

🏵 Browse through your hymnal, and look at a few familiar hymns. You will see the name and date the **lyrics** were written, along with the name of the **tune**, its composer, and the date it was written. The lyrics and the tune may have been composed centuries apart.

In Lesson 12.1, you entered information on hymns. Now we will explain what you entered more fully. In the hymnal, you probably noticed numbers separated by periods for each hymn. These numbers indicate the **metrical notation.** This is measured by the number of beats in a line without regard to the stress patterns. The number of beats usually corresponds to the number of syllables in the line. A hymn with the metrical notation 8.8.8.8 is one that has four lines of eight syllables in each stanza:

> All pe-ople that on earth do dwell
>
> Sing to the Lord with cheer-ful voice.
>
> Him serve with fear, His praise forth tell;
>
> Come ye be-fore Him and re-joice.

> — lyrics based on Psalm 100, by William Kethe, 1561

Most hymnals have a Metrical Index that lists tunes by meter. You will find many metrical notations listed there, but three are used so often that they have names: **Long Meter** (8.8.8.8), **Short Meter** (6.6.8.6), and **Common Meter** (8.6.8.6). These are often abbreviated to **LM**, **SM**, and **CM**.

🏵 What is the metrical notation and name for "The Spacious Firmament on High"?

🏵 In your hymnal, find one example of each of these meters. Note the name of the hymn, the author, the name of the tune, and the metrical notation (including name) in your Writer's Journal.

Writer's Journal

You probably also noticed that there are variations on these common meters. Some of these meters are **Doubled**, so there are eight lines following the metrical pattern, such as 8.6.8.6.8.6.8.6. Sometimes these meters have a **Refrain**, a recurring phrase or line, that follows each stanza, but that has a different metrical pattern. Some meters will have **Alleluias** with a different metrical pattern following each stanza.

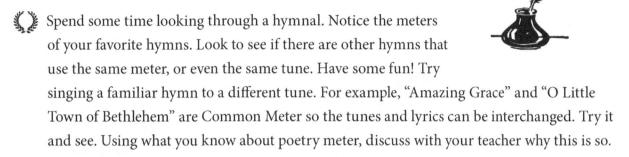

Prose & Poetry
Handbook

◯ Make the entry indicated below in the Figures division.

   ◆ Refrain P&P 73: Skip a line after the last entry, add <u>Refrain</u> and
     its definition.

◯ Spend some time looking through a hymnal. Notice the meters
   of your favorite hymns. Look to see if there are other hymns that
   use the same meter, or even the same tune. Have some fun! Try
   singing a familiar hymn to a different tune. For example, "Amazing Grace" and "O Little
   Town of Bethlehem" are Common Meter so the tunes and lyrics can be interchanged. Try it
   and see. Using what you know about poetry meter, discuss with your teacher why this is so.

SCANSION AND ANALYSIS: THE SPACIOUS FIRMAMENT ON HIGH

◯ Scan and analyze the poetic form of the stanzas below.

   A. Scan the lines. Note there are some added unstressed syllables in a few feet, as well as
      some elision.

   B. Mark the end rhyme. Name the rhyme scheme:

   C. Write the stanza name, along with any form/genre designation that may apply:

The spacious firmament on high,

Wth all the blue ethereal sky,

And spangled heavens, a shining frame,

Their great Original proclaim.

The unwearied sun from day to day

Does his Creator's power display;

And publishes to every land

The work of an almighty hand.

Lesson 22.2

Language Logic

SYNTAX – SENTENCE ELEMENTS

 Study/review these lessons in *Sentence Sense.*

II. Syntax – The Sentence

- ◆ 9.2D Kinds of Elements
- ◆ 9.4B and 9.4C Simple and Complete Subjects *Note that we have been identifying grammatical (simple) subjects and predicates throughout this course when we underline the subject and double underline the verb.*
- ◆ 9.5.B and 9.5C Simple and Complete Predicates

DIAGRAMMING & PARSING

Writer's Journal

 In your Writer's Journal, copy this sentence. Mark the prepositional phrases, subjects, and verbs. Bracket the clauses. Classify the sentence as simple, compound, complex, or compound-complex. Then diagram it. Refer to *Sentence Sense* as needed.

Soon as the evening shades prevail,

The moon takes up the wondrous tale,

And nightly to the listening earth

Repeats the story of her birth;

While all the stars that round her burn,

And all the planets, in their turn,

Confirm the tidings, as they roll

And spread the truth from pole to pole.

 Orally parse these words with your teacher, using the charts in *Sentence Sense* to guide you.

shades, prevail, nightly. listening, of her birth, while, burn, confirm, tidings

Lesson 22.3

Eloquent Expression

COPIA OF CONSTRUCTION: SENTENCE STRUCTURE – POSITION OF WORDS, PHRASES, AND CLAUSES

Adjective elements can be moved within the sentence, but in a limited way. They almost always stay very near the noun or pronoun that they modify. In English prose, descriptive adjectives are usually placed immediately before the noun that they modify, but they can also be placed after (what figure of speech is this?).

> Your delightful letter has arrived.

> Your letter, delightful to me, arrived.

In the second sentence, the addition of the words *to me* clarifies that it is an adjective, and not the name of the letter.

Relocating a participial phrase to the beginning of a sentence is an effective device to vary your sentence opening words. Remember to always avoid dangling participles!

> Erasmus, having received your letter, was filled with great joy.

> Having received your letter, Erasmus was filled with great joy.

Moving clauses around in the sentence is another effective way to vary opening words and sentence structure. Clauses that are adjective elements usually need to remain close to the noun or pronoun they modify in order to avoid dangling.

> Your letter was filled with glad tidings, which brought joy to Erasmus.

> Your letter, which brought joy to Erasmus, was filled with glad tidings.

Notice that moving this clause makes it modify a different noun. The meaning is changed slightly; in the first sentence it is the tidings in the letter that bring joy, in the second it is the letter itself. Always check to make sure your revised sentence expresses your meaning accurately.

Adverb elements can be moved more freely, but again, always check the meaning:

> I received your letter joyfully.

> Joyfully, I received your letter.

I received your letter <u>with great joy</u>.

<u>With great joy</u>, I received your letter.

<u>When it arrived</u>, your letter brought joy to Erasmus.

Your letter, <u>when it arrived</u>, brought joy to Erasmus.

Your letter brought joy to Erasmus <u>when it arrived</u>.

Paraphrase each sentence, moving adjective and adverb elements to a different positions. Add commas and adjust other words if needed. Be careful to check that the resulting sentences retain the same sense and are grammatically correct.

For without friends no one would choose to live, though he had all other goods; even rich men and those in possession of office and of dominating power are thought to need friends most of all; for what is the use of such prosperity without the opportunity of beneficence, which is exercised chiefly and in its most laudable form towards friends?

Writer's Journal

Lesson 22.4

Classical Composition

PROGYMNASMA NARRATIVE: PLOT OBSERVATION – THEON'S SIX AND SUMMARY
Observe and summarize Homer's *Odyssey*, Book Twenty. Refer to the instructions and example in the Appendix under "Narrative Plot Observation" and "Example Narrative Plot Observation."

Complete the steps for Plot Observation – Theon's Six on the original narrative and in your Writer's Journal.

Writer's Journal

Write a one paragraph summary of this book, following the steps for Plot Observation – Summary. Work either in your Writer's Journal or on the computer. Add this summary to your running file of *Odyssey* summaries, and save the file.

HYMN COMPOSITION

Write your own hymn in imitation of the lines that you diagrammed from the hymn "The Spacious Firmament on High" in Lesson 22.2.

Writer's Journal

◯ Copy the lines into your Writer's Journal. If you have trouble getting started, try copying the diagram skeleton and using it to begin to construct your own lines. List possible rhyming words, and write words and phrases to fit the meter. Use a rhyming dictionary and a thesaurus as needed.

◯ When you are satisfied with your imitation, type the final version on the computer. Title it, add your byline, and note below your poem that it is an imitation of "The Spacious Firmament On High."

Lesson 22.5

Reflection & Review

Commonplace Book

COMMONPLACE BOOK

◯ Enter in your Commonplace Book:

- ◆ a favorite passage or two from your reading in Homer's *Odyssey*
- ◆ an example or two of epithet and/or epic simile
- ◆ a few lines of poetry from your anthology (identify meter)
- ◆ examples from your reading of other figures you have learned
  (see Figures and Literary Devices list in *Poetics & Progym I* Appendix)

BOOK OF CENTURIES

◯ Record in your Book of Centuries:

- ◆ Joseph Addison

MEMORY WORK

GRAMMAR
FLASHCARDS

Continue to review each set once a week (more if needed):

- Parts of Speech – *Bards & Poets* Review
- Sentence Terms – *Bards & Poets* Review
- Noun Terms – *Poetics & Progym I*
- Verb Terms – *Poetics & Progym I*
- Modifier Terms – *Poetics & Progym I*
- Pronoun Terms – *Poetics & Progym I*
- Figures – Set #1 – *Poetics & Progym I*
- Figures – Set #2 – *Poetics & Progym I*
- Figures – Set #3 – *Poetics & Progym I*

☙

"THE ADMIRABLE LIGHT OF TRUTH"

from INSTITUTES OF THE CHRISTIAN RELIGION
by John Calvin

Therefore, in reading profane authors, the admirable light of truth displayed in them should remind us, that the human mind, however much fallen and perverted from its original integrity, is still adorned and invested with admirable gifts from its Creator. If we reflect that the Spirit of God is the only fountain of truth, we will be careful, as we would avoid offering insult to him, not to reject or condemn truth wherever it appears. In despising the gifts, we insult the Giver. How, then, can we deny that truth must have beamed on those ancient lawgivers who arranged civil order and discipline with so much equity? Shall we say that the philosophers, in their exquisite researches and skilful description of nature, were blind? Shall we deny the possession of intellect to those who drew up rules for discourse, and taught us to speak in accordance with reason? Shall we say that those who, by the cultivation of the medical art, expended their industry in our behalf were only raving? What shall we say of the mathematical sciences? Shall we deem them to be the dreams of madmen? Nay, we cannot read the writings of the ancients on these subjects without the highest admiration; an admiration which their excellence will not allow us to withhold. But shall we deem anything to be noble and praiseworthy, without tracing it to the hand of God? Far from us be such ingratitude; an ingratitude not chargeable even on heathen poets, who acknowledged that philosophy and laws, and all useful arts were the inventions of the gods. Therefore, since it is manifest that men whom the Scriptures term carnal, are so acute and clear-sighted in the investigation of inferior things, their example should teach us how many gifts the Lord has left in possession of human nature, notwithstanding of its having been despoiled of the true good.

— BOOK II

CR

Lesson 23.1

Prose & Poetry

LITERARY ELEMENTS IN PROSE: JOHN CALVIN ON READING PAGAN AUTHORS

In the third century after Christ, Tertullian posed the question, "What hath Jerusalem to do with Athens?" This question has been echoed throughout the ages of Christendom, and is still being asked today, usually without the figurative language: "Why should Christians read the pagan classics?" Our selection is sixteenth century pastor and theologian John Calvin's answer to that question.

1 **Read**
   ◆ Read the selection aloud, preferably in a group setting. **Delight** in the well-chosen words.

2 **Inquire**
   ◆ Does the **title** give any hint as to the content or message of the passage? If this work was published by the author in a larger book or anthology, does that title give any hint?
   ◆ Look up the meaning of any words in the work that are not familiar to you; conduct a complete Vocabulary Study for **key words.** What does Calvin mean by *profane*? It has a different connotation today than it did in his day. Do a little etymology research so that you understand his meaning. Neither he nor we are suggesting that you make a habit of reading authors who use foul and offensive language!
   ◆ Research unfamiliar persons, places, or things mentioned in the work.
   ◆ State your first impression of the author's **message**.

3 **Observe the Invention, Arrangement, and Style**
   ◆ What is the topic of this passage? Outline its main points.
   ◆ **Point of View** Identify the **person** (P&P 50)

♦ Identify the **Figures** – both **figures of speech** and **figures of description** (See the list of figures in the Appendix.) Why did the author choose these particular figures?

4 Investigate the Context

♦ Research a bit about the author. Make notes in your Writer's Journal about John Calvin's

Writer's Journal

- **Origin** – Who were the author's parents/ancestors? Where was his homeland?
- **Historical Time Period** – When did the author live?
- **Influences** What education, training, people, events, books, or ideas shaped the author's thinking?

♦ **Rhetorical Situation** (P&P 2) Research Calvin's *Institutes* to see what his overall aim was. Answer the questions below based on the passage under study.

- **Exigency** – What is the issue, problem, or situation to be addressed? How does the author want the reader to respond?
- **Audience** – Who is the author addressing in order to change or persuade?
- **Constraint** What are the requirements based on the audience and the genre?

5 Respond

♦ State the message of the passage. Revisit your first impression. Has your interpretation changed?

♦ Paraphrase, summarize and/or write a précis of this passage.

6 Connect the Thoughts

♦ Does this passage remind you of other things you have **Read** in Scripture, literature, history, etc?

♦ Does this passage remind you of any proverbs or other well-known quotations? If so, enter these in your Commonplace Book.

Commonplace Book

7 Profit and Delight

♦ What are the sources of **delight** in this work?

♦ What **wisdom** does this work furnish?

♦ **Discuss** this work **in community** with family, friends, classmates.

♦ **Memorize** a portion of this work and recite it before an audience.

THE ODYSSEY

THE ODYSSEY OF HOMER

❂ Read

- *The Odyssey of Homer,* Book Twenty-One

❂ As you read, continue to mark the text and make notes:

- Literary concepts and terms you observe in the narrative. Do any of your earlier thoughts need revision?
- Instances of **epic simile**.
- **Epithets** to add to your running list.
- Passages reflecting on the value of **hearth and home**.

Writer's Journal

❂ Discuss this week's reading with your teacher, along with all your notes and observations. Narrate the main action of the book, and discuss any parts you did not understand. How was this reading **delightful**? What **wisdom** does this reading furnish?

Lesson 23.2

Language Logic

DIAGRAMMING & PARSING

❂ In your Writer's Journal, copy this sentence. Mark the prepositional phrases, subjects, and verbs. Bracket the clauses. Classify the sentence as simple, compound, complex, or compound-complex. Then diagram it. Refer to *Sentence Sense* as needed. Hint: Although you might think at first that the pronoun *us* in this sentence is the direct object of *should remind*, it is in fact an indirect object, telling to whom the reminder is "given."

Writer's Journal

So, what is the direct object of *should remind*? Also, *fallen* and *perverted* are both modified by *however much* and by *from its original integrity*. You may need to be creative in showing these relationships. See the answer key if you just cannot figure it out.

Therefore, in reading profane authors, the admirable light of truth displayed in them should remind us, that the human mind, however much fallen and perverted from its original integrity, is still adorned and invested with admirable gifts from its Creator.

Orally parse these words with your teacher, using the charts in *Sentence Sense* to guide you.

Therefore, reading, admirable, should remind, however, from its original integrity, is adorned, gifts, its

Lesson 23.3

Eloquent Expression

COPIA OF CONSTRUCTION: SENTENCE STRUCTURE – WORDS, PHRASES, CLAUSES

An **adjective element** is a word or group of words that modifies a noun or pronoun. Adjective elements can be constructed as **words, phrases**, or **clauses**. Study the underlined adjective elements in the sentences below. Notice how the same thought can be expressed with a word, a phrase, or a clause.

Erasmus, joyful, received your letter.

Filled with joy, Erasmus received your letter.

Erasmus, who was filled with joy, received your letter.

You probably already do this kind of switch without even thinking about it when you convert possessive nouns and pronouns, **words** that are adjective elements, to a **phrase** using the preposition *of*. (With pronouns, remember to make sure the antecedent is clear!)

Your letter pleased me greatly. That letter of yours pleased me greatly.

The contents of the letter pleased me. The letter's contents pleased me.

An **adverb element** is a word or group of words that modifies a verb (or verbal!), an adjective, or another adverb. Adverb elements may also be constructed as **words, phrases**, or **clauses**.

Your letter brought Erasmus joy immediately.

Your letter brought Erasmus joy upon its arrival.

Your letter brought Erasmus joy when it arrived.

So here is yet another tool for writing excellent sentences and adding interest to your narrative: experiment with switching words, phrases, and clauses for adjective and adverb elements. The lists below show the different types of words, phrases, and clauses that can be adjectival and adverb elements.

ADJECTIVE ELEMENTS
Words
- ✓ Adjective
- ✓ Possessive Noun or Pronoun
- ✓ Appositive
- ✓ Participle

Phrases
- ✓ Prepositional Phrase
- ✓ Appositive Phrase
- ✓ Participial Phrase
- ✓ Infinitive Phrase

Clauses
- ✓ Relative Clause

ADVERB ELEMENTS
Words
- ✓ Adverb

Phrases
- ✓ Prepositional Phrase
- ✓ Infinitive Phrase

Clauses
- ✓ Adverbial Clause

Paraphrase each sentence two times by changing words to phrases and clauses, phrases to words and clauses, and clauses to words and phrases.

1. The profane authors sometimes display an admirable light of truth.

2. The Spirit of God is the only fountain of truth.

3. We must give that admiration which their excellence will not allow us to withhold.

Writer's Journal

LITERARY IMITATION

Work with the sentence that you diagrammed in Language Logic. Copy the **diagram skeleton**, construct a new sentence, and write the new sentence below the diagram. The topic of your new sentence is the relation between habit and character formation.

Lesson 23.4

Classical Composition

PROGYMNASMA NARRATIVE: PLOT OBSERVATION – THEON'S SIX AND SUMMARY

Observe and summarize Homer's *Odyssey*, Book Twenty-One. Refer to the instructions and example in the Appendix under "Narrative Plot Observation" and "Example Narrative Plot Observation."

- Complete the steps for Plot Observation – Theon's Six on the original narrative and in your Writer's Journal.

Writer's Journal

- Write a one paragraph summary of this book, following the steps for Plot Observation – Summary. Work either in your Writer's Journal or on the computer. Add this summary to your running file of *Odyssey* summaries, and save the file.

ANECDOTE/PROVERB ELABORATION AND THE EXPOSITORY ESSAY

An **essay** is a common academic assignment. The English word essay has its roots in the Latin word *exigere*, which literally means *to drive out*, but is often translated *measure, weigh, test,* or *examine*. This is precisely what essays are designed to do in the academic setting – to cause you to measure, weigh, test, and examine ideas about a given topic. The word **expository** also comes to us from the Latin, meaning "to set forth." An **expository essay** is one which puts forth or presents information, analysis, or explanation pertaining to your topic.

An expository essay is a good tool for evaluating a student's comprehension of a topic, so in addition to being a stand-alone writing assignment, expository writing shows up frequently in the form of essay questions on an exam. Standardized testing and college applications also utilitze the expository essay to evaluate a student's composition skills.

The ancient Anecdote/Proverb elaboration provides excellent invention and arrangement guidelines for an expository essay. Academic writing has some particular style conventions that must be observed, and we will highlight some of those requirements as we go. But remember that while academic writing is important, it is limited to your academic career. Beyond that, style conventions vary greatly. Our goal at Cottage Press is to produce ready scribes for every writing need, so remember this cardinal principle of composition: *Know your audience!* Adjust your style accordingly.

Just like a fable or a narrative, every academic essay will have a beginning (introduction), a middle (body), and an end (conclusion). The **introduction** tells what the main point or message of your essay will be. The **body** supports your main point with logical reasoning, illustrations, and analogies to make your main point more clear and concrete. The **conclusion** restates your main point and often goes on fix the reader's attention on a larger purpose, such as an exhortation or encouragement to change his/her thinking and/or behavior.

In more colloquial terms, you

"tell 'em what you're gonna tell 'em;

tell 'em;

then tell 'em what you told 'em."

The introduction "tells 'em what you are gonna tell 'em," the body "tells 'em," and the conclusion "tells 'em what you told 'em."

This chart shows how the topics of the ancient Anecdote/Proverb elaboration may help with invention – arrangement for an academic essay.

The Academic Essay, Classically Considered

	ANCIENT ANECDOTE (PROVERB) ELABORATION
I. INTRODUCTION	Encomion Paraphrase
II. BODY	Cause Contrast Comparison Example Authority*
III. CONCLUSION	Authority* Exhortation

Authority may be effective in the body and/or in the conclusion.

Prose & Poetry
Handbook

◯ Enter the following item in the Rhetoric Section.

♦ The Academic Essay, Classically Considered, P&P 17: (Copy the
   completed chart in the Appendix, not the one in this lesson!)
   Title The Academic Essay, Classically Considered.
   Construct the entire chart, with the column headings at the top
   and the row headings on the side, but only fill out the topics
   in the Anecdote Proverb column for now. Leave room for all
   the rest of the topics, which you will complete as you work through the following levels of
   Poetics & Progym.

EXPOSITORY ESSAY FROM ANECDOTE ELABORATION

◯ Study this example academic expository essay, rewritten from a Proverb elaboration. Notice
   how some of the ancient elaboration paragraphs are combined and some sentences are
   struck for the sake of concision.

Consider the Consequences and Act Accordingly

The fables of Aesop offer invaluable insights into human behavior. His simple, yet unforgettable
stories have endured through the ages. Though only a slave in ancient Greece, Aesop continues to
influence the English language to this day, since many of the pithy proverbs that conclude his fables
have become idiomatic, encouraging people everywhere to tell the truth, avoid temptation, resist
pride, and much more. Aesop's wisdom is aptly displayed in the words "Look before you leap."
Careful consideration before pursuing a particular course of action is prudent.

One must consider possible adverse consequences of a particular action to avoid unexpected
pitfalls. This is true not only when making decisions in matters of great importance, but also in
seemingly small or mundane matters. In either situation, unanticipated outcomes may prove
costly or even dangerous. Further, those who rush into an action without due consideration are left
without resource when unexpected obstacles surface. Aesop clearly had these things in mind when
he called for the necessity of thinking ahead.

A person who plans before committing to a course of action will avoid running out of resources
or facing unintended consequences. What person in his right mind would begin to build a house
without first making a careful blueprint? He must budget the necessary funds and forsee possible
hindrances. In the same way, a comprehensive plan is the crucial first step for any course of action.

In the fable that gave rise to this proverb, Aesop himself provides the perfect illustration. A goat
came upon a well into which a fox had fallen. The goat inquired of the fox whether the water was

good. Seeing a way of escape, the crafty fox encouraged the goat to come and see for himself. The foolish goat, impulsively heedless of everything but his thirst, jumped into the well. Whereupon the fox promptly vaulted onto the goat's back and used him as a ladder to escape, leaving the goat stranded in the well.

Other revered thinkers have echoed Aesop's wisdom in this matter. The great American statesman Benjamin Franklin echoed Aesop's warning when he said, "By failing to plan, you are planning to fail." The nineteenth century author of the French literary masterpiece *Les Miserables*, Victor Hugo, also agreed when he said "Caution is the eldest child of wisdom." Indeed, every thinking person must agree with this judicious advice of Aesop: evaluate each and every course of action with great care, and act accordingly.

Rework your Anecdote elaboration on Plutarch's definition of charater into a modern five-paragraph persuasive essay with the topic.

What is the effect of habit on character formation?

A. Open the file with your final elaboration of "Plutarch said character is habit long continued."

B. Create the introduction paragraph. Combine your Encomion and Paraphrase paragraphs into a one-paragraph introduction. Include the quoted anecdote (state the proverb/anecdote), a praise of the one who said it (Encomion), and an explanation of what habit and character are in general terms (Paraphrase). End the introduction with a **thesis statement** expressing connection between habit and character.

C. Create three body paragraphs. Choose the strongest topics from your Proverb elaboration for your body paragraphs. For instance, you may choose your Cause, Comparison, and Example paragraphs. Alternately, you may combine some paragraphs, such as Cause and Contrast. For this essay, use the Authority paragraph as part of your conclusion. Paragraphs in this essay should be roughly the same length. Each of your body paragraphs should be no less than three sentences, and no longer than five.

D. Create a one-paragraph conclusion by combining Authority with Exhortation.

E. Develop a title for your essay. You may use the title from your elaboration, or make up a new one. Use parallelism, antithesis, and/or alliteration. Include a heading for your essay, following this format:

ভ

SENECA ON FRIENDSHIP
from SENECA, EPISTLES

You have sent a letter to me through the hand of a "friend" of yours, as you call him. And in your very next sentence you warn me not to discuss with him all the matters that concern you, saying that even you yourself are not accustomed to do this; in other words, you have in the same letter affirmed and denied that he is your friend. Now if you used this word of ours in the popular sense, and called him "friend" in the same way in which we speak of all candidates for election as "honourable gentlemen," and as we greet all men whom we meet casually, if their names slip us for the moment, with the salutation "my dear sir," – so be it. But if you consider any man a friend whom you do not trust as you trust yourself, you are mightily mistaken and you do not sufficiently understand what true friendship means. Indeed, I would have you discuss everything with a friend; but first of all discuss the man himself. When friendship is settled, you must trust; before friendship is formed, you must pass judgment.

Those persons indeed put last first and confound their duties, who, violating the rules of Theophrastus, judge a man after they have made him their friend, instead of making him their friend after they have judged him. Ponder for a long time whether you shall admit a given person to your friendship; but when you have decided to admit him, welcome him with all your heart and soul. Speak as boldly with him as with yourself.

As to yourself, although you should live in such a way that you trust your own self with nothing which you could not entrust even to your enemy, yet, since certain matters occur which convention keeps secret, you should share with a friend at least all your worries and reflections. Regard him as loyal, and you will make him loyal. Some, for example, fearing to be deceived, have taught men to deceive; by their suspicions they have given their friend the right to do wrong. Why need I keep back any words in the presence of my friend? Why should I not regard myself as alone when in his company?

There is a class of men who communicate, to anyone whom they meet, matters which should be revealed to friends alone, and unload upon the chance listener whatever irks them. Others, again, fear to confide in their closest intimates; and if it were possible, they would not trust even themselves, burying their secrets deep in their hearts. But we should do neither. It is equally faulty to trust everyone and to trust no one. Yet the former fault is, I should say, the more ingenuous, the latter the more safe. In like manner you should rebuke these two kinds of men, – both those who always lack repose, and those who are always in repose. For love of bustle is not industry, – it is only the restlessness of a hunted mind. And true repose does not consist in condemning all motion as merely vexation; that kind of repose is slackness and inertia. Therefore, you should note the following saying, taken from my reading in Pomponius: "Some men shrink into dark corners, to such a degree that they see darkly by day." No, men should combine these tendencies, and he who reposes should act and be who acts should take repose. Discuss the problem with Nature; she will tell you that she has created both day and night. Farewell.

— VOLUME I, EPISTLE III, LOEB CLASSICAL LIBRARY

℃ℛ

Lesson 24.1

Prose & Poetry

THE ACADEMIC ESSAY: THESIS STATEMENT

Academic expository or argumentative essays generally require a **thesis statement**. This is a sentence or two at the end of the introduction stating the central idea of your paper. It is the organizing theme of your essay. It is the main way that you "tell 'em what you're gonna tell 'em."

 Locate the thesis statement in the example essay from Lesson 23. It is the final sentence of the introductory paragraph. Underline it and write *thesis statement* in the margin next to it.

Everything else in the essay should relate in some way to your thesis statement. A good thesis statement should be:

- ◆ stated as a proposition
- ◆ specific, concrete, and literal
- ◆ supported by the rest of the essay

A **proposition** is a declarative statement that affirms or denies something about the subject. State plainly what you plan to prove in the rest of your essay. As a general rule, you should not refer to the essay or paper itself or use first person pronouns to state your thesis.[1] The affirmation or denial in your thesis statement should be specific and concrete. *Planning ahead is good* would be a poor thesis statement because it is vague and abstract. Avoid using metaphorical language; state your thesis using literal terms with no ambiguity or double meaning (hence, a proverb is generally not an appropriate thesis statement). Finally, you must support your thesis statement by developing and explaining by means of logical reasoning, evidence, and examples in the rest of the essay.

When you first begin planning an essay, you will find it helpful to construct a working thesis statement to focus your thoughts. It may well be necessary to tweak or even completely rewrite your thesis as you write, but it will give you a good starting point.

THE ACADEMIC ESSAY: TOPIC SENTENCES

Every paragraph in your essay should include a topic sentence that identifies its main idea. Each topic sentence should relate clearly to the thesis statement. The topic sentence is often the first or last sentence of the paragraph.

---

1 My son had one professor who required his students to use the words *In this paper I will demonstrate* as the beginning of the thesis statement. In a case like this, it is prudent to suspend the general rule.

Writer's
Journal

Locate the topic sentences in each body paragraph of the
example essay from Lesson 23. Underline the sentence and write
topic sentence in the margin next to each. In your Writer's
Journal, copy the thesis statement, followed by the topic
sentences from the body paragraphs. Notice how the thesis
statement and the topic sentences give a mini-outline of your
essay.

Prose & Poetry
Handbook

Enter the following items in the Rhetoric Section.

◆ Thesis Statement, P&P 19: Subtitle THESIS STATEMENT and add
"A good thesis statement should be" followed by the list of three
points. As you come across excellent thesis statements in your
reading and studies, add them to this page for inspiration.

◆ Topic Sentences, P&P 20: Subtitle TOPIC SENTENCES and then
add the definition. As you come across excellent topic sentences
in your reading and studies, add them to this page for inspiration.

LITERARY ELEMENTS IN PROSE: SENECA'S EPISTLE ON FRIENDSHIP

1 Read
◆ Read the selection aloud, preferably in a group setting. **Delight** in the
well-chosen words.

2 Inquire
◆ Look up the meaning of any words in the work that are not familiar to
you; conduct a complete Vocabulary Study for **key words.** What is an
epistle?

◆ Research unfamiliar persons, places, or things mentioned in the passage.

◆ State your first impression of the author's **message**.

3 Observe the Invention, Arrangement, and Style
◆ What is the topic of this passage? Outline its main points. Can you identify a **thesis
statement**? **topic statements**? If so, include those in your outline.

◆ **Point of View** Identify the **person** (P&P 50).

◆ Identify the **Figures** – both **figures of speech** and **figures of description** (See the list of
figures in the Appendix.) Why did the author choose these particular figures?

4 Investigate the Context

Writer's Journal

- ◆ Research a bit about the author. Make notes in your Writer's Journal about Seneca's
    - ■ **Origin** – Who were the author's parents/ancestors? Where was his homeland?
    - ■ **Historical Time Period** – When did the author live?
    - ■ **Influences** What education, training, people, events, books, or ideas shaped the author's thinking?
- ◆ **Rhetorical Situation** (P&P 2)
    - ■ **Exigency** – What is the issue, problem, or situation to be addressed? How does the author want the reader to respond?
    - ■ **Audience** – Who is the author addressing in order to change or persuade?
    - ■ **Constraint** What are the requirements based on the audience and the genre?

5 Respond

- ◆ State the message of the passage. Revisit your first impression. Has your interpretation changed?
- ◆ Paraphrase, summarize and/or write a précis of this passage.

6 Connect the Thoughts

- ◆ Does this selection remind you of other things you have **Read** in Scripture, literature, history, etc?
- ◆ Does this selection remind you of any proverbs or other well-known quotations? If so, enter these in your Commonplace Book.

Commonplace Book

7 Profit and Delight

- ◆ What are the sources of **delight** in this work?
- ◆ What **wisdom** does this work furnish?
- ◆ **Discuss** this work **in community** with family, friends, classmates.
- ◆ **Memorize** a portion of this work and recite it before an audience.

READ THE SELECTION ALOUD ONCE MORE

Writer's Journal

Though this epistle understandably does not follow all of the requirements for a modern academic essay, it is possible to identify a thesis statement in the first paragraph and topic sentences in the others, although you may not find all of them in the expected position. Underline and label the thesis statement and the topic sentences in this letter. Then list them in order in your Writing Journal. Do they give an accurate outline of the letter?

THE ODYSSEY

THE ODYSSEY OF HOMER

Read

◆ *The Odyssey of Homer*, Book Twenty-Two

As you read, continue to mark the text and make notes:

◆ Literary concepts and terms you observe in the narrative. Do any of your earlier thoughts need revision?
◆ Instances of **epic simile**.
◆ **Epithets** to add to your running list.
◆ Passages reflecting on the value of **hearth and home**.

Writer's Journal

Discuss this week's reading with your teacher, along with all your notes and observations. Narrate the main action of the book, and discuss any parts you did not understand. How was this reading **delightful**? What **wisdom** does this reading furnish?

Lesson 24.2

Language Logic

SYNTAX – CLASSES OF ELEMENTS

◯ Study/review these lessons in *Sentence Sense*.

II. Syntax – The Sentence
- ◆ 9.6B Classification of Phrases
- ◆ 9.7C Classification of Clauses

DIAGRAMMING & PARSING

Writer's Journal

◯ In your Writer's Journal, copy these sentences. Mark the prepositional phrases, subjects, and verbs. Bracket the clauses. Classify the sentence as simple, compound, complex, or compound-complex. Then diagram each one. Refer to *Sentence Sense* as needed.

1. When friendship is settled, you must trust; before friendship is formed, you must pass judgment.

2. It is equally faulty to trust everyone and to trust no one.

◯ Orally parse these words with your teacher, using the charts in *Sentence Sense* to guide you.

is settled, must trust, judgment, It, is, equally, faulty, to trust

Lesson 24.3

Eloquent Expression

COPIA OF CONSTRUCTION: SENTENCE STRUCTURE – ADJECTIVE AND ADVERB ELEMENTS

Some sentences can switch adverb elements with adjective elements to express the same, or a similar, thought.

Erasmus, joyful, received your letter.

Erasmus joyfully received your letter.

Erasmus received your letter, which filled him with joy.

When Erasmus received your letter, he was filled with joy.

First identify the class of each sentence (simple, compound, complex, compound-complex). Then, in your Writer's Journal, paraphrase the sentences by switching adverbial elements with adjective elements and vice versa.

But if you consider any man a friend whom you do not trust as you trust yourself, you are mightily mistaken and you do not sufficiently understand what true friendship means. Indeed, I would have you discuss everything with a friend; but first of all discuss the man himself. When friendship is settled, you must trust; before friendship is formed, you must pass judgment.

Writer's Journal

LITERARY IMITATION

Work with one of the sentences that you diagrammed in Language Logic. Copy the **diagram skeleton**, construct a new sentence, and write the new sentence below the diagram. The topic of your new sentence should be based on your recent reading in history or literature, or it may be a theological or philosophical reflection on a different virtue.

Lesson 24.4

Classical Composition

PROGYMNASMA NARRATIVE: PLOT OBSERVATION – THEON'S SIX AND SUMMARY

Observe and summarize Homer's *Odyssey*, Book Twenty-Two. Refer to the instructions and example in the Appendix under "Narrative Plot Observation" and "Example Narrative Plot Observation."

Complete the steps for Plot Observation – Theon's Six on the original narrative and in your Writer's Journal.

Writer's Journal

Write a one paragraph summary of this book, following the steps for Plot Observation – Summary. Work either in your Writer's Journal or on the computer. Add this summary to your running file of *Odyssey* summaries, and save the file.

EXPOSITORY ESSAY: HABIT AND CHARACTER

Continue working on your academic expository essay.

A. In your Writer's Journal, copy or create the thesis statement for the essay you began in Lesson 23. Make sure that it is stated as a proposition and is specific, concrete, and literal. Identify or write a topic statement for each body paragraph you plan to include in your essay. List all of these below your thesis statement. Does each topic sentence relate clearly to the thesis? Does this list give an accurate representation of what you will cover in your essay? If not, revise your thesis statement and topics sentences to meet these requirements.

Writer's Journal

B. Open the file with your academic essay from Lesson 23 on habit and character. Incorporate your revised thesis statement and topic sentences. Check to make sure:

- Paragraphs are roughly the same length.
- Body paragraphs should be no less than three sentences, and

no longer than five.

C. Revise your elaboration using the checklist below. Work through the checklist once on your own, and then a second time with your writing mentor, making notes on the print copy of your essay. A few items have been changed or added to this checklist to meet the modern requirements. See particularly Flow of Ideas, Point of View, and Tone in paragraph editing, and Verbs and Level of Formality in final details. Transfer all additions and corrections from your print copy to the computer file.

D. Save and print the document.

Editor's Pen – The Big Picture

✓ Invention and Arrangement:

    I. **Introduction** (one paragraph based on Encomion and Paraphrase; ends with thesis statement)

    II. **Body** (three paragraphs – proofs based on Cause, Contrast, Comparison, and/or Example)

    III. **Conclusion** (one paragraph based on Authority and Exhortation)

✓ Thesis Statement

    ◆ stated as a proposition

    ◆ specific, concrete, and literal

◆ supported by the rest of the essay

✓ Length: five paragraphs of three to five sentences each

✓ Title & Header: includes parallelism, antithesis, and/or alliteration

✓ Figures of speech (at least one instance of each): *parallelism, antithesis*

✓ Figures of speech (one or the other) *asyndeton, polysyndeton*

Editor's Pen – Zoom 5x: Paragraphs

Refer to Copia In Your Writing (Prose & Poetry Handbook or Appendix) as needed

✓ Flow of Ideas: *logical, not repetitive;*

✓ Tone: *objective, not overly emotional or superlative (the best! the most!, etc.)*

✓ Content: *supports thesis statement*

✓ Topic sentence: *clearly relates to the thesis statement and points to paragraph content*

✓ Length: *neither too wordy nor too short*

✓ Sentence class by use: *effective use*

✓ Sentence openers: *varied*

✓ Sentence length and class by form: *varied, avoid overuse of exclamatory sentences*

✓ Verb Tense: *consistent*

✓ Pronouns clear: *easily identified antecedents*

✓ Point of View: *3rd person; avoid 1st and 2nd*

Editor's Pen – Zoom 10x: Sentences
Refer to Copia In Your Writing (Prose & Poetry Handbook or Appendix) as needed

✓ Complete thought expressed

✓ Subject and predicate agree in number

✓ Correct capitalization and punctuation

　◆ No comma splices!

✓ Items in a series constructed in parallel form

Editor's Pen – Fine Focus: Words

✓ Word choices varied; word meanings clear; consider denotation AND connotation

　◆ Verbs: *strong, specific, fitting, mostly active (vs. passive); appropriate adverbs if needed*

　◆ Nouns: *clear, descriptive; appropriate adjectives if needed*

　◆ Dialogue: *n/a except for Authority*

　◆ Level of Formality: *no contractions, no informal language, no slang or overused words (lots of, cool, awesome), acronyms adequately explained*

✓ Correct spelling

✓ Final read-through

POETRY COMPOSITION

Write your own limerick. For content, use Seneca's epistle on friendship or another selection from literature or history that you have read recently.

1. Copy the lines into your Writer's Journal. Remember that a limerick is a quintain written in anapestic meter; lines 1, 2, and 5 are trimeter, lines 3 and 4 are dimeter; rhyme scheme is usually AABBA.

2. List possible rhyming words, and write words and phrases to fit the meter. Use a rhyming dictionary and a thesaurus as needed.

Writer's Journal

3. When you are satisfied with your limerick, type the final version version on the computer. Title it and add your bylineNote below your poem that it is based on an epistle from Seneca.

Reflection & Review

Commonplace
Book

COMMONPLACE BOOK

Enter in your Commonplace Book:

- ◆ a favorite passage or two from your reading in Homer's *Odyssey*
- ◆ an example or two of epithet and/or epic simile
- ◆ a few lines of poetry from your anthology (identify meter)
- ◆ examples from your reading of other figures you have learned
  (see Figures and Literary Devices list in *Poetics & Progym I* Appendix)

BOOK OF CENTURIES

Record in your Book of Centuries:

- ◆ Seneca

MEMORY WORK

GRAMMAR
FLASHCARDS

Continue to review each set once a week (more if needed):

- ◆ Parts of Speech – *Bards & Poets* Review
- ◆ Sentence Terms – *Bards & Poets* Review
- ◆ Noun Terms – *Poetics & Progym I*
- ◆ Verb Terms – *Poetics & Progym I*
- ◆ Modifier Terms – *Poetics & Progym I*
- ◆ Pronoun Terms – *Poetics & Progym I*
- ◆ Figures – Set #1 – *Poetics & Progym I*
- ◆ Figures – Set #2 – *Poetics & Progym I*
- ◆ Figures – Set #3 – *Poetics & Progym I*

ℭ

BEN FRANKLIN ON COMPOSITION
from his Autobiography

About this time I met with an odd volume of the Spectator. It was
the third. I had never before seen any of them. I bought it, read it over
and over, and was much delighted with it. I thought the writing excellent,
and wished, if possible, to imitate it. With this view I took some of the
papers, and, making short hints of the sentiment in each sentence, laid
them by a few days, and then, without looking at the book, try'd to
compleat the papers again, by expressing each hinted sentiment at length,
and as fully as it had been expressed before, in any suitable words that
should come to hand. Then I compared my Spectator with the original,
discovered some of my faults, and corrected them. But I found I wanted
a stock of words, or a readiness in recollecting and using them, which I
thought I should have acquired before that time if I had gone on making
verses; since the continual occasion for words of the same import, but
of different length, to suit the measure, or of different sound for the
rhyme, would have laid me under a constant necessity of searching for
variety, and also have tended to fix that variety in my mind, and make
me master of it. Therefore I took some of the tales and turned them
into verse; and, after a time, when I had pretty well forgotten the prose,
turned them back again. I also sometimes jumbled my collections of hints
into confusion, and after some weeks endeavored to reduce them into the
best order, before I began to form the full sentences and compleat the
paper. This was to teach me method in the arrangement of thoughts.
By comparing my work afterwards with the original, I discovered many
faults and amended them; but I sometimes had the pleasure of fancying
that, in certain particulars of small import, I had been lucky enough to
improve the method of the language, and this encouraged me to think I
might possibly in time come to be a tolerable English writer, of which I
was extremely ambitious. My time for these exercises and for reading was

at night, after work or before it began in the morning, or on Sundays, when I contrived to be in the printing-house alone, evading as much as I could the common attendance on public worship which my father used to exact of me when I was under his care, and which indeed I still thought a duty, thought I could not, as it seemed to me, afford time to practise it.

∝

Lesson 25.1

Prose & Poetry

LITERARY ELEMENTS IN PROSE: BEN FRANKLIN ON COMPOSITION

1 **Read**
  ◆ Read the passage aloud, preferably in a group setting. **Delight** in the well-chosen words.

2 **Inquire**
  ◆ Does the **title** give any hint as to the content or message of the poem? If this work was published by the author in a larger book or anthology, does that title give any hint?
  ◆ Look up the meaning of any words in the work that are not familiar to you; conduct a complete Vocabulary Study for **key words.**
  ◆ Research unfamiliar persons, places, or things mentioned in the work.
  ◆ State your first impression of the author's **message**.

3 **Observe the Invention, Arrangement, and Style**
  ◆ What is the topic of this passage? Outline its main points. Can you identify a **thesis statement**? **topic statements**? If so, include those in your outline.
  ◆ **Point of View** Identify the **person** (P&P 50)
  ◆ Identify the **Figures** – both **figures of speech** and **figures of description**. (See the list of figures in the Appendix.) Why did the author choose these particular figures?

4 Investigate the Context

- ◆ Research a bit about the author. Make notes in your Writer's Journal about Benjamin Franklin's

    - ■ **Origin** – Who were the author's parents/ancestors? Where was his homeland?
    - ■ **Historical Time Period** – When did the author live?
    - ■ **Influences** What education, training, people, events, books, or ideas shaped the author's thinking?

- ◆ **Rhetorical Situation** (P&P 2)

    - ■ **Exigency** – What is the issue, problem, or situation to be addressed? How does the author want the reader to respond?
    - ■ **Audience** – Who is the author addressing in order to change or persuade?
    - ■ **Constraint** What are the requirements based on the audience and the genre?

Writer's Journal

5 Respond

- ◆ State the message of the passage. Revisit your first impression. Has your interpretation changed?
- ◆ Paraphrase, summarize and/or write a précis of this passage.

6 Connect the Thoughts

- ◆ Does this passage remind you of other things you have **Read** in Scripture, literature, history, etc?
- ◆ Does this poem remind you of any proverbs or other well-known quotations? If so, enter these in your Commonplace Book.

Commonplace Book

7 Profit and Delight

- ◆ What are the sources of **delight** in this work?
- ◆ What **wisdom** does this work furnish?
- ◆ **Discuss** this work **in community** with family, friends, classmates.
- ◆ **Memorize** a portion of this work and recite it before an audience.

THE ODYSSEY

◯ Read as indicated below.

◯ Read

- *The Odyssey of Homer*, Book Twenty-Three

◯ As you read, continue to mark the text and make notes:

- Literary concepts and terms you observe in the narrative. Do any of your earlier thoughts need revision?
- Instances of **epic simile**.
- **Epithets** to add to your running list.
- Passages reflecting on the value of **hearth and home**.

Writer's Journal

◯ Discuss this week's reading with your teacher, along with all your notes and observations. Narrate the main action of the book, and discuss any parts you did not understand. How was this reading **delightful**? What **wisdom** does this reading furnish?

Lesson 25.2

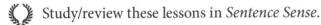

Language Logic

CONTRACTED SENTENCES

◯ Study/review these lessons in *Sentence Sense*.

II. Syntax – The Sentence
- 9.17A Sentence Contractions
- 9.17B Ellipsis

III. Sentence Diagramming – Figures of Speech: Schemes, Tropes
- 25.1 Ellipsis
- 26.1 Similes

DIAGRAMMING & PARSING

In your Writer's Journal, copy these sentences. Mark the prepositional phrases, subjects, and verbs. Bracket the clauses. Classify the sentence as simple, compound, complex, or compound-complex. Then diagram each one. Refer to *Sentence Sense* as needed.

1. Evils have been more painful to us in prospect than in actual

   pressure. — "Spectator," No. 505

2. With many a weary step, and many a groan,

   Up the high hill he heaves a huge round stone; — Pope's Odyssey, Book XI

Orally parse these words with your teacher, using the charts in *Sentence Sense* to guide you.

(2) many (first use), heaves

Lesson 25.3

Eloquent Expression

FIGURE OF SPEECH – ELLIPSIS

The omission of a word, phrase, or clause in a sentence is called **ellipsis**. It is so common in our both spoken and written speech that you may not notice it until you try to diagram the sentence! You just studied many of the ways to do this grammatically in *Harvey's Grammar* (Lesson 203). Review those if needed.

Reading maketh a full man, conference a ready man, and writing an exact man. — Francis Bacon, "Of Studies"

Books are the carriers of civilization. Without books, history is silent, literature dumb, science crippled, thought and speculation at a standstill. — Barbara Tuchman

Fairest Cordelia, that art most rich, being poor; most choice, forsaken, and most loved, despised. — William Shakespeare, *King Lear*

There are some promotions in life, which, independent of the more substantial rewards they offer, require peculiar value and dignity from the coats and waistcoats connected with them. A field-marshal has his uniform; a bishop his silk apron; a counsellor his silk gown; a beadle his cocked hat. — Charles Dickens, *Oliver Twist*

🏵 Discuss the examples of ellipsis with your teacher. Can you identify any additional figures? Scan selections from earlier lessons in this book to see if they contain this figure.

🏵 Enter the following item in the Figures division of your Prose & Poetry Handbook.

Prose & Poetry Handbook

   ◆ Ellipsis, P&P 81: Just below your last entry, write <u>Ellipsis</u>, and add the definition and an example.

LITERARY IMITATION

🏵 Work with the sentence that you diagrammed in Language Logic. Copy the **diagram skeleton**, construct a new sentence, and write the new sentence below the diagram. The topic of your new sentence is friendship.

Writer's Journal

Lesson 25.4

Classical Composition

PROGYMNASMA NARRATIVE: PLOT OBSERVATION – THEON'S SIX AND SUMMARY
Observe and summarize Homer's *Odyssey*, Book Twenty-Three. Refer to the instructions and example in the Appendix under "Narrative Plot Observation" and "Example Narrative Plot Observation."

🏵 Complete the steps for Plot Observation – Theon's Six on the original narrative and in your Writer's Journal.

Writer's Journal

🏵 Write a one paragraph summary of this book, following the steps for Plot Observation – Summary. Work either in your Writer's Journal or on the computer. Add this summary to your running file of *Odyssey* summaries, and save the file.

EXPOSITORY ESSAY FROM ANECDOTE ELABORATION

Rework your Anecdote elaboration on Homer's thoughts about friendship into a modern five-paragraph persuasive essay with the topic.

What are the benefits of true friendship?

A. Open the file with your final elaboration of "Homer said a friend is one '. . . who bore a brother's part, And claim'd by merit, not by blood, the heart.'"

B. Create the introduction paragraph. Combine your Encomion and Paraphrase paragraphs into a one-paragraph introduction. Include the quoted anecdote (state the proverb/anecdote), a praise of the one who said it (Encomion), and an explanation of friendship in general terms (Paraphrase). End the introduction with a **thesis statement** expressing the benefits of friendship.

C. Create three body paragraphs. Choose the strongest topics from your Proverb elaboration for your body paragraphs. For instance, you may choose your Cause, Comparison, and Example paragraphs. Alternately, you may combine some paragraphs, such as Cause and Contrast. For this essay, use the Authority header as part of your conclusion. Paragraphs in this essay should be roughly the same length. Each of your body paragraphs should be no less than three sentences, and no longer than five.

D. Create a one-paragraph conclusion by combining Authority with Exhortation.

E. Develop a title for your essay. You may use the title from your elaboration, or make up a new one. Use parallelism, antithesis, and/or alliteration. Include a heading for your essay, following this format:

> Title (with parallelism, antithesis, and/or alliteration)
> Student Name
> Date

F. In your Writer's Journal, copy the thesis statement from this essay. Make sure that it is stated as a proposition and is specific, concrete, and literal. Identify the topic statements for each body paragraph. List all of these below your thesis statement. Does each topic sentence relate clearly to the thesis? Does this list give an accurate representation of what you will cover in your essay? If not, revise your thesis statement and topics sentences to meet these requirements.

Writer's Journal

G. Incorporate your revised thesis statement and topic sentences into the essay on your computer. Check to make sure:

   ◆ Paragraphs are roughly the same length.
   ◆ Body paragraphs should be no less than three sentences, and no longer than five.

H. Save and print your essay.

🏅 Revise your elaboration using the checklist below. Work through the checklist once on your own, and then a second time with your writing mentor, making notes on the print copy of your narrative. Transfer all additions and corrections from your print copy to the computer file. Save and print the document.

Editor's Pen – The Big Picture

✓ Invention and Arrangement:

   I. **Introduction** (one paragraph based on Encomion and Paraphrase; ends with thesis statement)

   II. **Body** (three paragraphs – proofs based on Cause, Contrast, Comparison, and/or Example)

   III. **Conclusion** (one paragraph based on Authority and Exhortation)

✓ Thesis Statement

   ◆ stated as a proposition
   ◆ specific, concrete, and literal
   ◆ supported by the rest of the essay

✓ Length: five paragraphs of three to five sentences each

✓ Title & Header: includes parallelism, antithesis, and/or alliteration

✓ Figures of speech (at least one instance of each): *parallelism, antithesis, ellipsis*

✓ Figures of speech (one or the other) *asyndeton, polysyndeton*

Editor's Pen – Zoom 5x: Paragraphs

Refer to Copia In Your Writing (Prose & Poetry Handbook or Appendix) as needed

✓ Flow of Ideas: *logical, not repetitive;*

✓ Tone: *objective, not overly emotional or superlative (the best! the most!, etc.)*

✓ Content: *supports thesis statement*

✓ Sentence openers: *varied*

✓ Sentence length and class by form: *varied, avoid overuse of exclamatory sentences*

✓ Verb Tense: *consistent*

✓ Topic sentence *clearly relates to the thesis statement and points to paragraph content*

✓ Length: *neither too wordy nor too short*

✓ Sentence class by use: *effective use*

✓ Pronouns clear: *easily identified antecedents*

✓ Point of View: *3rd person; avoid 1st and 2nd*

Editor's Pen – Zoom 10x: Sentences

Refer to Copia In Your Writing (Prose & Poetry Handbook or Appendix) as needed

✓ Complete thought expressed

✓ Subject and predicate agree in number

✓ Correct capitalization and punctuation
  ◆ No comma splices!

✓ Items in a series constructed in parallel form

Editor's Pen – Fine Focus: Words

✓ Word choices varied; word meanings clear; consider denotation AND connotation
  ◆ Verbs: *strong, specific, fitting, mostly active (vs. passive); appropriate adverbs if needed*
  ◆ Nouns: *clear, descriptive; appropriate adjectives if needed*
  ◆ Dialogue: *n/a except for Authority*
  ◆ Level of Formality: *no contractions, no informal language, no slang or overused words (lots of, cool, awesome), acronyms adequately explained*

✓ Correct spelling

✓ Final read-through

Lesson 25.5

Reflection & Review

Commonplace Book

COMMONPLACE BOOK

 Enter in your Commonplace Book:

- ◆ a favorite passage or two from your reading in Homer's *Odyssey*
- ◆ an example or two of epithet and/or epic simile
- ◆ a few lines of poetry from your anthology (identify meter)
- ◆ examples from your reading of ellipsis
- ◆ examples from your reading of other figures you have learned (see Figures and Literary Devices list in *Poetics & Progym I* Appendix)

BOOK OF CENTURIES

 Record in your Book of Centuries:

- ◆ Benjamin Franklin

MEMORY WORK

GRAMMAR FLASHCARDS

 Review to mastery:

- ◆ Figures – Set #4 – *Poetics & Progym I*

 Continue to review each set once a week (more if needed):

- ◆ Parts of Speech – *Bards & Poets* Review
- ◆ Sentence Terms – *Bards & Poets* Review
- ◆ Noun Terms – *Poetics & Progym I*
- ◆ Verb Terms – *Poetics & Progym I*
- ◆ Modifier Terms – *Poetics & Progym I*
- ◆ Pronoun Terms – *Poetics & Progym I*
- ◆ Figures – Set #1 – *Poetics & Progym I*
- ◆ Figures – Set #2 – *Poetics & Progym I*
- ◆ Figures – Set #3 – *Poetics & Progym I*

ය

ON FIRST LOOKING INTO CHAPMAN'S HOMER

Much have I travell'd in the realms of gold,
   And many goodly states and kingdoms seen;
   Round many western islands have I been
Which bards in fealty to Apollo hold.
Oft of one wide expanse had I been told
   That deep-brow'd Homer ruled as his demesne;
   Yet did I never breathe its pure serene
Till I heard Chapman speak out loud and bold:
Then felt I like some watcher of the skies
   When a new planet swims into his ken;
Or like stout Cortez when with eagle eyes
   He star'd at the Pacific—and all his men
Look'd at each other with a wild surmise—
   Silent, upon a peak in Darien.

— JOHN KEATS

ය

Lesson 26.1

Prose & Poetry

LITERARY ELEMENTS IN THE POEM: ON FIRST LOOKING INTO CHAPMAN'S HOMER

1 Read

- Follow along and listen carefully as the poem is read aloud, OR read it aloud yourself. Read it at least two or three times. **Delight** in the meter, the rhyme, and the images.

2 Inquire

- Does the **title** give any hint as to the content or message of the poem? If this work was published by the poet in a larger book or anthology, does that title give any hint?

- Are there any unfamiliar persons, places, or things mentioned in the poem? Discuss these with your teacher. Suggestions: *John Keats, Chapman's Homer, Apollo, Cortez (Did Cortez discover the Pacific? Who did? Why did Keats name Cortez here?), Darien*

- Look up the meaning of any words in the work that are not familiar to you; conduct a complete Vocabulary Study for **key words.** Suggestions: *fealty, demesne, ken, stout*

- Was there any part of the poem you did not understand? If so, discuss this with your teacher and classmates.

3 Observe the Invention, Arrangement, and Style

- **Lyrical Elements**
  - What does the poet describe?
  - Does the poet make you see, hear, smell, taste, or touch anything?
  - Does the poet compare something in the poem to some other thing?

- **Narrative Elements** Does this poem tell a story? If so, observe the
  - **Setting** When and where does this story take place?
  - **Characters** Who is (are) the main character(s) in this story?
  - **Conflict** What is the main problem or crisis for the character(s)?
  - **Resolution** Is the problem solved? If so, how? If not, why not?
  - **Sequence** Is this story told *ab ovo*, or *in medias res*, or some other way?
  - **Point of View** Identify the **person** (and **level of omniscience** if applicable).

- **Figures** Look for figures of speech and figures of description. (See Appendix for the list of figures taught in *Poetics & Progym*.) Why did the poet choose these particular figures?

4 Investigate the Context

Writer's Journal

- ◆ Research a bit about the poet. Make notes in your Writer's Journal about John Keats's

    - ■ **Origin** Who were the poet's parents/ancestors? Where was his homeland?

    - ■ **Historical Time Period** When did the poet live? What events happened around the time that the poet lived?

    - ■ **Influences** What education, training, books, ideas, and other people or events shaped the poet's thinking?

- ◆ **Rhetorical Situation**

    - ■ **Exigency** – What is the issue, problem, or situation to be addressed?

    - ■ **Audience** – Who is the author addressing in order to change or persuade?

    - ■ **Constraint** What are the requirements based on the audience and the occasion?

- ◆ **Identify the poem's Literary Genre**

    - ■ **Genre by literary period** In which century (time period) and country was this work written?

    - ■ **Genre by poetic/narrative category** Is this poem chiefly **lyrical** (describes an event, or a person, or a feeling, or a time and place, etc., but it does not tell a particular story) or **narrative** (tells a story)? If narrative, is it primarily **non-fiction** (a story that really happened) or **fiction** (a story told as if it really happened)?

5 Connect the Thoughts

Commonplace Book

- ◆ Does this poem remind you of other poems, or of stories with similar plots, messages, or characters?

- ◆ Does this poem remind you of any proverbs or other well-known quotations? If so, enter these in your Commonplace Book.

6 Profit and Delight

- ◆ **Delight** What are the sources of delight in this poem?

- ◆ **Wisdom** What wisdom does this poem furnish?

- ◆ **Read** the poem to your teacher with expression and proper pauses.

- ◆ **Read** other works by this poet. These are readily available online or in an anthology of English verse. Here are a few of his most well-known poems: "A Thing of Beauty: Endymion" (read the excerpt from Book I online at Poetry Foundation), "Written on a Summer Evening," "Ode to Autumn," "Ode on a Grecian Urn," "Ode to a Nightingale," "His Last Sonnet."

◆ **Memorize** this poem and recite it before an audience.

SCANSION AND ANALYSIS: ON FIRST LOOKING INTO CHAPMAN'S HOMER

Scan and analyze the poetic form of the stanzas below.

A. Scan the lines. You will find at least one extra unstressed syllable.

B. Mark the end rhyme. Name the rhyme scheme:

C. Write the stanza name, along with any form/genre designation that may apply:

Much have I travell'd in the realms of gold,

    And many goodly states and kingdoms seen;

    Round many western islands have I been

Which bards in fealty to Apollo hold.

Oft of one wide expanse had I been told

    That deep-brow'd Homer ruled as his demesne;

    Yet did I never breathe its pure serene

Till I heard Chapman speak out loud and bold:

Then felt I like some watcher of the skies

    When a new planet swims into his ken;

Or like stout Cortez when with eagle eyes

    He star'd at the Pacific—and all his men

Look'd at each other with a wild surmise—

    Silent, upon a peak in Darien.

THE ODYSSEY

◯ Read

   ◆ *The Odyssey of Homer,* Book Twenty-Four

◯ As you read, continue to mark the text and make notes:

   ◆ Literary concepts and terms you observe in the narrative. Do any of your earlier thoughts need revision?
   ◆ Instances of **epic simile**.
   ◆ **Epithets** to add to your running list.
   ◆ Passages reflecting on the value of **hearth and home**.

Writer's Journal

◯ Discuss this week's reading with your teacher, along with all your notes and observations. Narrate the main action of the book, and discuss any parts you did not understand. How was this reading **delightful**? What **wisdom** does this reading furnish?

Lesson 26.2

Language Logic

DIAGRAMMING AND PARSING

◯ In your Writer's Journal, copy these sentences. Mark the prepositional phrases, subjects, and verbs. Bracket the clauses. Classify the sentences as simple, compound, complex, or compound-complex. Then diagram each one. Refer to *Sentence Sense* as needed. If you have trouble with the word *serene*, look it up in the dictionary to check its parts of speech.

Writer's Journal

Much have I travell'd in the realms of gold,

   And many goodly states and kingdoms seen;

Round many western islands have I been

Which bards in fealty to Apollo hold.

Oft of one wide expanse had I been told

That deep-brow'd Homer ruled as his demesne;

Yet did I never breathe its pure serene

Till I heard Chapman speak out loud and bold.

❦ Orally parse these words with your teacher, using the charts in *Sentence Sense* to guide you.

Much, Have travell'd, goodly, in fealty, Oft, his, serene

Lesson 26.3

Eloquent Expression

Writer's
Journal

LITERARY IMITATION

❦ Work with the stanza that you diagrammed in Language Logic. Copy the **diagram skeleton**, construct a new sentence, and write the new sentence below the diagram. Base your new sentence on Odysseus and his homecoming. Write it in the first person as if Odysseus were speaking. Do not worry about rhyme and meter.

Lesson 26.4

Classical Composition

PROGYMNASMA NARRATIVE: PLOT OBSERVATION – THEON'S SIX AND SUMMARY
Observe and summarize Homer's *Odyssey*, Book Twenty-Four. Refer to the instructions and example in the Appendix under "Narrative Plot Observation" and "Example Narrative Plot Observation."

💮 Complete the steps for Plot Observation – Theon's Six on the original narrative and in your Writer's Journal.

Writer's Journal

💮 Write a one paragraph summary of this book, following the steps for Plot Observation – Summary. Work either in your Writer's Journal or on the computer. Add this summary to your running file of *Odyssey* summaries, and save the file.

PROGYMNASMA NARRATIVE: HIERARCHICAL OUTLINE OF THE ODYSSEY

Now, the moment you have been waiting for throughout this course! You get to see the fruits of your labor come together into one comprehensive outline and summary of *The Odyssey*. In this exercise, you will take the plot observation work you have done for Homer's *Odyssey* throughout this course, and create a formal outline of the entire book. You will format this as a **hierarchical alphanumeric outline**. *Hierarchical* means that the outline is structured to show relationships between the overall plot and the individual plot points and sub-points. *Alphanumeric* means that numbers and letters within the outline create the hierarchical structure. When outlining, keep two principles in mind:

◆ Every point or sub-point on the outline must have at least one other point or sub-point to accompany it. If you have a point I., you must have at least a point II. If you have a sub-point A., you must have at least a sub-point B.; if you have a (sub-)sub-point 1., you must have a 2.; etc.

◆ Each level on the outline should be grammatically parallel with the other items at the same level, but they do not necessarily need to be parallel with items at other levels. For example, the points numbered I., II., III., etc. might all have the grammatical structure Noun-Prepositional Phrase, while the sub-points numbered A., B., and C. might be structured Participle-Object.

A. Create a one-level outline that captures the action of the entire *Odyssey* in twenty-four captions, one per book.

◆ Briefly review your plot observations for each book.
◆ Write a caption for each book, using Roman numerals to structure the outline. Format each caption as a title, using capital letters for all words except some articles and prepositions. The first word of

a title is always capitalized, even if it is an article or a preposition. Make your book captions *parallel*—each with the same grammatical format.

◆ Save and print your one-level outline.

B. Create a two-level outline that divides the action of the entire *Odyssey* into a beginning, a middle, and an end. Before you begin this step, review the following sections in Lesson 4.1 Prose & Poetry: Plot Structure – Beginning, Plot Structure – Middle, and Plot Structure – End.

   ◆ Mark up the print copy of your one-level outline, dividing the action of the entire book into a beginning, a middle, and an end. Refer back to Lesson 4.1 as you consider the components that might be included in each division. Expect that the middle will contain a good deal more action than the beginning or the end.

   ◆ Create a new document and make an outline with main points Beginning, Middle, and End numbered I., II., and III, and the book captions as sub-points under each, numbered A., B., C., etc. Use the cut and paste function to make this faster and easier. Again, expect that you will have significantly more book titles under Middle than you will under either Beginning or End.

   ◆ Add parallel captions to Beginning, Middle, and End, and add to the outline with the format Beginning: [Caption], Middle: [Caption], End: [Caption].

   ◆ Save and print your two-level outline.

C. Create a condensed three-level outline of the entire *Odyssey*. Note that as you work through this step, you may find that you need to adjust your captions somewhat. Feel free to do so in order to get a well-structured parallel outline that accurately summarizes the plot of the *Odyssey*.

   ◆ Mark up the print copy of your two-level outline, grouping the book captions into divisions of related actions, while keeping the original narrative order intact. For each grouping, create a caption that reflects the content of the actions each contain. These grouping captions should all be parallel with one another. Again, you will have more groupings under Middle than you will under Beginning and End, but you must have at least two groupings under each.

   ◆ Create a new document and make an outline with main points Beginning, Middle, and End, along with their captions, numbered I., II., and III. Insert your new book grouping captions as sub-points under each labeled A., B., C., etc. Finally, insert your book captions, numbered 1., 2., 3., etc. as sub-points under the appropriate grouping captions.

- Balance the structure of the outline by dividing the Middle (Point II.) into two or three points, creating new captions and shifting the numbers so that you have four or five Roman numerals in all. Create parallel captions for the new divisions reflecting the content listed under each.
- Save and print your completed three-level outline.

Lesson 26.5

Reflection & Review

COMMONPLACE BOOK

Enter in your Commonplace Book:

Commonplace Book

- a favorite passage or two from your reading in Homer's *Odyssey*
- an example or two of epithet and/or epic simile
- a few lines of poetry from your anthology (identify meter)
- examples from your reading of other figures you have learned (see Figures and Literary Devices list in *Poetics & Progym I* Appendix)

BOOK OF CENTURIES

Record in your Book of Centuries:

- John Keats, George Chapman (translator of Homer)

MEMORY WORK

GRAMMAR
FLASHCARDS

🏵 Review to mastery:

- Figures – Set #4 – *Poetics & Progym I*

🏵 Use the combine and test features at Quizlet for an online or printed quiz over Figure Set #4. If you wish, use combine set features to include previous figure sets.

🏵 Continue to review each set once a week (more if needed):

- Parts of Speech – *Bards & Poets* Review
- Sentence Terms – *Bards & Poets* Review
- Noun Terms – *Poetics & Progym I*
- Verb Terms – *Poetics & Progym I*
- Modifier Terms – *Poetics & Progym I*
- Pronoun Terms – *Poetics & Progym I*
- Figures – Set #1 – *Poetics & Progym I*
- Figures – Set #2 – *Poetics & Progym I*
- Figures – Set #3 – *Poetics & Progym I*

Lesson 27

ℭℛ

ULYSSES

It little profits that an idle king,
By this still hearth, among these barren crags,
Match'd with an aged wife, I mete and dole
Unequal laws unto a savage race,
That hoard, and sleep, and feed, and know not me.
I cannot rest from travel: I will drink
Life to the lees: All times I have enjoy'd
Greatly, have suffer'd greatly, both with those
That loved me, and alone, on shore, and when
Thro' scudding drifts the rainy Hyades
Vext the dim sea: I am become a name;
For always roaming with a hungry heart
Much have I seen and known; cities of men
And manners, climates, councils, governments,
Myself not least, but honour'd of them all;
And drunk delight of battle with my peers,
Far on the ringing plains of windy Troy.
I am a part of all that I have met;
Yet all experience is an arch wherethro'
Gleams that untravell'd world whose margin fades
For ever and forever when I move.
How dull it is to pause, to make an end,
To rust unburnish'd, not to shine in use!
As tho' to breathe were life! Life piled on life
Were all too little, and of one to me

Little remains: but every hour is saved

From that eternal silence, something more,

A bringer of new things; and vile it were

For some three suns to store and hoard myself,

And this gray spirit yearning in desire

To follow knowledge like a sinking star,

Beyond the utmost bound of human thought.

This is my son, mine own Telemachus,

To whom I leave the sceptre and the isle,—

Well-loved of me, discerning to fulfil

This labour, by slow prudence to make mild

A rugged people, and thro' soft degrees

Subdue them to the useful and the good.

Most blameless is he, centred in the sphere

Of common duties, decent not to fail

In offices of tenderness, and pay

Meet adoration to my household gods,

When I am gone. He works his work, I mine.

There lies the port; the vessel puffs her sail:

There gloom the dark, broad seas. My mariners,

Souls that have toil'd, and wrought, and thought with me—

That ever with a frolic welcome took

The thunder and the sunshine, and opposed

Free hearts, free foreheads—you and I are old;

Old age hath yet his honour and his toil;

Death closes all: but something ere the end,

Some work of noble note, may yet be done,

Not unbecoming men that strove with Gods.

The lights begin to twinkle from the rocks:

The long day wanes: the slow moon climbs: the deep

Moans round with many voices. Come, my friends,

'T is not too late to seek a newer world.

Push off, and sitting well in order smite

The sounding furrows; for my purpose holds

To sail beyond the sunset, and the baths

Of all the western stars, until I die.

It may be that the gulfs will wash us down:

It may be we shall touch the Happy Isles,

And see the great Achilles, whom we knew.

Tho' much is taken, much abides; and tho'

We are not now that strength which in old days

Moved earth and heaven; that which we are, we are;

One equal temper of heroic hearts,

Made weak by time and fate, but strong in will

To strive, to seek, to find, and not to yield.

—ALFRED, LORD TENNYSON

℞

Lesson 27.1

Prose & Poetry

LITERARY ELEMENTS IN THE POEM: TENNYSON'S ULYSSES

1 **Read**
  ◆ Follow along and listen carefully as the poem is read aloud, OR read it aloud yourself. Read it at least two or three times. **Delight** in the meter, the rhyme, and the images.

2 **Inquire**
  ◆ Does the **title** give any hint as to the content or message of the poem? If this work was published by the poet in a larger book or anthology, does that title give any hint?

◆ Are there any unfamiliar persons, places, or things mentioned in the poem? Discuss these with your teacher.

◆ Look up the meaning of any words in the work that are not familiar to you; conduct a complete Vocabulary Study for **key words.** Be sure to check the archaic meaning of *temper* that Tennyson used here.

◆ Was there any part of the poem you did not understand? If so, discuss this with your teacher and classmates.

3 Observe the Invention, Arrangement, and Style

◆ **Lyrical Elements**

  ▪ What does the poet describe?

  ▪ Does the poet make you see, hear, smell, taste, or touch anything?

  ▪ Does the poet compare something in the poem to some other thing?

◆ **Narrative Elements** Does this poem tell a story? If so, observe the

  ▪ **Setting** When and where does this story take place?

  ▪ **Characters** Who is (are) the main character(s) in this story?

  ▪ **Conflict** What is the main problem or crisis for the character(s)?

  ▪ **Resolution** Is the problem solved? If so, how? If not, why not?

  ▪ **Sequence** Is this story told *ab ovo*, or *in medias res*, or some other way?

  ▪ **Point of View** Identify the **person** (and **level of omniscience** if applicable).

◆ **Figures** Look for figures of speech and figures of description. (See Appendix for the list of figures taught in *Poetics & Progym*.) Why did the poet choose these particular figures?

4 Investigate the Context

◆ Research a bit about the poet. Make notes in your Writer's Journal about Tennyson's

  ▪ **Origin** Who were the poet's parents/ancestors? Where was his homeland?

  ▪ **Historical Time Period** When did the poet live? What events happened around the time that the poet lived?

  ▪ **Influences** What education, training, books, ideas, and other people or events shaped the poet's thinking?

◆ **Rhetorical Situation**

  ▪ **Exigency** – What is the issue, problem, or situation to be addressed?

  ▪ **Audience** – Who is the author addressing in order to change or persuade?

  ▪ **Constraint** What are the requirements based on the audience and the occasion?

Writer's Journal

◆ **Identify the poem's Literary Genre**
  ▪ **Genre by literary period** In which century (time period) and country was this work written?
  ▪ **Genre by poetic/narrative category** Is this poem chiefly **lyrical** (describes an event, or a person, or a feeling, or a time and place, etc., but it does not tell a particular story) or **narrative** (tells a story)? If narrative, is it primarily **non-fiction** (a story that really happened) or **fiction** (a story told as if it really happened)?

5 **Connect the Thoughts**
◆ Does this poem remind you of other poems, or of stories with similar plots, messages, or characters?
◆ Does this poem remind you of any proverbs or other well-known quotations? If so, enter these in your Commonplace Book.

Commonplace Book

6 **Profit and Delight**
◆ **Delight** What are the sources of delight in this poem?
◆ **Wisdom** What wisdom does this poem furnish?
◆ **Read** the poem to your teacher with expression and proper pauses.
◆ **Read** other works by this poet.
◆ **Memorize** this poem and recite it before an audience.

SCANSION AND ANALYSIS: ULYSSES

Scan and analyze the poetic form of the stanzas below.

A. Scan the lines. You will find some missing unstressed syllables and some elision as you scan.

B. Mark the end rhyme. Name the rhyme scheme:

C. Write the stanza name, along with any form/genre designation that may apply:

The lights begin to twinkle from the rocks:

The long day wanes: the slow moon climbs: the deep

Moans round with many voices. Come, my friends,

'T is not too late to seek a newer world.

Push off, and sitting well in order smite

The sounding furrows; for my purpose holds

To sail beyond the sunset, and the baths

Of all the western stars, until I die.

It may be that the gulfs will wash us down:

It may be we shall touch the Happy Isles,

And see the great Achilles, whom we knew.

Tho' much is taken, much abides; and tho'

We are not now that strength which in old days

Moved earth and heaven; that which we are, we are;

One equal temper of heroic hearts,

Made weak by time and fate, but strong in will

To strive, to seek, to find, and not to yield.

Lesson 27.2

Language Logic

DIAGRAMMING & PARSING

In your Writer's Journal, copy this sentence. Mark the prepositional phrases, subjects, and verbs. Bracket the clauses. Classify the sentence as simple, compound, complex, or compound-complex. Then diagram it. Refer to *Sentence Sense* as needed.

Writer's Journal

We are not now that strength which in old days

Moved earth and heaven; that which we are, we are;

One equal temper of heroic hearts,

Made weak by time and fate, but strong in will

To strive, to seek, to find, and not to yield.

Orally parse these words with your teacher, using the charts in *Sentence Sense* to guide you.

We, are, that, which, Made weak, To strive, not

Lesson 27.3

Eloquent Expression

COPIA OF CONSTRUCTION: SCHEMES – ALLITERATION AND ANASTROPHE

Alliteration (Lesson 9) is often used in writing poetry. But it is also used very often in prose, so subtly that we hardly notice it unless we are looking for it. Because alliterative phrases are often memorable, it is an excellent device for a title or a key point you wish to make.

What you wrote has brought me the deepest delight.

I am plenteously pleased in your lovely letter.

Your letter smoothed the brows of my spirit.

Synonyms and antonyms will probably be the best source when you are searching for alliterative words. You have been working with alliteration in your essay titles and captions, but you should also look for opportunity to use it in the body of your writing as well.

Anastrophe (Lesson 9) is best used sparingly in your writing, but it can be effective if you want to highlight or emphasize a particular point.

Most delighted was Erasmus with your letter.

Look back over your earlier compositions. Choose a sentence that could be improved by alliteration, and one that could be improved with anastrophe. Copy the originals into your Writer's Journal, along with your revisions.

Writer's Journal

POETICS & PROGYM I

Lesson 27.4 ◆ 337

Work with the stanza that you diagrammed in Language Logic. Copy the **diagram skeleton**, construct a new sentence, and write the new sentence below the diagram. Base your new sentence on your impression of Homer's *Odyssey* as a whole.

Writer's
Journal

Lesson 27.4

Classical Composition

PROGYMNASMA NARRATIVE: SUMMARY OF HOMER'S ODYSSEY

Remember, you have already done most of the work as you wrote summaries for each book! All you need to do now is assemble those into a narrative, and add a few descriptive details.

Write a summary of Homer's *Odyssey*:

A. Open the file with the précis paragraph of the *Telemachia* that you wrote in Lesson 7. This will form a prologue to the wanderings of Odysseus. Copy and paste this précis as the first paragraph of your summary in a new document.

B. Open the file with your summaries of all twenty-four books of the Odyssey. Cut and paste these into the new document below the one-paragraph précis of the *Telemachia*.

C. Keep your printed three-level outline handy as you work. Revise and rework your summary paragraphs into a smoothly flowing narrative. In general, you should have about one paragraph for each Roman numeral on your outline, although some in the middle may need two. Condense and combine sentences. Paragraphs should be no less than six and no more than ten sentences. Pay attention to transitions between actions. Create a title for your narrative, using alliteration, parallelism, and/or antithesis. Format a heading for your document, then save and print it.

D. Ask your writing mentor to check that the assignment is complete. Print and file the document.

EDITOR'S PEN: SUMMARY OF THE ODYSSEY

Revise your summary using the checklist below. Work through the checklist once on your own, and then a second time with your writing mentor, making notes on the print copy of your narrative. Transfer all additions and corrections from your print copy to the computer file. Save and print the document.

Editor's Pen – The Big Picture

✓ All important plot elements included
✓ All major characters represented correctly
✓ Sequence: *similar to the original*
✓ Length: six to seven paragraphs
✓ Title & Header: includes parallelism, antithesis, and/or alliteration
✓ Figures of speech (at least one instance of each): *parallelism, antithesis, ellipsis*
✓ Figures of speech (one or the other) *asyndeton, polysyndeton*

Editor's Pen – Zoom 5x: Paragraphs

✓ Formatting: *proper indentation*
✓ Length: *eight to ten sentences*
✓ Sentence class by use: *effective use*
✓ Sentence openers: *varied*
✓ Dialogue: *none or very limited*
✓ Verb Tense: *consistent (may use historical present)*
✓ Pronouns clear: *easily identified antecedents*
✓ Person for Nouns & Pronouns: *3rd person*

Editor's Pen – Zoom 10x: Sentences

✓ Complete thought expressed
✓ Subject and predicate agree in number
✓ Correct capitalization and punctuation
  ◆ No comma splices!
✓ Items in a series constructed in parallel form

Editor's Pen – Fine Focus: Words

✓ Word choices varied; word meanings clear; consider denotation AND connotation

  ◆ Verbs: *strong, fitting; appropriate adverbs if needed*

  ◆ Nouns: *clear, descriptive; appropriate adjectives if needed*

  ◆ Dialogue: *dialogue tags varied if appropriate*

✓ Correct spelling

✓ Final read-through

Lesson 27.5

Reflection & Review

Commonplace Book

COMMONPLACE BOOK

 Enter in your Commonplace Book:

  ◆ one stanza of another hymn (identify poetic & hymn meter)

  ◆ examples from your reading of other figures you have learned (see Figures and Literary Devices list in *Poetics & Progym I* Appendix)

BOOK OF CENTURIES

 Record in your Book of Centuries:

  ◆ Alfred, Lord Tennyson

MEMORY WORK

Review all sets for a comprehensive final exam:

- Parts of Speech – *Bards & Poets* Review
- Sentence Terms – *Bards & Poets* Review
- Noun Terms – *Poetics & Progym I*
- Verb Terms – *Poetics & Progym I*
- Modifier Terms – *Poetics & Progym I*
- Pronoun Terms – *Poetics & Progym I*
- Figures – Set #1 – *Poetics & Progym I*
- Figures – Set #2 – *Poetics & Progym I*
- Figures – Set #3 – *Poetics & Progym I*
- Figures – Set #4 – *Poetics & Progym I*

☙

COLLECT FOR THE FOURTH SUNDAY IN EASTER

O ALMIGHTY God, who alone canst order the unruly wills and affections of sinful men: Grant unto thy people, that they may love the thing which thou commandest, and desire that which thou dost promise; that so, among the sundry and manifold changes of the world, our hearts may surely there be fixed, where true joys are to be found; through Jesus Christ our Lord. Amen.

— BOOK OF COMMON PRAYER, 1928

☙

Lesson 28

Classical Composition

THE BOOK OF COMMON PRAYER

Our selection for this lesson comes from *The Book of Common Prayer*. The Prayer Book, as it was commonly known, was written primarily by Thomas Cranmer, Archbishop of the Church of England. Published in 1549, the beautiful language patterns and expressions of *The Book of Common Prayer* helped to shape the English language to this day, alongside Shakespeare and the King James Version of the Bible. This collect from the 1928 revision is one of my favorite prayers, and I pray it often for myself and for others dear to me. As you finish *Poetics & Progym I*, it is my prayer for you.

In this final lesson, you will use the skills you have learned in Prose & Poetry, Language Logic, Eloquent Expression, and Classical Composition throughout this book to complete the following brief compositions.

PROGYMNASMA NARRATIVE: THE ODYSSEY – PRÉCIS #1 AND PRÉCIS #2

Condense your summary to write a one paragraph précis of the entire epic. Refer to Lesson 7-8 if you need a refresher on the précis. Then you will condense it further to a one sentence précis.

A. Open the file with your summary and save it under a new name. Obviously, you will need to remove many details of the storyline. Though this paragraph will be concise, make sure the narrative flows smoothly and eloquently.

B. Essentially, you will write a one-paragraph summary of your summary. Though this paragraph will be concise, make sure the narrative flows smoothly and eloquently, using these tips for condensing a narative:

  ◆ Remove any dialogue, description, and repetition.
  ◆ Whittle down the remaining sentences using the sentence combination devices you have learned.
  ◆ Wherever possible, substitute single words for phrases or clauses.
  ◆ If you have items in a series joined by a conjunction, look for a way to express the same idea with a single word or phrase.
  ◆ The scheme of ellipsis may be helpful in condensing your summary.

C. When you are satisfied with your one paragraph précis, begin work on your one sentence précis. Open the file with your one-paragraph précis and save it under a new name. The challenge here is to refine your précis even further to express the central essence of *The Odyssey* in a single sentence. Take the time to make this a perfect sentence that gets at the heart of the story. Your one sentence précis must capture just the essence of the story, with little to no detail.

EDITOR'S PEN: THE ODYSSEY PRÉCIS #1

Revise your one-paragraph précis using the checklist below. Work through the checklist once on your own, and then a second time with your writing mentor, making notes on the print copy of your narrative. Transfer all additions and corrections from your print copy to the computer file. Save and print the document.

Editor's Pen – The Big Picture

✓ All major plot elements accounted for
✓ All characters represented correctly
✓ Sequence: *linear from the beginning*
✓ Length: *one paragraph*
✓ Point of View: *3rd person*
✓ Figure of speech: *asyndeton, ellipsis*

Editor's Pen – Zoom 5x: Paragraphs

✓ Formatting: *proper indentation*
✓ Length: *neither too wordy nor too short*
✓ Sentence class by use: *effective use*
✓ Sentence openers: *varied*
✓ Dialogue: *none*
✓ Verb Tense: *consistent (may use historical present)*
✓ Pronouns clear: *easily identified antecedents*
✓ Person for Nouns & Pronouns: *consistent and appropriate*

Editor's Pen – Zoom 10x: Sentences

✓ Complete thought expressed
✓ Subject and predicate agree in number
✓ Correct capitalization and punctuation
   ◆ No comma splices!
✓ Items in a series constructed in parallel form

Editor's Pen – Fine Focus: Words

✓ Word choices varied; word meanings clear; consider denotation AND connotation
   ◆ Verbs: *strong, fitting; appropriate adverbs if needed*
   ◆ Nouns: *clear, descriptive; appropriate adjectives if needed*
   ✓ Correct spelling
✓ Final read-through

EDITOR'S PEN: THE ODYSSEY PRÉCIS #2

Revise your one-sentence précis using the checklist below. Obviously, there is no need for Big Picture and Paragraph editing since your précis is only one sentence. Work through the checklist once on your own, and then a second time with your writing mentor, making notes on the print copy of your narrative. Transfer all additions and corrections from your print copy to the computer file. Save and print the document.

Editor's Pen – Zoom 10x: Sentences

✓ Complete thought expressed

✓ Subject and predicate agree in number

✓ Correct capitalization and punctuation
   ◆ No comma splices!

Editor's Pen – Fine Focus: Words

✓ Word choices varied; word meanings clear; consider denotation AND connotation
   ◆ Verbs: *strong, fitting; appropriate adverbs if needed*
   ◆ Nouns: *clear, descriptive; appropriate adjectives if needed*
   ✓ Correct spelling

✓ Final read-through

LITERARY ANALYSIS ESSAY: THE ODYSSEY

Now we are going to take all those literary terms we have been learning throughout this course and apply them to Homer's great epic. The purposes and uses of this type of essay are similar to the poetry analysis essay (Lesson 14). Read this example essay, written by a college student. The requirements of the assignment include using the particular terms in italic type and at least one instance of parallelism and one of antithesis.

The Lion, the Witch, and the Wardrobe is a beloved work of *fantasy fiction* written by *English author and apologist C.S. Lewis*. The story is told in *third person* and in straightforward *linear narrative*. The air raids on London during World War II provide the *context* for the book's opening chapters. To escape the bombing, the *protagonists* Peter, Susan, Edmund, and Lucy Pevensie are sent to live in the country home of an eccentric professor. While exploring the house, Lucy discovers a wardrobe which leads to *Narnia*, a magical land filled with snowy forests, talking animals, and sinister evils *(parallelism)*.

Her discovery of this mysterious land is the *catalyst* for their further adventures, as her brother Edmund also enters this world and meets the story's *antagonist*, the beautiful but evil-hearted White Witch, who keeps an icy grip on the land of Narnia and hates humans. Through deceptive promises, she tempts Edmund to bring the rest of his siblings to her castle, sparking the *conflict* of the narrative. Edmund's betrayal puts his siblings and himself in danger, and the *action rises* as Peter, Susan, and Lucy, with the help of talking beavers, evade the White Witch and seek help from the great lion, Aslan, the true ruler of Narnia. In order to rescue the traitor Edmund, Aslan allows himself to be slain by the White Witch. The White Witch's deep magic was done, but Aslan's deeper magic will prevail *(antithesis)*. In the *climactic* moment death begins to work backwards, and Aslan is restored to life. The *falling action* is swift, as Aslan totally defeats the White Witch and her evil forces, restores Narnia, and makes the four children its kings and queens. They have a long and happy reign, and the story *resolves* with them quietly slipping through the wardrobe and back into England, finding that no time has passed while they were gone.[1]

A note about verb tenses in literary analysis: Remember, when writing about a literary work, it is customary to use the historical present tense when referring to the content of the work. (See *Sentence Sense*, 3.7C, Rem. 2.) Circle each verb in the literary essay example above, and note its tense. The author uses the past participle when referring to the past act of writing the book itself, but as she begins to deal with the content of the work, the verbs are all present tense: *provide*, *are sent*, *discovers*, etc. to refer to the content of the story.

 Make literary analysis notes for Homer's *Odyssey*. Use the Literature section in your Prose & Poetry Handbook as a guide. In your Writer's Journal, make notes about each of the following elements:

- ◆ Literary Context (P&P 30)
- ◆ Literary Genre (P&P 31)
- ◆ Subgenre (see P&P 36)
- ◆ Setting – Time and Place (P&P 40)
- ◆ Point of View (P&P 50)
- ◆ Sequence (P&P 48)
- ◆ Basic Plotline – identify these elements in the narrative plot (P&P 41-43)
  - ■ Exposition – Protagonist(s), Antagonist(s), Conflict, Catalyst
  - ■ Middle – Rising Action, Climax, Falling Action
  - ■ End – Denouement (Resolution)

1 Essay by Patrick Henry College intern Sarah Watterson, 2013. Used by permission of the author.

✦ Use your notes to write a brief literary analysis essay (about 300 words) of Homer's *Odyssey*. In your essay, make sure that you identify each of the literary elements listed above, using bold type to denote the literary terms you use. Include the following in your essay:

- at least one instance of parallelism and one of antithesis (underline and note the figure in parentheses as in the example essay)
- use of historical present tense when referring to content of the work
- a header, properly formatted: the title, your name, and the date

✦ Revise your essay using the checklist below. Work through the checklist once on your own, and then a second time with your writing mentor, making notes on the print copy of your narrative. Transfer all additions and corrections from your print copy to the computer file. Save and print the document.

Editor's Pen – The Big Picture

✓ Invention and Arrangement: *all required literary elements included in bold type*
✓ Length: *around 300 words; similar to example*
✓ Title & Header: *properly formatted*
✓ Figures of speech (at least one instance of each): *parallelism, antithesis*
✓ Figures of speech (one or the other) *asyndeton, polysyndeton*

Editor's Pen – Zoom 5x: Paragraphs

Refer to Copia In Your Writing (Prose & Poetry Handbook or Appendix) as needed

✓ Flow of Ideas: *logical, not repetitive*
✓ Tone: *objective, not overly emotional or superlative (the best! the most!, etc.)*
✓ Length: *neither too wordy nor too short*
✓ Sentence class by use: *effective use*
✓ Sentence openers: *varied*
✓ Sentence length and class by form: *varied, avoid overuse of exclamatory sentences*

✓ Verb Tense: *historical present when referring to content of the work*
✓ Pronouns clear: *easily identified antecedents*
✓ Point of View: *3rd person*

Editor's Pen – Zoom 10x: Sentences

Refer to Copia In Your Writing (Prose & Poetry Handbook or Appendix) as needed

✓ Complete thought expressed

✓ Subject and predicate agree in number

✓ Correct capitalization and punctuation

   ◆ No comma splices!

✓ Items in a series constructed in parallel form

Editor's Pen – Fine Focus: Words

✓ Word choices varied; word meanings clear; consider denotation AND connotation

   ◆ Verbs: *strong, specific, fitting, mostly active (vs. passive); appropriate adverbs if needed*

   ◆ Nouns: *clear, descriptive; appropriate adjectives if needed*

   ◆ Dialogue: *n/a except for Authority*

   ◆ Level of Formality: *no contractions, no informal language, no slang or overused words (lots of, cool, awesome), acronyms adequately explained*

✓ Correct spelling

✓ Final read-through

POETRY COMPOSITION #1

Imitate the meter and rhyme scheme of these lines from "On First Looking Into Chapman's Homer" (Lesson 26). For content, use Odysseus and his homecoming. Write in the first person, as if Odysseus were speaking.

Much have I travell'd in the realms of gold,

   And many goodly states and kingdoms seen;

   Round many western islands have I been

Which bards in fealty to Apollo hold.

Oft of one wide expanse had I been told

   That deep-brow'd Homer ruled as his demesne;

   Yet did I never breathe its pure serene

Till I heard Chapman speak out loud and bold.

1. Copy the lines into your Writer's Journal. You diagrammed these lines in Lesson 26. If you have trouble getting started, try copying that diagram skeleton and using it to begin to construct your own lines.

2. List possible rhyming words, and write words and phrases to fit the meter. Use a rhyming dictionary and a thesaurus as needed.

3. When you are satisfied with your imitation, type the final version on the computer. Title it, add your byline, and and note below your poem that it is an imitation of "On First Looking Into Chapman's Homer."

POETRY COMPOSITION #2

Write a poem summary/précis of *The Odyssey*. The length should be at least six to ten lines, and you may use any meter, rhyme, and stanza form you prefer. A limerick or lines of iambic pentameter may be the simplest forms to try first.

1. Work in your Writer's Journal. Choose your meter and begin to write your lines. If you get stuck, choose lines from another poem to imitate.

2. List possible rhyming words, and write words and phrases to fit the meter. Use a rhyming dictionary and a thesaurus as needed.

3. When you are satisfied with your poem, type the final version version on the computer. Title it, add your byline, and and note the original below your poem if it is an imitation.

4. Memorize your poem and recite it before an audience.

Lesson 28.5

Reflection & Review

Commonplace Book

COMMONPLACE BOOK

Enter in your Commonplace Book:

- ◆ a favorite passage or two from your reading in Homer's *Odyssey*
- ◆ an example or two of epithet and/or epic simile
- ◆ a few lines of poetry from your anthology (identify meter)
- ◆ examples from your reading of other figures you have learned (see Figures and Literary Devices list in *Poetics & Progym I* Appendix)

BOOK OF CENTURIES

Record in your Book of Centuries:

- ◆ Thomas Cranmer, *Book of Common Prayer*

MEMORY WORK

GRAMMAR FLASHCARDS

Review all sets for a comprehensive final exam:
- ◆ Parts of Speech – *Bards & Poets* Review
- ◆ Sentence Terms – *Bards & Poets* Review
- ◆ Noun Terms – *Poetics & Progym I*
- ◆ Verb Terms – *Poetics & Progym I*
- ◆ Modifier Terms – *Poetics & Progym I*
- ◆ Pronoun Terms – *Poetics & Progym I*
- ◆ Figures – Set #1 – *Poetics & Progym I*
- ◆ Figures – Set #2 – *Poetics & Progym I*
- ◆ Figures – Set #3 – *Poetics & Progym I*
- ◆ Figures – Set #4 – *Poetics & Progym I*

Use the combine and test features at Quizlet for an online or printed quiz over all sets studied in this course.

APPENDIX

Writer's Journal

This composition book will be the place to put exercises, vocabulary studies, outlines and first drafts, dictation, and most other exercises. When you see an image like the one to the right, you are to do the work in your Writer's Journal. This notebook is simple to use. Start at the beginning of the book with Lesson 1. At the top of the first page, write the title:

Lesson 1 - The Dog and His Master's Dinner

Then, just add the exercises as you get to them in the text. The final few pages of the book will be reserved for several lists you will be prompted to make over the course of *Poetics & Progym*.

Commonplace Book

Sir, if you will be so good as to favor me with a blank book, I will transcribe the most remarkable occurrences I meet with in my reading, which will serve to fix them upon my mind. — John Quincy Adams, age 10, in a letter to his father

The Commonplace Book is the place to record beautiful literary passages in books that you are reading or studying. As you move through the levels of *Poetics & Progym*, you will have more liberty in choosing your commonplace entries. In addition, any time you are asked to find an example of a particular grammar structure or figure of speech in your reading, the Commonplace Book is the place to put it.

When you see an image like the one to the right, you are to make an entry in your Commonplace Book as instructed. A habit of reading with a pen in hand will make this much easier. Mark passages that you may wish to add to your commonplace directly in the book (with your parents' permission). If you would rather not write in the book, you could use a few index cards as a bookmark that you may make notes on, or stick 10-12 sticky notes to the back cover, and mark pages with passages that you might add to your Commonplace Book with a flag and a note.

Later, transfer entries into your commonplace book in your best handwriting, and with appropriate attribution. Begin your Commonplace Book right at the beginning of the notebook, and add entries straight through from front to back. If you like, you may make a title page that includes the date you begin it (and later you can add the date you complete it). You might also copy the quote above from John Quincy Adams on the title page.

Commonplace entries should include the date of entry. In the attribution, include the title of the story or poem, the author, and the book in which the passage is found. Note that for handwritten entries, the title of a book will be underlined; chapter, fable, and poem titles will be placed in quotes. For a Scripture passage, include the verse reference. Sometimes you will be instructed to make a note or label a particular type of passage.

I prefer to leave the left-hand page blank, partly because it is neater, and partly because I often go back and make notes on previous entries. Consider also developing your own personal flourish to place between entries, as in the sample entries below. Make your Commonplace Book attractive and neat, and make commonplacing a lifelong habit.

September 8, 2014

A thirsty Crow found a Pitcher with some water in it, but so little was there that, try as she might, she could not reach it with her beak, and it seemed as though she would die of thirst within sight of the remedy. At last she hit upon a clever plan. She began dropping pebbles into the Pitcher, and with each pebble the water rose a little higher until at last it reached the brim, and the knowing bird was enabled to quench her thirst.

Necessity is the mother of invention.

— Aesop's Fables, "The Crow and the Pitcher," by V.S. Jones

CR

September 22, 2014

Dark brown is the river,
    Golden is the sand.
It flows along for ever,
    With trees on either hand.
—Robert Louis Stevenson, "Where Go the Boats?" A Child's Garden of Verses

CR

October 23, 2014

Therefore whosoever heareth these sayings of mine, and doeth them, I will liken him unto a wise man, which built his house upon a rock: And the rain descended, and the floods came, and the winds blew, and beat upon that house; and it fell not: for it was founded upon a rock.

And every one that heareth these sayings of mine, and doeth them not, shall be likened unto a foolish man, which built his house upon the sand: And the rain descended, and the floods came, and the winds blew, and beat upon that house; and it fell: and great was the fall of it.

— A parable of Jesus, Matthew 7:24-27, King James Version

ख

January 18, 2015

There is no frigate like a book — Emily Dickinson, "A Book" [simile]

ख

March 25, 2015

There were stars staring in a black frosty sky overhead.

— C. S. Lewis, The Silver Chair [personification]

ख

There is a time for work and a time for play. — moral from "The Ants and the Grasshopper. (Similar messages: Ecclesiates 3, Pilgrims at Plymouth and the settlers at Jamestown)

ख

Vocabulary Study

Our knowledge is proportional to the number of words we understand, each conveying
a different thought, and our own power of producing thought and feeling in others
depends on the number of words that we can properly and promptly use.

— Erastus Otis Haven, *Rhetoric: A Textbook*

Practice Vocabulary Study not just in *Poetics & Progym*, but in all of your school subjects, and
with all of your reading. This is an excellent study skill to use in every area that you study, as
vocabulary is often the key to understanding a given subject.

STEPS FOR VOCABULARY STUDY

A. **Literary Context** Write the sentence (or at least the clause) containing the word to be
   studied. Underline the word.

B. **Spelling Analysis** Print the word again, dividing it into syllables, and including
   spelling markings based on the phonics method you have learned. If you have not
   learned a phonics marking method, copy the dictionary pronunciation.

C. **Part of Speech Identification** Note the part of speech according to the context of the
   word in the literary selection. For example, *trust* is listed in the dictionary as both a
   noun and a verb; determine how it is being used in the poem to know which word to
   enter.

D. **Definition** Write the dictionary definition that best fits the word in the context of the
   literary selection.

E. **Etymology** On the next line, note the etymology of the word from the dictionary. In
   the front of the dictionary, there should be a key to the abbreviations and symbols used
   to note etymology. These will vary from dictionary to dictionary. For example, you may
   see something like *<ME plesaunt <OF plaisant*. This means the word as it is used today
   was derived from a Middle English word that was in turn derived from an Old French
   word.

F. **Synonyms** and **Antonyms** On the next line write *syn:* and then make a list of
   synonyms (words having the same or nearly the same meaning) for the word from
   the dictionary. Below that, write *ant:*, and make a list of antonyms (words having an
   opposite meaning). You may find many synonyms and/or antonyms for a given word,
   but try to choose the ones that relate to the context as the vocabulary word.

A good dictionary will usually list several synonyms for each entry. For additional synonyms, ask your teacher to show you how to use a thesaurus. Keep one handy on your desk at all times! If you do not have a print thesaurus, there are some good ones available online, like thesaurus.com. Always use caution with online resources, and ask your teacher at home to help you avoid internet dangers and temptations.

G. **Literary Quotation** On the next line, copy a quotation from a different source that uses this word. Some good sources would include: the Bible, literary works, or the speeches, prayers, and letters of historical figures. Be sure to include an attribution.

A bible concordance is always a good place to start. Try the King James Version for lovely literary quotations. Some dictionaries, like *Webster's 1828 Dictionary*, include a quality literary quotation for most words. A reference like like *Bartlett's Quotations* is handy for this as well - and you can probably find a free or inexpensive one online or in your local used bookstore.

If you do not have a print resource, ask your teacher at home for permission and help in using an online resource like biblegateway.org or bartleby.com. I cannot repeat this too often—always use caution with online resources!

After completing these steps, discuss your findings with your teacher at home , and review the Word Usage notes in the dictionary for each word. Some possibilities for consideration include:

✓ Is this a word that is frequently misspelled or misunderstood? Does this word have any **homonyms** (words that sound the same but have a different spelling)? Does this word have any words that are frequently confused with it, such as *affect* and *effect*, or *then* and *than*? Are there any tips to help you remember the correct spelling and usage?

✓ Did you learn anything new about this word?

✓ Is the way the word is used in the literary selection "artfully varied from ordinary speech"? If so, it may be a figure of speech, and you should consider the literal meaning vs. the figural meaning of the word.

✓ Can this word be used as other parts of speech? If so, how does the meaning change?

✓ Discuss the synonyms and antonyms for the word. What effect would it have if one of the synonyms you have chosen was used in the literary selection in place of the original? What if you used an antonym with a negative expression before it in place of the original?

EXAMPLE VOCABULARY STUDY

Oh I do think it the <u>pleasantest</u> thing ever a child can do! — "The Swing" by Robert Louis Stevenson

Note: The dictionary does not have an entry for *pleasantest*, so it is necessary to remove the suffix -est, and define the root word).

ple̲a sant, adj., giving or affording pleasure; enjoyable

syn: agreeable, delightful, pleasing amusing enjoyable

ant: disagreeable, gloomy, sad, unpleasant

late 14th century, <ME plesaunt <OF plaisant "pleasant, pleasing agreeable"

"The lines have fallen for me in pleasant places; indeed, I have a beautiful inheritance." — Psalm 16:6, KJV

EXAMPLE VOCABULARY STUDY DISCUSSION

For this word, you might want to discuss the spelling. How can you remember that pleasant uses **ea** to spell the short sound of **e** /ĕ/? Perhaps if you think about the verb from which this adjective is derived, *to please*, it will be easier to remember.

You might also discuss the suffix -**est**. Usually when we want to make the superlative form of a multi-syllable adjective, we use the adverb *most* in front of the positive form of the adjective: *most pleasant*. Try that out in the poem. Think about why Robert Louis Stevenson might have chosen to use *pleasantest* instead. Think about who is speaking in this poem: young children often might not pick up little nuances in language usage, so the word *pleasantest* lends child-likeness to the language of the poem.

Theon's Six Narrative Elements

This chart lists questions and prompts to help you analyze the elements that Theon identified as fundamental to a narrative. *Bards & Poets* students will note that this chart is more comprehensive. Not every question will be answered in every narrative, but the questions are designed to help you thoroughly observe a narrative.[1]

PERSON   For each character in this Action, does the author give any information about the character's:

  ✓ Origin – parents, ancestors, or nation?

  ✓ Nature – physical characteristics?

  ✓ Disposition – personality characteristics?

  ✓ Training – upbringing or education?

  ✓ Age?

  ✓ Fortune – of wealth or circumstances?

  ✓ Morality?

  ✓ Action – the way he behaves?

  ✓ Speech – how does he/she talk?

  ✓ Death – Do we learn anything about this person's death or its consequences?

ACTION   Does the author indicate if the narrative (or action) was:

  ✓ Great or small?

  ✓ Dangerous or not?

  ✓ Possible or impossible?

  ✓ Necessary or unnecessary?

  ✓ Advantageous or not?

  ✓ Just or unjust?

  ✓ Honorable or dishonorable?

PLACE   Where does this narrative (or action) take place? Inside or outside? Country, continent, planet, universe?

  ✓ Size – how big is the place?

  ✓ Distance – is it near a city, town, or other well-known geographical location?

  ✓ Sacred or unhallowed – does the place have a religious significance?

  ✓ Ownership – to whom does the place belong?

  ✓ Deserted or inhabited?

  ✓ Strong (defended) or insecure (undefended)?

  ✓ Physical Characteristics – flat or mountainous? dry or wet? barren or wooded?

TIME   For the narrative (or action), what does the author tell us about:

    ✓ What has happened before?

    ✓ What is happening at present?

    ✓ What is going to happen after?

    ✓ What happened first, what happened second and so on?

    ✓ Were the person(s) and action(s) appropriate or fitting to life in the time period portrayed? Is this different from what is appropriate in our day?

    ✓ What is the date and season?

    ✓ What events are happening at the same time? — meeting? wedding? procession? festival? time of grief, time of joy? etc.

MANNER   How was the action in this narrative done? — willingly or unwillingly?

    ✓ If unwillingly – was it done in ignorance, by accident, or from necessity?

    ✓ If willingly – was it done by force, by deceit, or in secret?

CAUSE   Why was the action in this narrative done?

    ✓ To acquire goods?

    ✓ To escape evil?

    ✓ From friendship?

    ✓ Because of relationship: wife, husband, children, father, mother, friend, etc.?

    ✓ Out of the passions: love, hate, envy, pity, drunkenness, etc.?

Narrative Plot Observation

In each lesson of *Poetics & Progym I*, you will read one book of Homer's *Odyssey*, carefully observe the plot with Theon's Six, and then write a brief summary of the plot. After you read the first four books of the *Odyssey*, you will combine these summaries into a more detailed narrative retelling of those books in Lesson 6. Once you have finished reading the entire *Odyssey*, you will construct a hierarchical outline and write a four to six page summary in Lesson 27. Finally, you will write a one paragraph précis of the entire book, and then a one sentence précis in Lesson 28. Each step of this process offers opportunity to learn and hone the valuable composition and comprehension skills which were introduced and practiced in *Bards & Poets*. You will find examples of this process in the two sections beginning on page 362.

PLOT OBSERVATION – THEON'S SIX

Each of Theon's Six elements is important, but Action is particularly so because the entire narrative "is a clarification of an action."[2] Under Person, we name the story's characters. Under Action, we give the story's plot. Theon's other elements will add detail about the the plot. When we retell a story orally, we naturally recount the plot by telling which character does what action. The rest of Theon's Six helps add more detail.

Work in your Writer's Journal, and follow these steps to complete a plot observsation and summary for each book of Homer's *Odyssey*.

A. First, take a look at the big picture, following these steps:

Writer's Journal

- ◆ Person: List all the important characters, with a brief description of each.
- ◆ Action: List the major actions of the plot in the order they occur in the story. Your list should have no less than two, and no more than five. If possible, first number the actions in the margins of the book (Action 1, Action 2, Action 3, etc.). If the narrative includes any sections that do not detail an action, label them **Prologue**, **Epilogue**, **Explanation**, **Description**, **Summary**, **Author Comment**s, etc., and include them in your list.
- ◆ Place: Name and briefly describe the main place(s) where the action took place. Consult the questions listed for Theon's Six Elements in the Appendix and make notes about as many of the questions as the narrative answers.
- ◆ Time: Briefly describe the time period in which the action took place (this may be relative: before *x* or after *y*, or it may be more specific: one year later). Consult the

questions listed for Theon's Six Elements in the Appendix and make notes about as many of the questions as the narrative answers.

B. Use Theon's Six to observe the narrative plot. Consult the questions listed for Theon's Six Elements in the Appendix to complete this part of the assignment.

- ◆ Person: First, make notes on anything new you learn about Odysseus in this book. Then, make notes on up to three other characters that you meet in this book (there will usually be at least one other important character in each book). For each character, answer as many of Theon's Six questions about Person as you are able to answer directly from the narrative itself..

- ◆ Action: Create a numbered list with each of the actions you identified in order. If there are any sections of the narrative that do not detail an action, include these as well, and label them **Prologue**, **Epilogue**, **Explanation**, **Description**, **Summary**, **Author Comments**, etc.

- ◆ Under each action, answer Theon's Six questions about Time and Place if there are specifics attached to the action that you have not already detailed in Step A.

- ◆ Under each action, also answer as many of Theon's Six questions about Cause and Manner that the narrative answered.

- ◆ If you identified any sections that do not detail an action, add a brief note indicating the content of the section.

PLOT OBSERVATION – SUMMARY

A written summary is essentially a brief narration, or retelling, of the plot. The process of writing a summary is an aid to reading comprehension and retention. By limiting the length of the retelling, we are asking you to discriminate, or choose, only the most important details. You are responding to and even interacting with the author as you compose your summary. This is an important first step in entering the Great Conversation for yourself!

A. Review your notes and compose a one paragraph summary of the book that captures the main action, characters, and any other details from Theon's Six that are needful. You may either write this on the computer in a running file that you use for the entire *Odyssey*, or write each summary out by hand in your Writer's Journal, then transfer it to the running computer file.

B. Read over your summary to make sure you have not left out any essentials or included too many non-essentials. Revise as needed, and edit so that you have a smooth and eloquent summary paragraph.

PLOT OBSERVATION – HIERARCHICAL OUTLINE

An outline provides a strong foundation for a composition. It is—or should be—the first step in just about any kind of writing you will do, though often this will take the form of a simple list of points. Formal outlining is also an excellent skill for promoting comprehension of a narrative or any other kind of text, thus it is a crucial academic skill for all students to develop. In this exercise, you will take the plot observation work you have done for Homer's *Odyssey* throughout this course, and create a formal outline of the entire book. You will format this as a **hierarchical alphanumeric outline**. *Hierarchical* means that the outline is structured to show relationships between ther overall plot and the individual plot points and sub-points. *Alphanumeric* means that numbers and letters within the outline create the hierarchical structure. When outlining, keep two principles in mind:

- ◆ Every point or sub-point on the outline must have at least one other point or sub-point to accompany it. If you have a point I., you must have at least a point II. If you have a sub-point A., you must have at least a sub-point B.; if you have a (sub-)sub-point 1., you must have a 2.; etc.

- ◆ Each level on the outline should be grammatically parallel with the other items at the same level, but they do not necessarily need to be parallel with items at other levels. For example, the points numbered I., II., III., etc. might all have the grammatical structure Noun-Prepositional Phrase, while the sub-points numbered A., B., and C. might be structured Participle-Object.

A. Create a one-level outline that captures the action of the entire *Odyssey* in twenty-four captions, one per book.

   - ◆ Briefly review your plot observations for each book.
   - ◆ Write a caption for each book, using Roman numerals to structure the outline. Format each caption as a title, using capital letters for all words except some articles and prepositions. The first word of a title is always capitalized, even if it is an article or a preposition. Make your book captions *parallel*—each with the same grammatical format.
   - ◆ Save and print your one-level outline.

B. Create a two-level outline that divides the action of the entire *Odyssey* into a beginning, a middle, and an end. Before you begin this step, review the following sections in Lesson 4.1 Prose & Poetry: Plot Structure – Beginning, Plot Structure – Middle, and Plot Structure – End.

- Mark up the print copy of your one-level outline, dividing the action of the entire book into a beginning, a middle, and an end. Refer back to Lesson 4.1 as you consider the components that might be included in each division. Expect that the middle will contain a good deal more action than the beginning or the end.

- Create a new document and make an outline with main points Beginning, Middle, and End numbered I., II., and III., and the book captions as sub-points under each, numbered A., B., C., etc. Use the cut and paste function to make this faster and easier. Again, expect that you will have significantly more book titles under Middle than you will under either Beginning or End.

- Add parallel captions to Beginning, Middle, and End, and add to the outline with the format Beginning: [Caption], Middle: [Caption], End: [Caption].

- Save and print your two-level outline.

C. Create a condensed three-level outline of the entire *Odyssey*. Note that as you work through this step, you may find that you need to adjust your captions somewhat. Feel free to do so in order to get a well-structured parallel outline that accurately summarizes the plot of the *Odyssey*.

- Mark up the print copy of your two-level outline, grouping the book captions into divisions of related actions, while keeping the original narrative order intact. For each grouping, create a caption that reflects the content of the actions each contain. These grouping captions should all be parallel with one another. Again, you will have more groupings under Middle than you will under Beginning and End, but you must have at least two groupings under each.

- Create a new document and make an outline with main points Beginning, Middle, and End, along with their captions, numbered I., II., and III. Insert your new book grouping captions as sub-points under each labeled A., B., C., etc. Finally, insert your book captions, numbered 1., 2., 3., etc. as sub-points under the appropriate grouping captions.

- Balance the structure of the outline by dividing the Middle (Point II.) into two or three points, creating new captions and shifting the numbers so that you have four or five Roman numerals in all. Create parallel captions for the new divisions reflecting the content listed under each.

- Save and print your completed three-level outline.

Example Narrative Plot Observation

We will use this simplified retelling to illustrate the basic steps detailed above. The narrative retelling below, entitled "The Ransoming of Hector," is taken from the end of *The Iliad for Children* by Alfred Church. Patroclus, a Greek hero and close friend of Achilles, has been slain by Hector, a noble son of Priam, King of Troy. Achilles, in retribution, slays Hector. A possible scheme of listing the actions is noted to the left. There are, as always, other plausible ways to divide the narrative into actions. Sometimes, the end purpose for your observation will determine the way you divide actions. For example, this brief stand-alone narrative is similar to the narratives used for imitation in *Bards & Poets*, and would have been divided it into at least ten or twelve actions for retelling there. For our purposes in *Poetics & Progym I*, this would result in an outline and summary much longer and more detailed than we want to compile for the entire *Odyssey*. Therefore, for this example, we have divided the action into much larger chunks.

EXAMPLE NARRATIVE

Prologue

Action 1

The Greeks made a great mourning for Patroclus, and paid due honours to him, the body of Hector was shamefully treated, for Achilles caused it to be dragged daily about the tomb of his friend. Then Zeus sent for Thetis and said to her: "Go to the camp, and bid your son give up the body of Hector for ransom; it angers me to see him do dishonour to the dead."

So Thetis went to the tent of Achilles and found him weeping softly for his friend, for the strength of his sorrow was now spent. And she said to him: "It is the will of Zeus that you give up the body of Hector for ransom." And he said: "Let it be so, if the gods will have it."

Then, again, Zeus sent Iris his messenger to King Priam, where he sat in his palace with his face wrapped in his mantle, and his sons weeping round him, and his daughter and his daughters-in-law wailing in their chambers of the palace. Iris said to him: "Be of good cheer; I come from Zeus. He bids you take precious gifts wherewith to buy back the body of Hector from Achilles. Nor will Achilles refuse to give it up."

So Priam rose from his place with gladness in his heart. Nor would he listen to the Queen when she would have kept him back.

"I have heard the voice of the messenger of Zeus, and I will go. And if I die, what do I care? Let Achilles slay me, so that I hold the body of my son once more in my arms."

Then he caused precious things to be put into a wagon, mantles which had never been washed, and rugs, and cloaks, twelve of each, and ten talents of gold, and cauldrons and basins, and a great cup of gold which the Thracians had given him. Nothing of his treasures did he spare if only he might buy back his son. Then he bade his sons yoke the mules to the wagon. With many bitter words did he speak to them; they were cowards, he said, an evil brood, speakers of lying words, and mighty only to drink wine. But they did not answer him. Then Priam himself yoked the horses to the chariot, the herald helping. But before he went he poured out wine to Zeus, and prayed, saying: "Hear me, O Father, and cause Achilles to pity me; give me also a lucky sign that I may go on this business with a good heart."

So Zeus sent an eagle, a mighty bird, and it flew with wings outstretched over the city, on the right hand of the King.

Action 2

Then the King passed out of the gates. Before him the mules drew the wagon; these the herald drove. But Priam himself drove his horses. Then said Zeus to Hermes: "Go, guide the King, so that none of the Greeks may see him before he comes to the tent of Achilles." So Hermes fastened on his feet the winged sandals with which he flies, and he flew till he came to the plain of Troy. And when the wagon and the chariot were close to the tomb of Ilus, the herald spied a man (for Hermes had taken the shape of a man), and said to the King: "What shall we do? I see a man. Shall we flee, or shall we beg him to have mercy on us?" And the King was greatly troubled. But Hermes came near and said: "Whither do you go in the darkness with these horses and mules? Have you no fear of the Greeks? If any one should spy all this wealth, what then? You are old, and could scarcely defend yourselves. But be of good cheer; I will protect you, for you are like to my own dear father."

Priam answered: "Happy is he to have such a son. Surely the gods are with me, that I have met such a one as you."

Then said Hermes: "Tell me true; are you sending away these treasures for safe keeping, fearing that the city will be taken now that Hector is dead?"

Priam answered: "Who are you that you speak of Hector?"

Hermes said: "I am a Myrmidon, one of the people of Achilles, and often have I seen your son in the front of the battle."

Then the King asked him: "Is the body of Hector yet whole, or have the dogs and the vultures devoured it?"

Hermes answered: "It is whole, and without blemish, as fresh as when he died. Surely the gods love him, even though he be dead."

Then King Priam would have had the young man take a gift; but Hermes said: "I will take no gift unknown to my master. So to do would be wrong to him. But I will guide you to his tent, if you would go thither."

So he leapt into the chariot and took the reins. And when they came to the trench, where the sentinels were at their meal, Hermes caused a deep sleep to fall on them, and he opened the gate, and brought in the King with his treasures. And when they were at the tent of Achilles, the young man said: "I am Hermes, whom Father Zeus sent to be your guide. Go in and clasp him about the knees, and entreat him to have pity upon you." And he vanished out of his sight.

Action 3

Then Priam went to the tent, where Achilles, who had just ended his meal, sat at the table, and caught his knees and kissed his hands, yea, the very hands which had slain so many of his sons. He said: "Have pity on me, O Achilles, thinking of your own father. He is old as I am, yet it goes well with him, so long as he knows that you are alive, for he hopes to see you coming back from the land of Troy. But as for me, I am altogether miserable. Many sons have I lost, and now the best of them all is dead, and lo! I kiss the hands which slew him."

Then the heart of Achilles was moved with pity and he wept, thinking now of his own father and now of the dead Patroclus. At last he stood up from his seat and said: "How did you dare to come to my tent, old man? Surely you must have a heart of iron. But come, sit and eat and drink; for this a man must do, for all the sorrows that come upon him."

But the King said: "Ask me not to eat and drink while my son lies unburied and without honour. Rather take the gifts which I have brought, with which to ransom him."

But Achilles frowned and said: "Vex me not; I am minded to give back the body of Hector, but let me go my own way." Then Priam held his peace, for he feared to rouse the anger of Achilles. Then Achilles went forth from the tent, and two companions with him. First they took the gifts from the wagon; only they left two cloaks and a tunic wherewith to cover the dead. And Achilles bade the women wash and anoint the body, only that they should do this apart from the tent, lest Priam should see his son, and lament aloud when the body was washed and anointed, Achilles himself lifted it in his arms, and put it on a litter, and his comrades put the litter in the wagon.

When all was finished, Achilles groaned and cried to his dead friend, saying: "Be not angry, O Patroclus, that I have given the body of Hector to his father. He has given a noble ransom, and of this you shall have your share as is meet."

Action 4

Then he went back to his tent and said: "Your son, old man, is ransomed, and to-morrow shall you see him and take him back to Troy. But now let us eat and drink." And this they did. But when this had ended, they sat and looked at each other, and Achilles wondered at King Priam, so noble was he to behold, and Priam wondered to see how strong and how fair was Achilles.

Then Priam said: "Let me sleep, Achilles, for I have not slept since my son was slain." So they made up for him a bed, but not in the tent, lest, perhaps, one of the chiefs should come in and see him. But before he slept the King said: "Let there be a truce for nine days between the Greeks and the Trojans, that we may bury Hector." And Achilles said: "It shall be so; I will stay the war for so long."

But when the King slept, Hermes came again to him and said: "Do you sleep among your enemies, O Priam? Awake and depart, for although Achilles has taken ransom for Hector, what would not your sons have to pay for you if the Greeks should find you in the camp?"

Then the old man rose up. And the wise herald yoked the mules to the wagon and the horses to the chariot. And they passed through the camp of the Greeks, no man knowing, and came safe to the city of Troy.

Epilogue | On the ninth day the King and his people made a great burying for Hector, such as had never been seen in the land of Troy.

EXAMPLE PLOT OBSERVATION – THEON'S SIX

Person | Time

Zeus, king of the gods | During the Trojan War

Thetis, mother of Achilles | Place

Achilles, Greek warrior | Troy

Iris, messenger from Zeus

King Priam, father of Hector

Hermes, the messenger god

Action

Prologue: Greeks mourn for Patroclus, but mistreat the body of Hector

1. Zeus sends Priam to ransom Hector's body (Place: Priam's palace; Cause: Zeus is angry; Manner: Zeus sends help and encouragement to Priam willingly, Priam goes to Achilles willingly out of love for his son)

2. Priam journeys to the tent of Achilles accompanied by Hermes (Action of Priam is dangerous; Action of Hermes is necessary so that Priam arrives safely; Time: night; Place: between Troy and the Greek camp; Cause: Hermes helps Priam because he is "like my own dear father." Manner: Hermes helps Priam willingly)

3. Priam asks Achilles to give him Hector's body (Place: in the tent of Achilles; Time: same night; Action is dangerous and honorable; Manner: Priam humbles himself before Achilles willingly;

4. Achilles agrees to Priam's request (Place: in the tent of Achilles; Time: same night; Action is honorable; Cause: Achilles has great pity on Priam; Manner: Achilles is reluctant, but ultimately willing)

Epilogue: The Trojans bury Hector with great ceremony

EXAMPLE PLOT OBSERVATION: ONE-LEVEL HIERARCHICAL OUTLINE

For the outline examples we have divided the action in the Example Narrative into much smaller chunks than we used for the work with Theon's Six, in order give a comparable outline example of how to complete your captions for each book of the *Odyssey*.

I.	Impropriety of Greeks
II.	Anger of Zeus
III.	Message to Achilles
IV.	Message to Priam
V.	Obedience of Priam
VI.	Preparations by Priam
VII.	Sign from Zeus
VIII.	Orders for Hermes
IX.	Appearance of Hermes
X.	Advice from Hermes
XI.	Help from Hermes
XII.	Petition to Priam
XIII.	Pity of Achilles
XIV.	Acquiescence of Achilles
XV.	Gifts from Achilles
XVI.	Hospitality of Achilles
XVII.	Warning from Hermes
XVIII.	Journey to Troy
XIX.	Epilogue: Funeral of Hector

EXAMPLE PLOT OBSERVATION: TWO-LEVEL HIERARCHICAL OUTLINE

I. Beginning: Zeus Intervenes to Right a Wrong
    A. Prologue: Impropriety of Greeks
    B. Anger of Zeus
    C. Message to Achilles
    D. Message to Priam
II. Middle: Priam Travels to Ransom His Son
    A. Obedience of Priam
    B. Preparations by Priam
    C. Sign from Zeus
    D. Orders for Hermes
    E. Appearance of Hermes
    F. Advice from Hermes
    G. Help from Hermes
    H. Petition to Priam
    I. Pity of Achilles
    J. Acquiescence of Achilles
    K. Gifts from Achilles
    L. Hospitality of Achilles
    M. Warning from Hermes
III. End: Trojans Gather to Celebrate Their Champion
    A. Journey to Troy
    B. Epilogue: Funeral of Hector

EXAMPLE PLOT OBSERVATION: THREE-LEVEL HIERARCHICAL OUTLINE

I. Zeus Intervenes to Right a Wrong
    A. Hector's Body Is Dishonored
        1. Prologue: Impropriety of Greeks
        2. Anger of Zeus

   B. Zeus's Messengers Are Sent

     1. Message to Achilles

     2. Message to Priam

 II. Priam Travels to Ransom His Son

   A. Priam's Journey Is Approved

     1. Obedience of Priam

     2. Preparations by Priam

     3. Sign from Zeus

   B. Zeus's Provision Is Provided

     1. Orders for Hermes

     2. Appearance of Hermes

     3. Advice from Hermes

     4. Help from Hermes

 III. Achilles Responds to Priam's Appeal

   A. Hector's Body Is Ransomed

     1. Petition of Priam

     2. Pity of Achilles

     3. Acquiescence of Achilles

   B. Priam's Errand Is Concluded

     1. Gifts from Achilles

     2. Hospitality of Achilles

     3. Warning from Hermes

 IV. Trojans Gather to Celebrate Their Champion

   A. Achilles's Pity Is Shown

     1. Gifts from Achilles

     2. Hospitality of Achilles

   B. Priam's Errand Is Concluded

     1. Warning from Hermes

     2. Journey to Troy

     3. Epilogue: Funeral of Hector

Figures in Poetics & Progym I

Figures of Speech

- simile (Lesson 2)
- metaphor (Lesson 8)
- personification (Lesson 8)
- alliteration (Lesson 9)
- onomtopoeia (Lesson 9)
- anastrophe (Lesson 9)
- antithesis (Lesson 11)
- parallelism (Lesson 11)

- allusion (Lesson 15)
- biblical allusion (Lesson 15)
- idiom (Lesson 15)
- polysyndeton (Lesson 16)
- asyndeton (Lesson 17)
- refrain (Lesson 22)
- ellipsis (Lesson 25)

Figures of Description

- anemographia (Lesson 6)
- chronographia (Lesson 6)
- astrothesia (Lesson 6)

- topographia (Lesson 6)
- hydrographia (Lesson 6)

Other Literary Devices

- anecdote (Lesson 6)

- proverb (Lesson 6)

QUIZLET SETS

- Figures – P&P I Set #1: Lessons 1 – 6
- Figures – P&P I Set #2: Lessons 7 – 11
- Figures – P&P I Set #3: Lessons 12-18
- Figures – P&P I Set #4: Lessons 19-26

Eloquent Expression Through Copia

COPIA OF WORDS

✓ Synonyms and Antonyms (Lesson 1)

✓ Dialogue Tags – synonyms for *said* (Lesson 1)

✓ Nouns – varied, clear, specific, descriptive (Lesson 1)
   ◆ switch nouns/pronouns, common/proper, singular/plural (Lesson 1)
   ◆ switch gerund/infinitive (Lesson 5)

✓ Verbs – fitting and strong (Lesson 1)
   ◆ switch verb/verbal (Lesson 5)
   ◆ convert passive to active (Lesson 10)

✓ Modifiers (Lesson 1)
   ◆ add adjective (Lesson 1)
   ◆ add adverb (Lesson 1)
   ◆ add appositive noun (Lesson 7)

COPIA OF CONSTRUCTION

✓ Sentence Class by Use (Lesson 3)

✓ Opening Word (Lesson 3)

✓ Dialogue (Lesson 3)
   ◆ tag line position (Lesson 3)
   ◆ switch direct/indirect quotations (Lesson 3)

✓ Point of View (Lesson 3)

✓ Verb Tense (Lesson 3)

✓ Sentence Combination
   ◆ compound elements (Lesson 12)
   ◆ convert main verb to participle (Lesson 12)
   ◆ switch sentence classes by form (Lesson 18)

✓ Sentence Structure
   ◆ change position of words, phrases, and clauses (Lesson 22)
   ◆ switch subordinate/principal clauses (Lesson 21)
   ◆ switch words/phrases/clauses (Lesson 23)
   ◆ switch adjective/adverb elements (Lesson 24)

Leave a few lines here in your Prose & Poetry Handbook for future additions.

✓ Figures of Speech *Leave room for a future third column of figures.*
   ◆ parallelism (Lesson 13)   ◆ ellipsis (Lesson 26)
   ◆ antithesis (Lesson 14)   ◆ alliteration (Lesson 27)
   ◆ polysyndeton (Lesson 19)   ◆ anastrophe (Lesson 27)
   ◆ asyndeton (Lesson 19)

Grammar Terms & Definitions

Parts of Speech – *Bards & Poets* Review

Parts of Speech	1. Noun, 2. Pronoun, 3. Verb, 4. Adjective, 5. Adverb, 6. Preposition, 7. Conjunction, 8. Interjection
Noun	names a person, place, thing, or idea
Classes	common, proper
common	a name common to a class of persons, places, things, or ideas
proper	names a particular person, place, thing, or idea
Properties	gender, person, number, case
Property – Gender	masculine, feminine, common (either male or female), neuter (neither male nor female)
Property – Person	first person – the speaker, second person – spoken to, third person – spoken of
Property – Number	singular (only one), plural (more than one)
Verb	shows action, being, or state
Classes By Form	regular (past formed by adding -e or -ed), irregular (past formed some other way)
Classes By Use	transitive, intransitive, linking
Transitive	requires an object
Intransitive	does not require an object
Linking	joins the subject to a noun or adjective in the predicate
	forms of be: am, is, are, was, be, being, been
	verbs of sensing: taste, feel, smell, sound, look, appear
Auxiliaries	forms of be: am, is, are, was, be, being, been
	3 D's: do, does, did
	3 H's: have, has, had
	3 M's: may, might, must
Properties	person, number, tense, voice, mood
Property – Tense	the time of an action or event
Present	occurring or existing now
Present Perfect Tense	past but connected with the present and/or future
Past	occurring or existing before the present
Past Perfect Tense	ended or completed in the past
Future	yet to occur or exist
Future Perfect Tense	ended or completed before a certain future time
Verbal	derived from a verb; has both properties of a verb and of an adjective, a noun, or an adverb
Classes	participle, gerund, infinitive
Participle	verbal adjective
Gerund	verbal noun
Infinitive	verbal noun, adjective, or adverb; *to* + verb
Adjective	describes or defines a noun or pronoun
Classes	descriptive, definitive
Descriptive Adjective	describes a noun; telling what kind?
Definitive Adjective	limits or defines; telling which one? or how many?
Pronoun	"stands in" for a noun
Classes	personal, possessive, relative, interrogative
Antecedent	noun for which the pronoun "stands in"

Properties	gender, person, number, case
Adverb	modifies a verb, an adjective, or another adverb
Adverb Questions	where? when? why? how? to what extent?
Preposition	connects a noun or a pronoun to another word in the sentence

Common Prepositions	aboard	among	between	from	over	underneath
	above	around	beyond	in	past	until
	about	at	but	into	since	unto
	across	before	by	like	through	up
	after	behind	down	near	throughout	upon
	against	below	during	of	to	with
	along	beneath	except	off	toward	within
	amid	beside	for	on	under	without

Conjunction	connects words, phrases, clauses, or sentences
Classes	coordinate, subordinate, correlative
coordinate	joins elements of same rank or name
subordinate	joins elements of different ranks or names
correlative	coordinates or subordinates used in pairs
Interjection	shows sudden or strong emotion

Sentence Terms – *Bards & Poets* Review

Sentence	begins with a capital letter, ends with end punctuation, expressses a complete thought, has both a subject and a predicate
Subject	who or what the sentence is about
Predicate	what the subject is or does
Sentence Class by Use	declarative, interrogative, imperative, exclamatory
Declarative Sentence	makes a statement or gives information
Interrogative Sentence	asks a question
Imperative Sentence	tells or commands someone to do something
Exclamatory Sentence	expresses strong or sudden emotion
Phrase	a group of words working together in a sentence; does not have both a subject and a predicate
Clause	a group of words working together in a sentence; has both a subject and a predicate
Principal Clause	still makes complete sense if separated from the rest of the sentence
Subordinate Clause	does not make complete sense if separated from the rest of the sentence
Sentence Class by Form	simple, compound, complex, compound-complex
Simple Sentence	has one principal clause
Compound Sentence	has two or more principal clauses
Complex Sentence	has a principal clause and one or more subordinate clauses
Compound-Complex Sentence	has two or more principal clauses and one or more subordinate clauses
Basic Comma Rules	separate by commas: a series, a direct quotation, the salutation of an informal letter
Capitalization Rules	capitalize the first word of every sentence, proper nouns, titles, I, O!, dates and days of the week
Direct Quotation	relates what a speaker did or thought, repeating his/her actual words

Noun Terms – *Poetics & Progym I*, Lesson 6

Property – case	nominative, possessive, objective, absolute
Nominative	case used for a subject
Possessive	case which denotes ownership, authorship, origin, or kind
Objective	case used for an object
Absolute	case for independent use

Verb Terms – *Poetics & Progym I*, Lesson 10

Property – voice	form of the transitive verb showing whether the subject acts or is acted upon
Active Voice	the subject acts
Passive Voice	the subject is acted upon
Property – Mood	the manner in which action, being, or state is expressed
Indicative Mood	fact or actuality
Subjunctive Mood	doubtful or supposition
Potential Mood	power, necessity, liberty, duty, or liability
Imperative Mood	command, exhortation, entreaty, or permission
Infinitive Mood	expresses without affirming

Pronoun Terms – *Poetics & Progym I*, Lesson 16

Personal Pronouns	I, you, he, she, it, we, you, they, our, us, my, mine, your, his, him, her, its, their, them
Possessive Pronouns	mine, his, hers, ours, yours, theirs
Relative Pronouns	who, which, what, that
Interrogative Pronouns	who, which, what

Modifier Terms – *Poetics & Progym I*, Lesson 15

Articles	limit nouns without noting any qualities
Definite Article	the
Indefinite Articles	a, an
Degrees of Comparison	
Positive	simple quality or equal degree
Comparative	higher or lower degree
Superlative	highest or lowest degree

The Academic Essay, Classically Considered

	ANCIENT CLASSICAL ARGUMENT	ANECDOTE PROVERB	CONFIRMATION REFUTATION	COMMON-PLACE	ENCOMIUM INVECTIVE COMPARISON	RHETORICAL INVENTION
			PROGYMNASMATA			
I. INTRODUCTION	Exordium Narratio *Divisio*	Encomion Paraphrase	Discredit/Commend Storyteller (Proponent) Exposition of the Matter *(Slant Narrative)*		Prooemion *Origin *Nurture & Upbringing	*Appeal to Ethos* *Stasis Theory* *Common Topics* Definition Authority
II. BODY	Confirmatio Refutatio	Cause Contrast Comparison Example Authority*	Refutation/ Confirmation Headers •Clarity •Probability •Possibility •Credibility •Propriety •Profitability	Contrary *(From the Opposite)* Exposition *Maxim* Comparison Intention *(Way of Thinking)* Digression	*Origin *Nurture & Upbringing Deeds *Comparison	*Appeal to Logos* *Common Topics* Defintion Comparison Circumstance Relation Authority
III. CONCLUSION	Peroratio	Authority* Exhortation		Rejection of Pity *(Final Headings)* •Justice/Honor •Legality •Necessity •Possibility •Propriety •Expediency	*Comparison Exhortation/Prayer	*Appeal to Pathos* *Common Topic* Authority

*Authority may be used in either place, depending upon the needs of the essay.

Choice of format and topics depends upon **Rhetorical Situation**
   - Exigency – issue, problem, or situation to be addressed; cause of composition
   - Audience – those whom the author is addressing in order to change or persuade
   - Constraints – requirements based on the audience and the occasion; *kairos:* is this an opportune moment? is it fitting? Special Topics suited to occasion (*deliberative, judicial, or ceremonial*)

Proverbs & Anecdotes for Additional Elaborations
೧೩

A lie can travel halfway around the world while the truth is putting on its pants. — Mark Twain

A soft answer turneth away wrath: but grievous words stir up anger. — Proverbs 15:1

The man who will not read good books has no advantage over the man who cannot read. — Mark Twain

Socrates said that the unexamined life is not worth living.

Consider how much more you often suffer from your anger and grief than from those very things for which you are angry and grieved. — Marcus Aurelius

Julius Caesar avowed that he had rather be first in a village than second at Rome.

We are like dwarfs standing on the shoulders of giants; thanks to them, we see father than they. — Peter of Blois

When someone asked how can one become master of himself, Diogenes said, "When those things which he reproves in others he reproves even more in himself."

Ronald Reagan used to say, "Trust, but verify."

"The same sun which melts wax hardens clay. And the same Gospel which melts some persons to repentance hardens others in their sins" — Charles Spurgeon

If adversity hath killed his thousands, prosperity hath killed his ten thousands; therefore adversity is to be preferred. The one deceives, the other instructs; the one miserably happy, the other happily miserable. — Robert Burton (1577-1640, Oxford scholar)

Thomas Paine said, "Those who expect to reap the blessings of freedom must undergo the fatigue of supporting it."

If you read history you will find that the Christians who did most for the present world were precisely those who thought most of the next. — C. S. Lewis

A cheerful heart is good medicine, but a crushed spirit dries up the bones. — Proverbs 17:22

Prose & Poetry Handbook Sample Pages

We provide these sample pages to help you construct a Prose & Poetry Handbook as you progress through your studies in *Poetics & Progym I*. You will continue this handbook through *Poetics & Progym II* and *III*, so that you have a complete reference of all that you have learned about Rhetoric, Literature, Poetry, and Figures. This handbook will prove helpful to you now, as you work on compositions and comprehension in other disciplines like history, science, and (hopefully) even math. It will also prove valuable to you in the future as you encounter more challenging academic papers and readings, and perhaps will provide a reference for review if you sit for various Advanced Placement tests.

Of equal importance, as you record the things you are learning in this course in a systematic way, you are learning how to learn, which is the truly invaluable skill. To that end, it is imperative that you construct your handbook as you go—entering the concepts as you learn them; not blindly copying them all ahead of time, or at the last minute before they are due. Instead, follow the directions in the lessons, beginning with Lesson 1.1, where you are instructed to set up your Prose & Poetry Handbook.

RHETORIC   1

P&P I 1.1.4 — Rhetoric (literally, art of the orator) is the "faculty of discovering in any given case the available means of persuasion." – Aristotle, *Rhetoric* trans Rhys Roberts

CANONS OF RHETORIC

- Invention (Inventio)
- Arrangement (Dispositio)
- Style (Elocutio)
- Memory (Memoria)
- Delivery (Actio/Pronuntiatio)

RHETORIC   2
CANON OF INVENTION

P&P I 1.6.1 — RHETORICAL SITUATION

The context in which any written or spoken work is created – Lloyd Bitzer, "The Rhetorical Situation")

- <u>Exigency</u>: issue, problem, or situation to be addressed; cause of oratory or composition
- <u>Audience</u>: those whom the author is addressing; those whom the author wishes to change or persuade
- <u>Constraints</u>: requirements based on the audience (age, educational level, religious beliefs, and cultural factors) and the occasion (speech, essay, email, blog post, etc.); author's own character, ways of thinking and style; kairos: is this an opportune moment? is it fitting in this context?

RHETORIC
CANONS OF INVENTION AND ARRANGEMENT
10

P&P I
I.2.4

THE PROGYMNASMATA

Fable (MYTHOS LOGOS)

Retell a short fictional story illustrating a moral point
- Amplify
  - Add figures of description (enargia)
  - Invent dialogue (dialogismus)
- Slant
- Abbreviate

P&P I
I.3.4

Narrative

Retell an account or story, either fictional or non-fictional
- Clear articulation of the details - Theon's Six Components (Person, Action, Place, Time, Manner, Cause)
- Sequence – ab ovo, in medias res, reverse

RHETORIC
CANONS OF INVENTION AND ARRANGEMENT
11

P&P I
I.6.1

THE PROGYMNASMATA

Anecdote (CHREIA) and Proverb (Maxim)

- Anecdote "a recollection of a noteworthy statement, action, or combination of statement and action." – Libanius, tr Gibson
- Proverb "a pithy, universal statement" that seeks to persuade or dissuade the hearer from some course of action or thought. – Libanius, tr Gibson

Elaborate a proverb or anecdote, in this order:

1. Encomion: brief praise of the person represented as speaking or acting
2. Paraphrase: restate the anecdote (proverb) in your own words
3. Cause: rationale behind the words and/or action in the anecdote (proverb)
4. Contrast: consideration of contrasting words or action
5. Comparison: consideration of an analogous situation
6. Example: discussion of relevant illustration(s) from history or literature
7. Authority: wise person of the past that supports proverb/anecdote's wisdom
8. Exhortation: admire the wit and/or emulate the wisdom

RHETORIC
CANONS OF INVENTION AND ARRANGEMENT
17

P&P I
I.23.4

THE ACADEMIC ESSAY, CLASSICALLY CONSIDERED

PROGYMNASMATA

ANCIENT CLASSICAL ARGUMENT	ANECDOTE PROVERB	CONFIRMATION REFUTATION	COMMON PLACE	ENCOMIUM INVECTIVE COMPARISON	RHETORICAL INVENTION
I INTRODUCTION	Encomion				
	Paraphrase				
II BODY	Cause				
	Contrast				
	Comparison				
	Example				
	*Authority				
III CONCLUSION	*Authority				
	Exhortation				

* Headers should be placed where most effective for the particular composition

Choice of format and topics depends upon Rhetorical Situation
- Exigency - issue, problem or situation to be addressed, cause of composition
- Audience - those whom the author is addressing in order to change or persuade
- Constraints - requirements based on the audience and the occasion; kairos: is this an opportune moment? is it fitting? Special Topics suited to occasion (deliberative, judicial, or ceremonial)

RHETORIC
CANONS OF INVENTION AND ARRANGEMENT
19

P&P I
I.24.1

THESIS STATEMENT

A sentence or two at the end of the introduction stating the central idea of the essay, organizing theme of the essay

A good thesis statement should be
- stated as a proposition
- specific, concrete and literal
- supported by the rest of the essay

EXAMPLES OF EXCELLENT THESIS STATEMENTS
[Student should add these]

RHETORIC
CANONS OF INVENTION AND ARRANGEMENT

20

P&P I 1.24.1	TOPIC SENTENCES

Sentence in each body paragraph that identifies the main idea of the paragraph, and relates clearly to the thesis statement, often the first or last sentence of the paragraph

EXAMPLES OF EXCELLENT STATEMENTS

[Student should add these]

RHETORIC
CANON OF STYLE (ELOCUTION)

26

P&P I 1.1.3	COPIA

"an abundant and ready supply (or storehouse) of language" – Erasmus (trans. King)

COPIA OF WORDS

- Synonyms and Antonyms - consider connotation and denotation!
- Dialogue Tags - synonyms for said
- Nouns - varied, clear, specific, descriptive
  - switch noun antecedent/pronoun, common/proper, singular/plural, possessive/'of' phrase
  - switch gerund/infinitive
- Verbs - fitting and strong
  - switch main verb/participle
  - switch active to passive
- Modifiers
  - add adjective
  - add adverb
  - add appositive noun

RHETORIC
CANON OF STYLE (ELOCUTION)

27

P&P I 1.3.3	COPIA OF CONSTRUCTION

- Sentence Class By Use
- Opening Word
- Dialogue
  - tag line position
  - switch direct/indirect quotation
- Point of View
- Verb Tense

P&P I 1.4.3

- Sentence Combination
  - compound elements
  - convert main verb to participle
  - switch sentence class by form

Sentence Structure
- change position of words, phrases, and clauses
- switch subordinate/principal clauses
- switch words/phrases/clauses

[Nota Bene: Leave several lines for a few more in future books]

P&P I 1.23.4

Figures of Speech - Schemes of Construction
- parallelism
- antithesis
- polysyndeton
- asyndeton
- ellipsis
- alliteration
- anastrophe

[Nota Bene: Leave room for a third column of figures to be added in later books]

LITERATURE

30

P&P I 1.1.1	

"Literature belles-lettres and letters refer to artistic writings worthy of being remembered. In the broadest sense, literature includes any type of writings on any subject . . . usually, however, it means the body of artistic writings of a country or period that are characterized by beauty of expression and form and by universality of intellectual and emotional appeal." – Random House American English Dictionary, 2019

Middle English LITERATURE < Old French < Latin LITERATURA "writing, learning" < LITERATUS "learned, literate"– American Heritage Dictionary, 1975

"[Literature] is a fountain forever overflowing with the waters of wisdom and delight." – Percy Bysshe Shelley, A Defence of Poetry

LITERARY CONTEXT

TITLE
AUTHOR
- Origin – ancestor, homeland
- Historical time period
- Influences

P&P I 1.16.1

RHETORICAL SITUATION
(refer to Rhetoric, p. 2)

- Exigency
- Audience
- Constraints

| | LITERATURE | 31 |

P&P I
L 1.1

LITERARY GENRE

BROAD CATEGORIES
- Prose & Poetry
- Fiction & Non-Fiction
- Nation of Origin and Historical Time Period

SPECIFIC CATEGORIES
- Language
- Subject Matter
- Style

| | LITERATURE
NARRATIVE | 34 |

P&P I
L 2.1

"Narrative is language descriptive of things that have happened, or as though they have happened." – Theon, trans. Kennedy

- Synonyms: tale, story, account, chronicle
- Distinct from Exposition, which includes
  - Essay
  - Speech or sermon
  - Technical writing
  - Journalism (Investigative or Expositional)
  - Travel Guide

| | LITERATURE
NON-FICTION NARRATIVE | 35 |

P&P I
L 2.1

"Language descriptive of things that have happened." – Theon, trans. Kennedy

Non-fiction is written by an eyewitness to the event or by one who retells from sources who were eyewitnesses
- Actual people (characters)
- Actual times and places (setting)
- Actual actions, events and dialogues (plot)
- No fictional elements

Purpose of Non-Fiction: to provide a factual account of something that has happened.

Subcategories of Non-Fiction Narrative

- Biography
- Autobiography
- History
- Journalism (Narrative)

| | LITERATURE
FICTION NARRATIVE | 36 |

P&P I L
2.1

"Language descriptive of things as though they have happened." Theon, trans. Kennedy

May include
- People invented by the author (characters)
- Times and places invented by the author (setting)
- Actions, events or dialogues invented by the author (plot)
- Actual (historical) characters, setting, or plot elements

Purpose of Fiction (Perrine)
- Escape
- Interpretive – broadens, deepens, and sharpens our awareness of life

Subgenres of Fiction
- Fable
- Myth
- Legend
- Fairy Tale
- Historical Fiction
- Science Fiction
- Fantasy
- Allegory
- Novel

LITERATURE
NARRATIVE & THE CANONS OF RHETORIC

38

P&P I
1.2.1

INVENTION
- Characters (Person, Cause)
- Setting (Time, Place)
- Plot (Action, Manner)
- Plot Devices
- Theme (Message)
- Literary Devices

ARRANGEMENT
- Chronology - the order in which the story is told

STYLE
- Point of View
- Diction

LITERATURE
NARRATIVE INVENTION

39

P&P I
1.5.1

CHARACTERS

"Human life began, we are told, when God breathed life into a handful of dust and created Adam. Fictional life begins when an author breathes life into his characters and convinces us of their reality."—Perrine, Literature Structure Sound, and Sense

- Direct Characterization – the author "tells" about the character
- Indirect Characterization – the author "shows" the character through his/her own words and actions

CHARACTER TYPE
- Flat (Static): does not change throughout the story
- Stock (Stereotypical): immediately recognizable
- Rounded (Complex): multi-faceted ("many faces"); does not always act according to expectations
- Dynamic: undergoes significant personality or perspective change
- Bildungsroman: an entire story dedicated to moral, emotional, or spiritual development of a character, a "coming of age" story

LITERATURE
NARRATIVE INVENTION

40

P&P I
1.5.1

SETTING

The time and place in which the action of a narrative happens

- Historical
- Author's creation
- Blend

LITERATURE
NARRATIVE INVENTION

41

P&P I
1.4.1

PLOT

The plot of a narrative is its storyline. It is the structure or scheme into which the author has arranged each action and event making up the complete story (may or may not correspond to the temporal or chronological order of actions and events - see Narrative Arrangement)

PLOT STRUCTURE: BEGINNING
Also called Exposition or Introduction

Characters
- Protagonist: central character, whether sympathetic or not
- Antagonist: person(s) or thing(s)—circumstances, conventions, character traits (fatal flaw, besetting sin)— working in opposition to the protagonist

Conflict
- Internal: within the character
- External: from outside the character
- Thematic: conflict between competing ideals, virtue and vice, etc.

Catalyst: action or event that sets off the conflict

	LITERATURE	42
	NARRATIVE INVENTION	

P&P I L 4.1 — PLOT STRUCTURE: MIDDLE

Rising Action: conflict builds and characters and situations develop

Climax: turning point, decision is made

Falling Action: consequences

	LITERATURE	43
	NARRATIVE INVENTION	

P&P I L 4.1 — PLOT STRUCTURE: END

Denouement or final Resolution

- Consequences
- Reversal of fortune or situation
- Epiphany – revelation or aha! moment for character(s)

Types of Endings

- Happy
- Unhappy
- Indeterminate – no definite conclusion or complete resolution
- (Sequel set-up) – thanks to modern film-making...

	LITERATURE	44
	NARRATIVE INVENTION	

P&P I L 3.1 — PLOT STRUCTURE ELEMENTS - SIX BY THEON

- Person (Who?)
  Origin? Nature? Training? Disposition? Age? Fortune? Morality? Action? Speech? Manner of death? What followed death?

- Action (What?)
  Great or small? Dangerous or not dangerous? Possible or impossible? Easy or difficult? Necessary or unnecessary? Advantageous or not? Just or unjust? Honorable or dishonorable?

- Place (Where?)
  Size? Distance? Near city or town? Sacred or unhallowed? Whose property? Deserted or inhabited? Defended or not? Topography?

- Time (When?)
  What has gone by? What is present? What is going to be? What was first, second, etc? What is appropriate to life in our time? to ancient times? Special dates in private or public life? Season of the year? Time of day or night? Circumstances surrounding?

- Cause (Why?)
  To acquire good things? To escape from evil? From friendship? Because of or for wife or children? Out of passions: anger, love, hate, envy, pity, inebriation

- Manner (How?)
  Willingly: by force, secretly, or by deceit? OR unwillingly: in ignorance, by accident, or by necessity?

	LITERATURE	48
	NARRATIVE ARRANGEMENT	

P&P I L 4.1 — SEQUENCE

The order in which the events and actions are told within the narrative account

Terms used to describe narrative arrangement (these are not mutually exclusive; more than one may apply to a particular narrative):

- Chronological: linear arrangement of events from beginning to end in the order that they actually happened
- "ab ovo": from the egg (earliest causes)
- "in medias res": the narrative begins in the middle of things
- Flashbacks: an interruption in the present action to fill in details of previous events or actions; commonly takes the form of a character's reminiscence or an author's commentary
- Episodic: presents a series of mostly unrelated stories or scenes instead of a single unified plot
- Frame Narrative: shorter unrelated scenes, stories or episodes which are connected in the context of a larger, overarching story
- Reverse

- Stream of Consciousness

LITERATURE
NARRATIVE ARRANGEMENT
49

P&P I
I.3.1

STORY STRUCTURE

ACTION

The action in a narrative forms the plot.
- Physical
- Dialogue
- Thoughts related as a dialogue inside a character's mind

OTHER ELEMENTS
- Prologue
- Epilogue
- Background
- Explanation
- Description
- Summary
- Transition
- Author comments

ESSENTIAL ELEMENTS OF A NARRATIVE
- Essential Elements: must be present for the story to make sense or the message to be understood
- Non-essential Elements: give additional information or make actions more vivid, but could be removed with no change to the essential storyline

---

LITERATURE
NARRATIVE STYLE
50

P&P I
I.3.1

POINT OF VIEW

Narrator - literally one who tells; may be an "onlooker" or may be a character (major or minor) inside the story

Naming Point of View: Person + Level of Omniscience
- Person
  - First Person
  - Third Person
- Level of Omniscience
  - Omniscient: "all knowing" about the story and its characters, including all thoughts, feelings, and motives
  - Limited: knows only the thoughts, feelings, and motives of one (or only a very few) character(s)
  - Objective or Dramatic: reports only actions and dialogue, does not have access to (or does not relate) character's thoughts, feelings, or motives.

LITERATURE
LITERARY FORMS
53

P&P I
I.3.1

THE EPIC

a long narrative poem, featuring

INVENTION
- epic hero, "who embodies (despite imperfections) the ideals of the author's culture" – Ryken, Homer's The Odyssey
- epic feat or quest: action of great historical or mythical importance
- epic sweep: cosmic scope/setting "encompasses the whole earth, a supernatural world, and the afterlife" – Ryken, Homer's Odyssey
- often concerned with foundings or re-foundings of a civilization or culture
- supernatural intervention
- invocation of the Muse and a statement of purpose
- "An epic sums up what an entire age wants to say." – Ryken, Literary Forms in the Bible

ARRANGEMENT

in medias res

STYLE

Epic Style
- exalted, formal or "high" language
- epic simile - extended simile over several (or many!) lines
- epithets - repeated titles or descriptive phrases for persons, places or things
- periphasis or circumlocution - indirect or roundabout way of expressing something

---

POETRY
55

P&P I
I.10.1

A poem is a metrical composition, with an aim to please by addressing the imagination and sensibilities – Thomas Harvey, A Practical Grammar

1350-1400: ME poetrie < Medieval Latin poetria "poetic art" < Latin POETA "poet" derived from Greek: poetes "maker, creator" – American Heritage Dictionary, 1975

TERMS AND DEFINITIONS

Prosody: the study of meter, rhyme, and stanza forms in poetry

Versification: "the art of metrical composition" – Thomas Harvey, A Practical Grammar

Verse: a line of poetry - often incorrectly used in place of the term stanza, which refers to a grouping of verses (lines).

Prose: the ordinary form of speaking or writing without meter or rhyme, "having reference, mainly, to a clear and distinct meaning of the author's meaning" – Thomas Harvey, A Practical Grammar

Herodotus, the ancient Greek historian, coined the phrase "pedzos logos" to describe prose—language that walks on feet, where poetry rides in a winged chariot.

POETRY
POETIC METER

57

P&P I
L 11.1

DIVISIONS OF POETIC METER

- Quantitative meter that relies on the length of syllables and consequently, verses (lines); meter in classical Greek and Latin poetry.
- Qualitative meter that relies on patterns of stressed and unstressed intervals
  - Accentual: counts stresses in the verse; common meter in Old English poetry.
  - Accentual-Syllabic counts accents and syllables; most common meter in post-Renaissance English poetry

POETRY SCANSION

Process of analyzing the meter of a verse (line) in four steps--taken from Perrine, Sound and Sense:

1. marking stress (/ or sometimes --) and unstress (∪) syllables

2. dividing the lines into feet (|) with groups of stressed and unstressed syllables

3. identifying the metrical pattern (see below)

4. noting significant variations from the pattern

POETRY
POETIC METER

58

P&P I
L 11.1

METRICAL PATTERNS

Foot: basic unit used in scansion of verse.

FEET IN ENGLISH POETRY

- Iamb: breve-stress
- Trochee: stress-unstress
- Anapest: unstress-unstress-stress
- Dactyl: stress-unstress-unstress
- Pyrrhee: unstress-unstress
- Spondee: stress-stress
- Amphibrach: unstress-stress-unstress
- Molossus: stress-stress-stress

LINE NAMES (NUMBER OF FEET PER VERSE)

1. Monometer
2. Dimeter
3. Trimeter
4. Tetrameter
5. Pentameter
6. Hexameter
7. Heptameter
8. Octameter

NAMING VERSE

a. Make predominant foot name into an adjective
b. Follow with line name

POETRY
RHYME

62

P&P I
L 11.1

TERMS & DEFINITIONS

- Rhyme "a correspondence of sound in the last syllables of two or more lines succeeding each other immediately, or at no great distance"-- Thomas Harvey, A Practical Grammar
- Perfect rhyme: the final syllable's stress, vowel sound, and ending consonant sound (if there is one) are the same, e.g. talk/walk, town/crown
- Imperfect (slant) Rhyme: final syllables have the impression of rhyme either through sound or through sight, e.g. breathe/teeth, home/come
- Rhyme Scheme: the pattern of rhyme within a stanza. Mark with capital letters at the end of line using the same letter for lines that rhyme, e.g. ABBA, ABAB, ABA

POETRY
STANZA FORM

64

P&P I
L 11.1

TERMS & DEFINITIONS

Stanza: a grouping of verses (lines) in a pattern, which is often repeated throughout the poem.

# OF LINES	STANZA NAME
2	couplet
3	tercet, triplet
4	quatrain
5	quintain, cinquain, quintet
6	sextet, sextain, sexain, sixain, hexastich, sestet
7	septet
8	octave, octet

	POETRY	66
	POETIC FORM AND GENRE	

P&P I
L 12.1

Narrative Poetry: has a plot (complete story)

Lyrical Poetry: descriptive, without a plot

Closed Couplet: pair of rhymed lines that form a complete thought or syntactical unit (usually a sentence).

Heroic Couplet: pair of rhymed lines written in iambic pentameter

Triplet: three lines which rhyme AAA

Haiku: three line poem with 5 syllables, 7 syllables, 5 syllables (Japanese)

Terza Rima: tercet with interlocking rhyme e.g. ABA BCB CDC DED (Italian)

Quatrain Rhyme Schemes

- ABAB   cross-rhymed
- ABBA   envelope rhyme
- AAAA   mono-rhymed
- AAxA   rubai (Persian form) – x can vary
- AABB   heroic, elegiac couplet (Greek form)

Ballad: a narrative poem, usually a quatrain

Elegy: poem written in response to a death; in English poetry, often iambic pentameter cross-rhymed quatrains

Hymn: song of praise, often in quatrain form
- Short Meter: iambic trimeter in 1st, 2nd, and 4th lines, iambic tetrameter in the 3rd; noted by syllables: 6686
- Long Meter: four iambic tetrameters in each line; noted by syllables: 8888
- Common Meter: alternating lines of iambic tetrameter and iambic trimeter; noted by syllables: 8686

	POETRY	67
	POETIC FORM AND GENRE	

P&P I
L 13.1

Limerick: Quintain written in anapestic meter, lines 1, 2, and 5 are trimeter, lines 3 and 4 are dimeter, rhyme scheme is usually AABBA. Most limericks are meant to be amusing.

Rhyme Royale (Rime Royal or Troilus Stanza): seven lines of ten syllables, usually written in iambic pentameter; rhyme scheme is ABABBCC

Spenserian Stanza: nine line stanza; eight lines rhyming The ABABBCBCC; last line is an alexandrine (iambic hexameter)

Sonnet: fourteen line poem, usually in iambic pentameter. Rhyme scheme depends on the type of sonnet.

Petrarchan Sonnet: octave rhyming ABBAABBA plus sestet rhyming CDCDCD or CDECDE

Shakespearean Sonnet: three quatrains plus a couplet, rhyming ABAB CDCD EFEF GG

Spenserian Sonnet: similar to Shakespearean, with interlocking rhyme ABAB BCBC CDCD EE

Ode: A formulaic poem that addresses, exalts, and/or celebrates a person, place, thing or idea; stanza forms vary

Epic Poem: A long narrative poem written with epic conventions and in epic style. See list in Literary Forms, p. 54

Blank Verse: metrical verse with no rhyme

Free Verse: Lines closely following the natural rhythm of speech. Lines are not metrical and do not rhyme. Though a regular pattern of sound or rhythm may be discerned, the poet does not compose free verse in a particular meter.

	FIGURES	70
	FIGURES OF SPEECH	

P&P I
L 2.3

"A figure is a form of speech artfully varied from common usage."—Quintilian, Institutes of Oratory, trans. Butler

CLASSIFICATION OF FIGURES

This classification system is based on Edward Corbett's system in Classical Rhetoric for the Modern Student (Oxford University Press, 1990) with some additional categories from Gideon O. Burton at Silva Rhetoricae online.

Figures of speech subdivided into:
- Schemes: "Artful variation from the common arrangement of words."—Corbett, Classical Rhetoric
- Tropes: "Artful variation from the ordinary and principal meaning of a word."—Corbett, Classical Rhetoric

SCHEMES
- Words
- Construction
  - Balance
  - Word Order
  - Omission
  - Repetition

TROPES
- Comparison
- Wordplay
- Substitution
- Overstatement & Understatement
- Semantic Inversion

	FIGURES	73
	SCHEMES OF CONSTRUCTION	

REPETITION

P&P I
L 9.3

Alliteration: the repetition of the same sound at the beginning of two or more closely associated words or stressed syllables; e.g. "No guest on God's earth would he gladlier greet."

P&P I
L 16.3

Polysyndeton: repetition of a conjunction between words, phrases, or clauses; e.g. "But ye shall receive power, after that the Holy Ghost is come upon you: and ye shall be witnesses unto me both in Jerusalem, and in all Judaea, and in Samaria, and unto the uttermost part of the earth."—Acts 1:8

P&P I
L 22.3

Refrain: a recurring phrase or line

FIGURES
SCHEMES OF CONSTRUCTION

77

BALANCE

P&P I
1.11.3

Parallelism: the use of related elements similar in grammatical form or structure. These elements may be words, phrases, or clauses in pairs or in a series; e.g. "...we mutually pledge to each other our Lives, our Fortunes, and our sacred Honor."— The Declaration of Independence

P&P I
1.11.3

Antithesis: juxtaposition of contrasting ideas, often in parallel structure; e.g. "It was the best of times, it was the worst of times."—Charles Dickens, Tale of Two Cities

FIGURES
SCHEMES OF CONSTRUCTION

79

WORD ORDER

P&P I
1.9.3

Anastrophe: inversion of the usual or natural word order; e.g. "(Of) Arms and the man I sing"—Virgil, Aeneid; "Did ever dragon keep so fair a cave? ... fiend angelical!"—William Shakespeare, "Romeo and Juliet"

FIGURES
SCHEMES OF CONSTRUCTION

81

OMISSION

P&P I
1.17.3

Asyndeton: omission of conjunctions between clauses; e.g. "I came, I saw, I conquered"—Julius Caesar; "That government of the people, by the people, for the people shall not perish from the earth."—Abraham Lincoln, "The Gettysburg Address"

P&P I
1.25.3

Ellipsis: the omission of a word, phrase, or clause in a sentence; e.g. "Reading maketh a full man, conference a ready man, and writing an exact man."—Francis Bacon, "Of Studies"

FIGURES
TROPES OF COMPARISON

83

P&P I
1.2.3

Simile: explicit comparison between two things of unlike nature, using the words "like," "as" or "than"; e.g. "My luve is like a red, red rose"—Robert Burns

P&P I
1.8.3

Metaphor: implied comparison between two things of unlike nature; e.g. All the world's a stage and men and women merely players"—Shakespeare; "How frugal is the chariot [a book] that bears the human soul."—Emily Dickinson

Personification (Prosopopoeia): living characteristics are attributed to an abstract idea or inanimate thing, or human characteristics are attributed to a non-human thing.

- First-Degree Personification: qualities, including giving a gender to an object that is not inherently masculine or feminine; e.g. majestic tree, crafty fox, her anchor (ship's)
- Second-Degree Personification: actions; e.g. "Lands intersected by a narrow frith abhor each other."— William Cowper
- Third-Degree Personification: direct address; e.g. "O death, where is thy sting? O grave, where is thy victory?"—I Corinthians 15:55

P&P I
1.15.3

Allusion: a comparison using an indirect or figurative reference to a historical or literary source; e.g. "cry wolf for tell a lie (Aesop's Fables); He met his Waterloo (reference to Napoleon's downfall)

Biblical Allusion: an indirect or figurative reference to a biblical source; e.g. Good Samaritan (Luke 10), forbidden fruit (Genesis 3), turn the other cheek (Matthew 5)

Idiom: an allusion that has become common in everyday English usage; e.g. piece of cake for easy

	FIGURES TROPES OF WORDPLAY	86
P&P I I.9.3	<u>Onomatopoeia</u>: words whose sound echoes the sense, e.g. splash, bark, gush, lull	

	FIGURES FIGURES OF DESCRIPTION	94
P&P I I.6.3	A FIGURE OF DEFINITION is a vivid portrayal – "a bringing to life" in the mind's eye of the reader. Figures of description are classified by the thing they describe. <u>Anemographia</u>: vivid description of the wind. ‹Greek anemos: wind, e.g. "On stormy nights, when the wind shook the four corners of the house, and the surf roared along the cove and up the cliffs . . ." – Robert Louis Stevenson, <u>Treasure Island</u> <u>Chronographia</u>: vivid description of a particular time, an historical time period, or a recurring time period, such as a season or a particular time of day. ‹Greek chronos: time, e.g. "It was one of those March days when the sun shines hot and the wind blows cold: when it is summer in the light and winter in the shade" – Charles Dickens, <u>Great Expectations</u> <u>Astrothesia</u>: vivid description of the stars or the night sky ‹Greek astron: star, e.g. "Silently, one by one, in the infinite meadows of heaven,	Blossomed the lovely stars, the forget-me-nots of the angels." – Henry Wadsworth Longfellow "Evangeline: A Tale of Acadie" <u>Topographia</u>: the vivid description of a place. ‹Greek topos: place, e.g. "A damp mist rose from the river, and the marshy ground about, and spread itself over the dreary fields. It was piercing cold, too, all was gloomy and black." – Charles Dickens, Oliver Twist <u>Hydrographia</u>: vivid description of water. ‹Greek hydro: water, e.g. "Never in his life had he seen a river before – this sleek, sinuous, full-bodied animal, chasing and chuckling, gripping things with a gurgle and leaving them with a laugh, to fling itself on fresh playmates that shook themselves free, and were caught and held again. All was a-shake and a-shiver – glints and gleams and sparkles, rustle and swirl, chatter and bubble." – Kenneth Grahame, <u>The Wind in the Willows</u>	

Bibliography
∽

This Bibliography lists works that we have used in researching and creating this curriculum. Most of these are cited by short footnotes throughout the text. Most selections at the beginning of lessons are in the public domain, besides the full length excerpts of the progymnasmata translations, which are used by permission of the Society for Biblical Literature in Atlanta, Georgia.

"Aphthonius' Progymnasmata," translated by Malcolm Heath. http://www.rhetcomp.gsu.edu/—gpullman/2150/Aphthonius%20Progymnasmata.htm.

Aristotle. *The Rhetoric and Poetics of Aristotle*, trans. Rhys Roberts and Ingram Bywater. New York: Random House, 1954.

Aristotle. *Art of Rhetoric*, trans. John Henry Freese. Cambridge: Harvard University Press, 1926.

Bitzer, Lloyd. "The Rhetorical Situation." 1968. Accessed July 5, 2019. http://www.arts.uwaterloo.ca/~raha/309CWeb/Bitzer(1968).pdf

Corbett, Edward P. J. *Classical Rhetoric for the Modern Student*. New York: Oxford University Press, 1990.

Gideon O. Burt. Silva Rhetoricae, http://rhetoric.byu.edu/

Erasmus, *On Copia of Words and Ideas*, trans. Donald B. King. Milwaukee: The Marquette University Press, 1963.

Gibson, Craig A. *Libanius' Progymnasmata: Model Exercises in Greek Prose Composition and Rhetoric*. Atlanta, Society for Biblical Literature, 2008.

Harvey, Thomas W. *A Practical Grammar of the English Language: Revised Edition*. New York: Van Antwerp, Bragg & Co., 1868.

Harvey, Thomas W. *Elementary Grammar and Composition*. New York: American Book Compar, 1880.

Hock, Ronald F., and O'Neil, Edward N. *The Chreia and Ancient Rhetoric: Classroom Exercises*. Atlanta, Society for Biblical Literature, 2002.

Kennedy, George A. *Progymnasmata: Greek Textbooks of Prose Composition and Rhetoric.* Atlanta, Society for Biblical Literature, 2003.

Mills, Dorothy, *The Book of the Ancient Greeks: An Introduction to the History and Civilization of Greece from the Coming of the Greeks to the Conquest of Corinth by Rome in 146 B.C.* New York: G. P. Putnam's Sons, 1925.

Perrine, Laurence. *Liter.* San Diego: Harcourt Brace Jovanovich, 1988.

Perrine, Laurence. *Literature, Structure, Sound, and Sense.* San Diego: Harcourt Brace Jovanovich, 1988.

Perrine, Laurence. *Sound and Sense, An Introduction to Poetry* San Diego: Harcourt Brace College Publishers, 1992.

Perrine, Laurence. *Story and Structure.* San Diego: Harcourt Brace Jovanovich, 1988.

Quintilian. *Institutes of Oratory.* Translated by H. E. Butler. Hastings: Delphi Classics, 2015.

Ryken, Leland. *A Complete Handbook of Literary Forms in the Bible.* Illinois: Crossway, 2014.

Ryken, Leland. *Homer's The Odyssey.* Illinois: Crossway, 2013.

℘

COTTAGE PRESS

Classical Curriculum

with a

Charlotte Mason foundation
for Language Arts *& more*
~toward a life well read

Language Lessons for Children
Primer One & Primer Two

Charlotte Mason style gentle lessons in grammar and composition for early elementary students—the perfect preparation for more rigorous language arts in later years. Features copywork and narration lessons drawn from classic children's literature and poetry. Includes nature and picture study lessons each week.

Language Arts for Grammar Students
Language Arts for Intermediate Students

Grammar and composition lessons structured around the fable and narrative stages of the progymnasmata. Features selections for imitation from classic children's literature as well as a gentle introduction to several classics as well. Includes strong sentence diagramming component along with basic studies in poetry, literary terms, figures of speech, and figures of description.

Language Arts for Upper School
Poetics & Progym I, II, and III

Composition and introductory rhetoric structured around the classical progymnasmata. Selections from the classical literature are central to each lesson for imitation, comprehension, and literary analysis. Includes in-depth study of grammar, sentence diagramming, poetry, literary terms, figures of speech, and figures of description.

Historical Timeline Notebook
Book of Centuries

A blank timeline book for students to record the major events and people they encounter in their study of history, literature, science, art, and music. Each page has lined sections for lists and blank sections for sketching.

Cottage Press Classics
Poetry Readers

Based on Charlotte Mason's method of poetry study, each volume of the Poetry Readers series includes three or four poets, along with several selections from Shakespeare's sonnets and plays, providing more than enough poems for a full year's poetry study. Our six year cycle of poets will introduce students to many of the most beautiful and well-known poems in the English tongue.

Visit *cottagepresspublishing.net* to see our complete offerings.

06-13-2020